# THE REAL
## BILL SHANKLY

Outside the Shankly Gates,

I heard a Kopite calling

He said: 'Shankly they have taken you away'

But you left a great eleven

Before you went to heaven

Now it's glory round the Fields of Anfield Road . . .

THIS BOOK IS DEDICATED TO MY NAN ADA GILL
AND MY CHILDREN PANAYIOTIS AND RHIANNA,
MY HUSBAND ANGELOS AND TO MY BROTHER
STEPHEN, WHO I HAVE NEVER MET
BUT HOPE TO ONE DAY.

**KAREN ELIZABETH GILL**

**THE REAL BILL SHANKLY**
**ADDITIONAL SUPPORT/RESEARCH:**
KEN ROGERS, JAMES CLEARY,
DAVID RANDLES AND WILLIAM HUGHES
**PRODUCTION EDITOR:**
PAUL DOVE

Sport Media
A Trinity Mirror Business

**EXECUTIVE EDITOR:** KEN ROGERS **EDITOR:** STEVE HANRAHAN
**PRODUCTION EDITOR:** PAUL DOVE **ART EDITOR:** RICK COOKE
**SALES AND MARKETING MANAGER:** ELIZABETH MORGAN
**DESIGNERS:** LEE ASHUN, GLEN HIND,
COLIN SUMPTER, BARRY PARKER
**WRITERS:** DAVID RANDLES, GAVIN KIRK,
JOHN HYNES, CHRIS McLOUGHLIN

**PUBLISHED IN GREAT BRITAIN IN 2007 BY:** TRINITY MIRROR SPORT MEDIA,
PO BOX 48, OLD HALL STREET, LIVERPOOL L69 3EB.
ISBN 978-1905-26650-0

**MAIN PHOTOGRAPHS:** LIVERPOOL DAILY POST AND ECHO. TRINITY MIRROR.
**ADDITIONAL IMAGES** COURTESY OF THE SHANKLY FAMILY
AND THE LIVERPOOL FAMILY

PRINTED BY BROAD LINK ENTERPRISE LTD

I would like to take this opportunity to thank everyone who made the writing of this book possible.

First to my sister Pauline, whose organisational skills were of incalculable help in sorting out and cataloguing our granddad's personal items which are now in the hands of the Liverpool FC Museum. Also my sister Emma whose help was invaluable in the collecting of stories and photographs.

A big thanks to my Aunty Jean who gave me so much insight into my granddad's private life and generously loaned so many of his belongings to the Liverpool FC museum where they will be accessible to the people who really mattered most to Bill Shankly – the Liverpool fans.

Thanks to my cousins Jenny, Claire and Christopher for their input.

A huge thanks to my dad Victor Gill whose support and encouragement was instrumental in my not giving up the project and for the great stories he let me use almost word for word.

Through my dad I came into contact with supporter Chris Wood who was so helpful that the book was transformed by his contributions. Chris provided the Alan Rudkin photographs and was the link with Joe Neary that produced some remarkable 1965 FA Cup final homecoming pictures.

Thanks to my godfather Colin Taylor and his sons Michael and Stephen for sharing their special memories.

Many thanks to Kenny Quayle who was a great friend and neighbour of my granddad. He so kindly offered to share his stories, even after not hearing from me for about 30 years.

On the practical side, a great big thanks to Joanne Lavos who rescued me from typing this book with two fingers and helped me to finish everything on time.

Special thanks to Nick Edwards and Kate Donnelly for their encouragement and advice. Can I also acknowledge the help of Liverpool FC Museum Curator Stephen Done.

Of course, without Ken Rogers and his Sport Media editorial team this book simply would not exist. The biggest thanks of all go to the fans who took the time and trouble to send in their stories and photos. The response was overwhelming and helped to fill the pages of this book with warm memories of my granddad.

This book will hopefully provide everlasting memories for whole Shankly clan.

Last but not least, thanks to Nassos and all the members of the Hellenic branch of the Liverpool supporters club who were the catalyst for the whole project and helped me really appreciate and understand the true greatness of Bill Shankly.

**KAREN**

# CONTENTS

Artist's impression presented to Shankly by John Devereux from Kirkby

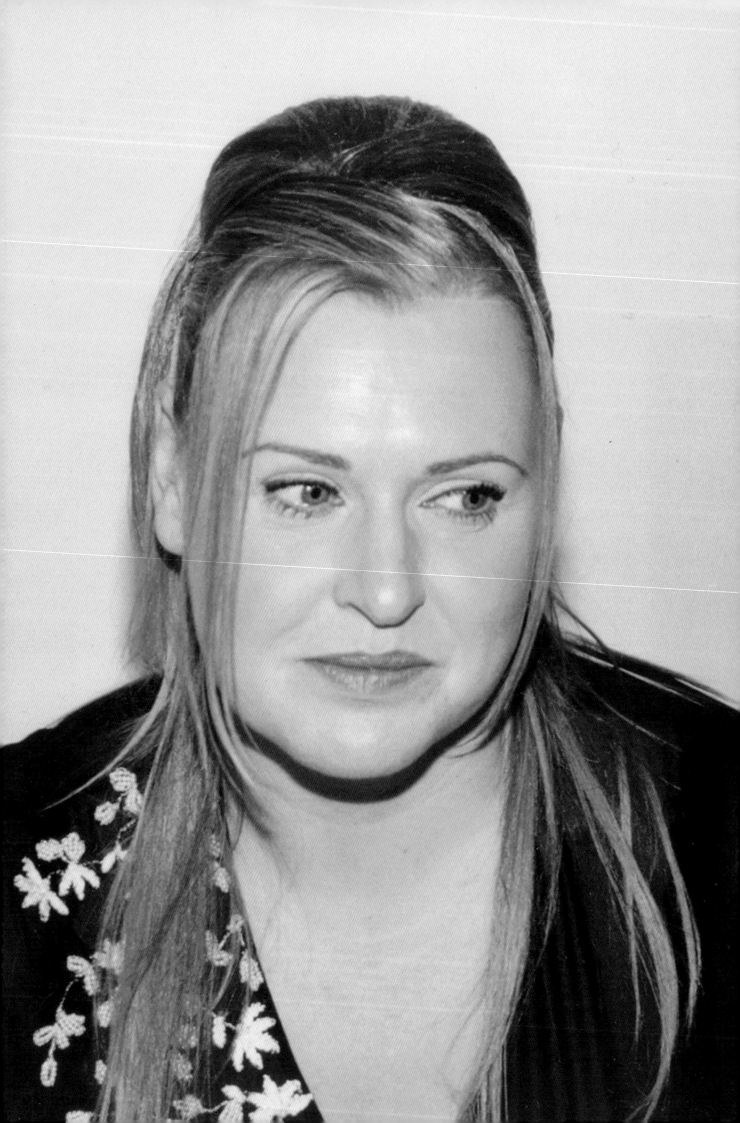

# Foreword

Mention the name Bill Shankly in any football setting and it is guaranteed to inspire an avalanche of stories, a mix of fact and folklore.

Here was the man who told us that football wasn't a matter of life and death, it was more important than that. It's fortunate that the great man did not live to witness the Hillsborough Disaster.

It would have devastated him and he would have been the first to rewrite his most famous quote and immerse himself in the grief of the fans because if ever there was a man of the people it was this fiercely proud manager of Liverpool.

His teams played simple football, beautiful football, but he was a complex character. Many people will know much more than me about the football genius of the gritty Scot from Glenbuck, but I would like to think that I have the inside story of THE REAL BILL SHANKLY and this is what this book is all about.

You see, he was my grandfather, or my Grandy as I called him.

As a child, I was in the heart of the Shankly household with Grandy and my grandmother Ness. For any Shankly female, it was difficult to make your mark, not just in a world of men, but a world of men's men. My Grandy didn't just eat, sleep and drink football. He used to dream about it as well.

He was probably the world's first 24 hours a day manager. His life was dominated by one thing – football.

Grandy was a remarkable individual who has fascinated and inspired me throughout my life. On the 25th anniversary of his death (he died on September 29, 1981) I was determined to publish this book to tell him how much we still love him and miss him (both his blood family and the family of football supporters he idolised).

This book ends a personal dream for me because I finally have a complete grasp of a truly amazing man who I am fiercely proud of. I was too young to truly understand the impact he made on people during his lifetime.

In the opening chapter of my book, I speak directly to Grandy because I know he is up there looking down on us and I want to say all the things I couldn't say when he was this larger than life character in my life.

I was only 16 when he died, but when I looked into the eyes of the fans and the dignitaries at his cathedral memorial service back in 1981, I knew his legacy would be with me forever.

The tribute on his Anfield statue declares: 'He made the people happy.'

We as a family had to take something of a backseat, but still have some incredible memories and stories that I want to share with you. I know they will inspire you, make you smile and at times fill you with emotion.

I have talked to my family, his friends and his football colleagues in my search to find THE REAL BILL SHANKLY. I have lived his exploits all over again by researching his life through the remarkable archive of the Liverpool Daily Post & Echo. I have also been talking to you, the fans, to truly understand the immense impact he had on his Red Army.

No book about Grandy would be complete without a significant supporters' section, putting the facts where before there was folklore.

The format is simple. The first part of the book is my inside story in which I tell you about the Bill Shankly the world did not see. At this point, we also begin to tell his amazing story from start to finish through the Liverpool Daily Post & Echo headlines and stories that appeared over two decades and more from the very first moment his name was linked with the club on 20 November, 1959.

These headlines also capture the mood in the city on 12 July, 1974 when the bombshell announcement was made that a football partnership made in heaven was finally over and that Bill Shankly was leaving Liverpool FC.

Finally, I let the fans take centre stage

and your stories are remarkable. Here was a football manager who didn't just open his heart to the people who followed Liverpool, but opened his wallet, his house, his whole being in a remarkable show of support in reverse.

My research highlighted many things. For instance, I found out that Bob Paisley had pleaded with him to change his mind about retiring in 1974 with the words: "You can't pack it in. It will kill you!"

Bob's prophetic statement had followed a story in the Liverpool Echo months earlier in February, 1974 in which chairman John Smith declared: "Bill Shankly has a job for life, but that decision is not for us to take, we are completely at Mr Shankly's disposal."

Of course, we now know that there was turmoil going on behind the scenes and that Nessie had pleaded with my Grandy to retire 12 months earlier as she feared for his health. That he refused at that time clearly upset her and she was as shocked as anyone when, in June 1974, he suddenly announced, while watching the TV, that it was all over.

It was mixed emotions for her. The first thought was absolute relief. The second was that retirement would be anything but a walk in the park for someone like Bill Shankly.

I feel extremely sad that I was only a child at that point and couldn't be supportive of my grandparents. I know how difficult the following years must have been because my Grandy described retirement as the equivalent of "damned hard labour" adding: "The word should be struck from the record!"

For my part, I want to make sure that the facts about the REAL BILL SHANKLY live forever.

Many books have been written before. I hope this one takes you on an inside track and perhaps reminds you why you are a dedicated Liverpudlian.

My Grandy could make anyone believe. He was very special.

**KAREN ELIZABETH GILL**

# Just one of the
# FAMILY

## KAREN GILL IS FIERCELY PROUD OF HER ROOTS. SHE SHOULD BE – SHE IS BILL SHANKLY'S GRANDDAUGHTER. THIS IS HER STORY OF HOW SHE GREW UP WITH AN ANFIELD GENIUS

Memories are made of this: Karen Gill (far right) pictured with 'Grandy' Bill Shankly, sister Pauline and (centre) sister Emma

BILL SHANKLY

Best Wishes

FROM THE

> Things weren't going too well in the winter of 1959 for Liverpool Football Club. Languishing in the Second Division, when manager Phil Taylor was sacked, the hunt for his successor began . . .

**20 November 1959**

### Hunt for new Reds boss – Shankly in the frame

### Liverpool's New Manager
### Shankly's Name Mentioned

While Liverpool chairman, Mr. T. V. Williams, and fellow-director Mr. S. C. Reakes, were making a signing in Scotland to-day speculation links the names of famous former players with the vacant managership at Anfield (writes Leslie Edwards).
The most recurring one is that of Huddersfield Town's former Scottish international half-back, Mr. Bill Shankly. The story goes that if Mr. Shankly applies for the position he stands a very

**Bill Shankly.**
good chance of getting it.

Echo sports editor Leslie Edwards, writing on 20 November 1959, conjured up the very first mention that a passionate Scot, working for Huddersfield Town, might be the man to lead the Reds out of the wilderness.

Liverpool had spent years trying to get out of the old Second Division. Edwards, a journalist with tremendous contacts inside Anfield, revealed that former Preston North End and Scotland star Bill Shankly was the man in the board's sights.

He wrote: 'While Liverpool chairman Mr T.V. Williams and fellow director Mr S.C. Reakes

# Dear Grandy . . .

It's taken me a long time to understand exactly who you were and what you meant and still mean to people.

You died when I was too immature to really appreciate you as a person but thanks to the events of the last few years I've begun to get some real insight into your character and the influence that you still exert even after a quarter of a century!

I feel so proud of you. I want to tell you I feel so lucky you were my granddad. I never got the opportunity to see you or speak to you before you died. It was just so out of the blue. We didn't even know you were in hospital. Then there was a phone call made to our school, we had to go home early. I remember it as if it were yesterday . . . one of the saddest days of our lives.

I've been reading a lot about you recently and there are many references to you as a "hero" or a "working class hero".

It might seem like an exaggeration to some people. I must admit that I felt a bit like that at first.

Then I looked the word up in the dictionary and the definition was hero; a person who is admired by many for his noble qualities or his bravery; chief male character in a story, poem or play.

Heroic; of a size larger than in real life. After doing my research and speaking to people from all over the world I can quite justifiably say that you meet the dictionary definition of the word.

You are one of the chief characters in the story of Liverpool Football Club; you were one of the chief characters in my story. You are admired by many for your noble qualities; honesty, fairness integrity and determination, qualities you demonstrated on many occasions.

Lastly, you were certainly larger than life and that's definitely one of the reasons you still command such respect even today. I feel so proud of you Grandy and this book is my gift to you on the 25th anniversary of your untimely death.

**Party time: Me (right) and sister Pauline with 'Grandy' Bill**

A fitting tribute: Me at Anfield's famous statue

'I FEEL SO PROUD OF YOU. I WANT TO
TELL YOU I FEEL SO LUCKY YOU WERE
MY GRANDDAD. I NEVER GOT THE
OPPORTUNITY TO SEE YOU OR
SPEAK TO YOU BEFORE YOU DIED.
IT WAS JUST SO OUT OF THE BLUE'

were making a signing in Scotland today, speculation links many famous names with the vacant managership at Anfield.

The most recurring one is that of Huddersfield Town's former Scottish international half-back Mr Bill Shankly. The story goes that if Mr Shankly applies for the position he stands a very good chance of getting it.

What lends strength to the rumour is the fact that Mr. Shankly was on the short list of candidates for the Liverpool post before the club elected to invite Mr Don Welsh to succeed Mr George Kay.

Mr Shankly, who played mostly with Preston North End, was manager at Carlisle and Grimsby before succeeding his former playing colleague at Preston, Andy Beattie, at Leeds Road.

But however much conjecture there is about the successor to Mr Phil Taylor, there can be no certainty about any name until applications arrive at their registered offices in Victoria Street.

Mr Lawson Martindale, one of the senior directors of the club, said today: "Any names mentioned in connection with the vacancy are only conjecture. There is no certainty about the matter; nor can there be until we have examined all the applications.

"We particularly desired secrecy.

'We are hopeful that we shall have many first-class men seeking the job, but we do not wish to cause any of them or their clubs embarrassment."'

**2 December 1959**

### Shankly to take over in a month

It was the Liverpool Daily Post and their correspondent Horace Yates who followed the theme through, claiming Shankly had been offered the job. Writing in his column "Sport As I See It", Yates declared:

# My search for the

Liverpool F.C.'s new manager, Mr Bill Shankly (left) being welcomed by Mr T. V. Williams, the club chairman, at Anfield yesterday when Mr Shankly officially took over.

MAKING N PROMISES

position of Mr W. Shankly, now with Huddersfield Town FC and eventually offered the management to him.

"Mr Shankly put the position before his board and after expressing their regret at the prospect of losing his services, they have agreed that Mr Shankly shall join Liverpool FC."

'For once in a way, the grapevine service has proved correct, for within two days of Mr Taylor's decision, Mr Shankly's name was being whispered as the likely man.

'The service apparently did not spread as far as Huddersfield, for I understand that when Mr Shankly asked for his release last night the intimation was like a bolt from the blue. It was almost the last thing in the world Town's directors were expecting.

'He had no contract with the club, but considers it only fair to Huddersfield that he should stay at Leeds Road for a month in

Why did I decide to write this book? Well there are a couple of reasons. First I'm at that "certain" age when I really want to discover why I am the way I am and what the deciding factors were in the shaping of my personality.

Naturally we look to the past and to our close relatives in order to do this. Most of the close relatives who could have told me more about my granddad and his influence have gone.

My mum, Barbara, died at the age of 46 so now that I'm of an age to appreciate her stories she's not here to tell them. Luckily, though I have discovered a whole new family. A family of Liverpool supporters who are just brimming with stories, eager to regale me with tales of his exploits and sayings. Apart from my own dear memories I have many other sources I can turn to; books where I can read about his amazing career as both footballer and manager, websites with thousands of dedications from loyal Liverpool fans all over the world.

I can soak up admiration and praise from doting fans here in Greece where I now live and be

proposed to by taxi drivers in Liverpool when I tell them who my granddad was! Secondly I want my children to know about Bill Shankly - not just because he was a chief character in my story - but because he played such an important role in other people's lives.

He not only achieved this in Liverpool where I was born and bred, but all over the world and that's no exaggeration. I'm not blowing things up out of proportion or trying to make my granddad larger than life. He just was and even if you attempt to tone things down or be modest about him, you can't. He defies such an approach.

I didn't really realize how much he meant to people until I went to live in another country. I had to travel halfway round the globe to truly understand the phenomenon of Shankly (I've always had to learn the hard way!).

I don't think when you're young you have the ability to appreciate somebody famous in the family. You kind of resent the intrusions. When you're a child you resent it because it means interruptions at mealtimes as there are fans at the door clamouring

Proud to hold the FA Cup with a Greek fan club stalwart

# real Bill Shankly

Home comforts: Bill in relaxed mood with Nessie

order to give the Yorkshire club the opportunity of making a new appointment before leaving them.

'When I spoke to Mr Shankly after his appointment, he told me: "I am very pleased and proud

to have been chosen as manager of Liverpool FC, a club of such great potential.

"I have known Mr Tom Williams a long time and have always considered him to be one of football's gentlemen. I am confident that we will be able to work well together.

"It is my opinion that Liverpool have a crowd of followers which rank with the greatest in the game. They deserve success and I hope in my small way to be able to do something towards helping them to achieve it.

"I make no promises except that from the moment I take over I shall put everything I have into the job I so willingly undertake.

"This appointment is a challenge to me. I rank it similar to that confronting Joe Mercer when he left Sheffield United for Aston Villa, and when Alan Brown left Burnley to go to Sunderland.

"These clubs, like Liverpool, are amongst the top grade teams in the football land. When the challenge was made to me I simply could not refuse to accept it.

"There is a job to be done, perhaps a big job, but with the co-operation of Mr Williams, the directors and staff I feel certain we shall see the task through together.

"I am not a lazy man. I like to get down to it and set the example which I want following from the top of the club to the bottom. I make few promises, but

---

for autographs or wanting to chat about such and such a player's performance.

When you're in hospital you hate it because even the nurses are going to lose interest in you the moment he appears in the ward. You can't really go shopping with them since you suddenly become surrounded by admiring crowds and the shopping spree has to be prematurely terminated.

When you're a teenager it's a great way to attract the opposite sex initially.

You name drop to impress but when they start pestering you to meet the "Man" or for tickets for the

match, the attraction begins to wear off!

Then one day he's gone, there's a great big empty space and an ache in your heart that never goes away and gets sharper every time you read his name or see his picture and believe me they pop up in the most unexpected places.

So it's now in retrospect that I can appreciate my granddad's achievements and really begin to feel that pride bursting out of me. Now I feel the need to understand what made him a hero. I once read that you can tell a man from the enemies he has. Well, I don't want to blow my granddad's trumpet (too much) but I honestly don't think he had

one of them is that everything I do I hope there will be patent common sense attached to it."

'Mr Shankly, strangely enough, saw his team beat his new club on Saturday, and his reaction to the game is interesting.

He said: "I must say that Huddersfield were a better side than Liverpool, but at least Liverpool did fight. The fact that Huddersfield were leading only 1-0 for most of the time kept Liverpool fighting. I was quite pleased with what I saw."'

Yates then gave a clear indication of the character of the new man who had set the agenda immediately with his references to the fans, his respect for them and what he wanted to do to make them happy. Yates' report continued:

'Mr Shankly has built his reputation as a canny Scot who prefers to make his stars rather than buy them, which has suited Huddersfield's copy book completely, for Huddersfield have never been one of the best supported sides, and on one occasion this season had fewer than 10,000 spectators for a home game.

"When I took over at Huddersfield three years ago," Mr Shankly said, "I had only a team of boys to go to work on. Indeed, they are still boys, most of them.

"I would not be human if I were not pleased with the way in which players like McHale, Law and Massie have advanced under my direction. I guided them from their junior beginnings to League football.

"My signings have been Ray Wood of Manchester United, who I consider to be the best goalkeeper in the Second Division today, and Derek Hawksworth. I don't think either of them have let me down."

'I told Mr Shankly that the burning ambition of every Liverpool supporter, as well as the club officials, was to see the club in Division One, and I asked him how he felt about that.

"Nobody realises more than I what a tough job that is likely to

any true enemies (I'll probably receive indignant letters from them all after this). I've read criticism levelled at him and the most biting and vitriolic was that he was prone to exaggeration.

Even his rivals from other teams had great respect for him and I'll never forget the sight of the streets lined with fans, paying their last respects on the day of his funeral.

Not just Liverpool fans, but fans with blue and white scarves and hats on, tears rolling down their faces. When I saw them it made me cry even more. I think that says a lot about him.

As I was saying before, I had to come halfway (maybe that's a slight exaggeration….a quarter of the way…please forgive me I am after all Shanks' granddaughter) round the world to understand the phenomenon.

Why? What exactly was the catalyst that made me decide to put pen to paper and write this eulogy? It was the year 2002. August. Hot here in Greece, which is where I've been living for the last 15 years.

We were at our house by the sea, having just returned from a two week visit to Liverpool to see the family, when I received a phone call from my brother-in-law informing me that

'THEY WANTED TO TALK TO THE WOMAN WHO HAD BEEN MARRIED TO HIM FOR 37 YEARS AND TO STAND IN THE ROOM WHERE HE HAD LIVED AND BREATHED. THIS WAS THEIR MECCA'

be, but I think we can do it. I have gained quite a lot of experience of Second Division football and know some of the difficulties."

'Mr Shankly is certain to be given plenty of freedom of action in trying to fashion the football future of Liverpool FC. When I asked him what sort of contract had been given, and the duration of it, he replied instantly: "I have no contract at all. I would not have one. If I cannot do the job then it is up to the people who employ me to do as they wish."

'The new manager's confidence and firm resolve are infectious. Nobody can be in his company for more than a few minutes and not realise that here is a rare driving force who will spare himself no pains to get done the job he has in view.

'The players will find him fair, friendly and always willing to help and advise, but in return he will demand a high price – the last possible ounce of effort each player is able to give.

'There will be no freewheeling. That much is certain. He works hard himself and will demand nothing less from those who serve under him.

'Bill Shankly achieved fame as a player with Preston North End. Born in Ayrshire, he was a member of the Glenbuck Cherrypickers team when invited to join Carlisle United in 1932. A year later he was signed by Preston and within a season was playing half back in their League team.

'He went to Wembley with Preston in 1937 and had to be

my grandmother Nessie had just passed away. I decided to fly straight back to Britain for the funeral, which I'm extremely glad I did, as it was to change my life for the better (and that's no exaggeration).

When we got to the funeral home to pay our last respects to Nessie, there was a huge wreath sitting in the corner which immediately caught my eye. There was a card attached conveying deep commiserations to the Shankly family. It was signed by the official LFC supporters club in Athens.

I was deeply touched by their gesture and decided to contact them

when I returned to Athens in order to thank them personally. When I did so you cannot imagine their reaction! The chairman Thomas Papanikolau and the general secretary Nassos Siotropos had been actively trying to track me down since visiting the Shankly home in 1997 when they had met with Ness.

They had enjoyed a cup of the famous herbal tea that Bill always used to drink, then had their photograph taken with my Nan. They had gone on this pilgrimage to Bellefield Avenue so that they could walk along the very same street that their hero had walked along. They

content with a losers' medal.

'The following year, Preston were there again, and this time were triumphant – against Huddersfield Town.

'Capped for Scotland against England in 1938, he played in all their international games the following season.

'After the war he was appointed manager of Carlisle United in 1949, before moving on to Grimsby Town two years later.

'It was in 1954 that he left to take over the managerial reins at Workington and then after one year as assistant manager of Huddersfield Town, he took over as manager when Andy Beattie retired in November 1956.'

**2 December 1959**

## Shankly starts at a great advantage

The Echo's Leslie Edwards was highly enthusiastic about Bill Shankly's arrival and pointed to the coincidences that augered well for the future.

He said: 'The Shankly appointment is one full of coincidences. It was Bill Shankly who was a favoured short-list candidate for the same post when George Kay became ill and could not continue in office seasons ago. On that occasion the Liverpool board had second thoughts and invited Don Welsh (who had not applied) to take the position.

'After the Welsh reign came

wanted to talk to the woman who had been married to him for 37 years and to stand in the room where he had lived and breathed.

This was their Mecca. Not only were they thrilled by the warm reception they received from Ness, but they were excited to learn that Bill Shankly's granddaughter actually lived in Athens. It seemed like a sign to them!

Upon their return to Greece they tried to find me . . . but their efforts bore no fruit. They had been too polite to ask my Nan for details and it would never have even entered my Nan's head to give my details out to some foreign men however nice they appeared to be.

So seven years later when I contacted them, it was another sign. I was cordially invited to their office in downtown Athens, where a "royal" reception awaited me.

The red carpet was well and truly rolled out. I was greeted with a huge bouquet of beautiful flowers,

photographed all evening, presented with honorary membership of the club and requested to cut a specially made cake with my granddad's face on it.

It goes without saying that I was bombarded with questions about my granddad and unceremoniously corrected whenever my feeble memory failed me (and it did so miserably). I always try not to say too much when I meet up with them as they truly do know a lot more about him than I do.

They worship my granddad. One of them asked me what it's like to have Bill Shankly's DNA! It was a bit overawing at first and I didn't feel very worthy of all the attention until I realized that I brought them closer in some way to their idol.

I didn't have to do anything to deserve their admiration. It was enough that Bill's blood was running through my veins. I began to feel the true power and influence of my granddad. Don't imagine that these

**Warm welcome: Nessie pictured with the Liverpool fans from Greece**

Grandy's girls: Pauline with me and our 'great' granddad!

Phil Taylor's. Now Bill Shankly, whom we remember as a non-stop bullet-headed Preston and Scotland international half-back gets his chance and it is a safe bet that come hell or high water, the team he selects will be the one he wants to see on the field of play. I fancy he will get his way, though he takes this £2,500 a year job without contract.

'In this respect he will start at a great advantage. No other Liverpool manager in history has ever been given "his head."

'Coincidence number two is the club's Scottish coach, Reuben Bennett, whose appointment at Anfield dated psychologically at all events from the heavy defeat at Huddersfield last season (Bennett arrived in late 1958, not long after Shankly's Huddersfield had inflicted a 5-0 defeat on the Reds). It will be a second association with a member of the famous footballing family of Shankly. He was on the staff with Bill Shankly's brother, Bob, at Third Lanark at the time he was offered his present Anfield position.

Thirdly, the long arm links the new Liverpool guv'nor with the player he transferred to Everton two years ago, Dave Hickson. So whatever the future holds for Liverpool fans, officials and Press, it certainly will not be dull.

If he has a fault it is that he is likely to be too conscientious. He's football daft, as they say and he spares neither himself nor anyone who does not give him 100 per cent effort.'

**11 December 1959**

## Shankly's Anfield mission

The local newspapers on Merseyside were quickly highlighting Shankly's early agenda. One report said:

'Liverpool's new manager Bill Shankly will start his Anfield activities tomorrow watching the reserves play Manchester City.

'He said last night that he had been hoping to be able to make

men and women are in their 60s.

They are all under 40 and some of them are teenagers. It was through them that on 12 March, 2005, I got to meet the legendary Ian Callaghan, who had been invited to Athens to celebrate the 10th anniversary of the supporters' club. That night was very special to me.

It was the night I felt inspired to write this book; it was the night I realised I wanted to help people remember my granddad. Since then my granddad's name just keeps popping up in the most unlikely of places. Later in the year, at my son's

school book fair, all the boys were pouring over a football book which I was eventually persuaded to buy.

Imagine my son's astonishment when he saw his great granddad staring out at him from the page dedicated to the greatest managers of all time.

Remember this was a Greek book so we didn't exactly expect him to be included.

Of course, it was something to boast about the next day at school. Another time a 15 year old student of mine (I'm an English teacher in Greece) asked me if Î had ever heard

the trip with the first team to Bristol for the match against Rovers, but as there were one or two business items to be dealt with this evening, he could not get clear in time.

"I am looking forward to seeing the reserves," Shankly said. "There is nothing like getting to know what there is in the second string at the earliest opportunity."

'To greet him at Anfield will be the club chairman, Mr T.V. Williams, who is anxious to see how the Scottish signing Tommy Leishman performs. Shankly expects to take over officially at Anfield on either Monday or Tuesday morning.

'He revealed that he had visited Liverpool this week to start the task of selecting living accommodation, and had seen premises at Formby. I gather that he will see property in other districts before arriving at a final decision.

'The last Liverpool team to be chosen without Mr Shankly's participation is that which he saw in action at Huddersfield a fortnight ago, and which was retained for last Saturday's home fixture with Ipswich Town.'

LIVERPOOL: Slater; Molyneux, Moran; Wheeler, White, Campbell; Morris, Hunt, Hickson, Melia, A'Court.

The reserve team against Manchester City will be: Lawrence; Jones, Byrne; Wilkinson, Nicholson, Leishman; Twist, Woodall, Arnell, Harrower, Morrissey.'

### 15 January 1960

## Liverpool plan drive on youth and schoolboys

The Liverpool Daily Post was encouraged to see that Bill Shankly was opening the gates of Melwood to potential local football talent. They reported:

'Just a month into his role at Anfield, Bill Shankly made a bid to encourage local youngsters to earn a place within the Reds'

of the great Bill Shankly who he'd just read about in his French book at school!

You can imagine how I felt.

It's one thing to be reminded of someone in the country where they lived and were well-known and another entirely to be reminded of him in a country far from home.

It's like I haven't lost him after all. It's as if I still have him with me, keeping an eye on me, letting me know he's still there.

I know that there are lots of people who don't really believe in all that "stuff."

I can be a bit of a sceptic myself, but I know that when you really believe something deep down then it is real.

Wasn't that my granddad's philosophy?

Believe in yourself and you can make things happen. Believe that you can do the impossible and it's more likely that you'll achieve your goals.

"Blind faith" is one of the principles on which religion is based and it's one of the basic tenets of the Shankly philosophy.

He had a lot of faith in Liverpool Football Club.

He had unshakeable faith in his players and he always tried to instil that faith into them so that they would believe in themselves.

Last but not least, he had tremendous faith in the people of Liverpool and as I've learned over the last year it was a feeling reciprocated in full.

*So this is not just a gift to you Grandy but it is also dedicated to your army, "Shankly's Army" in the hope that they will indeed keep marching on.*

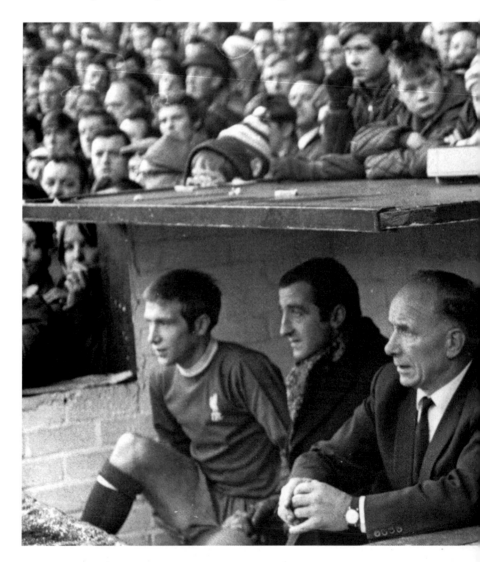

# As Ness played Scrabble, Shanks played Superman

Larger than life figures, of course, often make people feel uncomfortable and my granddad was no exception. I think it boils down to the fact that we ordinary mortals can't really understand all that passion and single-mindedness.

That kind of total unswerving devotion to one thing, demands a lot of energy and an endless supply of enthusiasm. Bill Shankly was never lacking in either. But as I said it sometimes made people uneasy.

My granddad did actually make some people feel as if they'd like to be somewhere else! My nanny Ada (my dad's mum) always said that if you didn't know anything about football you couldn't sit on your own

ranks.

'The gates to Anfield and Melwood are wide open on the orders of manager Bill Shankly, who plans to make one of the greatest appeals ever made to schoolboys and youths for miles

around Merseyside, to report for training and coaching, in a tremendous drive to put the soccer-playing youngsters through a fine toothcomb, to see that players of any potential are given every opportunity to develop it.

'Mr Shankly said that youngsters must not feel shy or embarrassed in any way in asking permission to attend training and coaching sessions. He declared: "If there is any talent at all in them, we will do our best to bring it out. They will be most welcome. The more the merrier."

'In these days it is not such a long step from school to League football, for seldom has there been greater opportunity to make the grade. With accomplished and experienced players so difficult to find and so costly to procure, Mr Shankly's attack on the problem may be only a little slower and certainly no less reliable in the end.

"We cannot have too many lads," he said "If we get enough of them we are sure to get a percentage of winners and in a city as soccer-conscious as Liverpool, and Merseyside generally, I cannot believe that the material we seek is not close at hand.

"Within three years of leaving school some of these boys could be in the first team, so that the

**A thoughtful Bill Shankly with Reuben Bennett, Gerry Byrne and Bobby Graham in the dugout**

policy is not quite so long-term as cynics might suggest.

"It is all very well to say that it is the ready-made material we want. Nobody would attempt to deny that, but when it becomes increasingly difficult to obtain, until today it is heartbreakingly difficult, this chase after youth seems to me to be the most reasonable alternative.

"Obviously we will keep our usual watch on the junior teams and hope that more and more Roger Hunts can be unearthed, but I would like to think that anybody who has any faith in himself at all and hankers after a soccer career, will give me the chance of helping him to attain that goal.

"Football is my life and I do not mind how much time I spend among these youngsters. If my efforts in this direction produce one first-team player a season, nobody would complain. In fact, I would think I had been well rewarded, but I have great hopes of Liverpool. I am confident they can produce a much better return than that.

"If we could achieve such impressive results at Leeds Road (Huddersfield Town), it should be much easier here in Liverpool, where the area is so vast and the numbers of lads who think, eat and sleep football are so great. To me the sky's the limit. I have very great hopes and I know these lads will not let me down.'"

**1959/60**

## Reds miss promotion by seven points

That first season 1959/60, ended with the Reds finishing third and missing promotion by seven

points (Aston Villa and Cardiff City were the top two), the run-in yielding nine points from 10 in the last five games. Shankly took

The women stuck together in the Shankly household! My mum Barbara, me, my nan and my sister Pauline

with him for long.

She would often sit in the living room of Bellefield Avenue racking her brains to think of some conversation opener, only to spurt out some ill-informed comment about some player or other, whereupon my granddad would launch into a long diatribe in order to enlighten her.

She used to dread Ness going into the kitchen to make a cup of tea and being left alone with him. He was without doubt a man's man and didn't have an awful lot to say to women.

You see, he was one of the old school who believed that women had no place in football and they certainly weren't expected to show anything beyond a polite interest in the game.

My nanny Ness was often made to feel jittery as well, especially on a match day. Throughout the 1960's, Saturday was match day for my granddad and Scrabble day for my Nan and her friends.

Often though, poor Ness couldn't quite settle down and get into the swing of her game. Her mind was on the outcome of another game. If they lost it would mean days of stony silence at the Bellefield home.

At best it would mean an extremely clean oven (I'm sure many of you are aware of the endearing trait, dating back to his Huddersfield days, of cleaning the oven after defeat. The object in question was given a vigorous scrubbing and some mild cursing could be heard. I'm sure it was his way of trying to obliterate the bitter taste of defeat).

On one particular day, it was a derby day in fact, Ness had been unable to concentrate on her game of Scrabble and had rushed home from her friend's in order to listen to the match results on the transistor radio. She heaved a sigh of relief. It was a draw. That wasn't too bad. A draw could be lived with, a draw could be endured.

Most men, on the other hand, felt a strong affinity to him and he himself felt more at home in the company of men. After all, his world was and always had been male orientated, from his days down the pit to his own football playing days and then his years as manager.

There were many men who were indispensable to him in his every day life; not just the ones we all know about, but the unsung heroes behind the scenes. He never forgot these

Working man: Shanks deep in thought at Melwood

charge for the first time on December 19th, 1959. He did not travel for the 2-0 win at Bristol Rovers on December 12. The resulting 4-0 defeat at the hands of Cardiff City in front of 27,291 at Anfield did little to inspire confidence.

The line-up that day was:

Bert Slater; Alan Jones, Ronnie Moran; Johnny Wheeler, Dick White, Robert Campbell; Fred Morris, Roger Hunt, Dave Hickson, Jimmy Melia, Alan A'Court.

Jones did not play again that season. A game later, a 3-0 defeat at Charlton Athletic resulted in Morris's last appearance of the season while Campbell also went out of the side, coming back in for the final five games.

Changes later that season saw Liddell return to the side, Tommy Leishman given an opportunity at No 6 (Liverpool won the return against the Addicks two days later, on December 28, 2-0) while Gerry Byrne (5 games) and Ian Callaghan (4 games) were given run-outs later on in the campaign. Ronnie Moran and Alan A'Court were the only ever-presents, while Roger Hunt and Dave Hickson were joint-top scorers with 21 goals.

Incidentally, the FA Cup campaign ended at the fourth-round stage, Manchester United winning 3-1 at Anfield.

### 1960/61

## Third again in first full season in charge

In what was Shankly's first full season in charge, the Reds finished third again in the old Second Division, six points behind runners-up Sheffield United and a point further behind champions Ipswich Town.

The season saw Billy Liddell bow out, playing only once against Brighton in September, while Ronnie Moran made the last of his 12 appearances that season in January.

Goalkeeper Bert Slater and

Dick White were ever presents and new signing from Sheffield United (only Shankly's second after Sammy Reid), winger Kevin Lewis, was top scorer with 19 goals.

New players brought into the team included Gordon Milne (16 appearances), signed for £16,000 from Preston, while Johnny Morrissey made 23 appearances, scoring five goals – although the young Ian Callaghan only made three appearances.

FA Cup defeat came again in the fourth round while Liverpool's first foray into the League Cup ended at home to Southampton.

## 1961/62

### Fortress Anfield and back to the big time

A home record of 18 wins and three draws from 21 games was the catalyst for Liverpool's return to the top flight after an eight-year absence (their last home defeat had been on the last day of 1960), romping home to the title eight points ahead of runners-up Leyton Orient and scoring 99 goals in the process. With eight players playing in 40 League games or more of the 42, the success was based on

consistency of selection as well as results. The summer signings of Ron Yeats and Ian St John proved key, as did the form of Roger Hunt, who scored 41 in 41 games. St John, who replaced Dave Hickson in the team, notched 18 in his first campaign while Jimmy Melia and Kevin Lewis also hit double figures.

Changes saw goalkeeper Bert Slater make his last appearance against Middlesbrough in

Team spirit: Shanks loved the camaraderie of the training ground

men even when they no longer worked together. He appreciated their valuable contribution and tried to show that appreciation in his own inimitable way. There was Eli Wass, the groundsman at Melwood training ground, for one.

Bill would always take the time to chat to Eli, usually over a cup of tea. Eli was extremely important to the smooth running of the training sessions and consequently he was extremely important to my granddad too. Bill tried to show his appreciation in many ways; if he had a suit or a pair of shoes that he no longer wore then he would pass them on to Eli. They were all tailored suits and Italian shoes. Only the best!

After the bombshell had been

dropped in 1974 (the year he went into retirement), my granddad would often pop along to Melwood. After all, it was only round the corner from Bellefield Avenue, and for 15 years it had been one of the most significant places in his life.

Eli would make him a cup of tea, they would chat about the old days and reminisce about the great players but it was a short-lived habit; it was making some people feel uncomfortable and maybe understandably so, but still, doesn't your heart go out to him when you put yourself in his shoes and imagine how he must have felt when he realised that he no longer belonged, that he was something of an unwanted presence?

# True Blue barber

Another important male figure was assigned the equally important task of grooming Mr. Shankly; Harold the barber! The venue: Rosthwaite Road, Tuebrook. None of the residents owned a car except the barber, so when there were two cars parked outside the shop people knew Bill Shankly was there and they wouldn't expect a haircut that day.

You see Harold would shut up shop so that he and Bill could talk shop. They would spend all morning talking football even though Harold was a dyed-in-the wool Evertonian (some people might find it incredible that Bill would entrust an Evertonian with the task of giving him a shave,

but it is true. My sister Pauline and I often sat on his knee while the deed was being done, so I know from first hand experience).

Harold had a favourite line that he loved to say to my granddad: "I'd cut your throat, but your damn blood's red as well!"

Generally speaking, I think he particularly warmed to people who weren't in awe of him, who stood up to him if they felt he was in the wrong and would just speak to him naturally. Funnily enough, children were often most comfortable in his presence and countless were the times that dinner would be interrupted by children asking if Mr Shankly was coming out to play.

February, with £18,000 signing from Burnley James Furnell playing the final 13 games of the season, while Johnny Wheeler's one game against Plymouth in December was his last in

**Roger Hunt: 41 in 41 games**

Liverpool colours. Similarly John Molyneux, who had made 39 appearances the previous season, made only three this time while Ian Callaghan began to establish himself in the second half of the campaign. Incidentally, only 17 players were used that season.

FA Cup progress was ended at the fifth-round stage, Preston proving one step too far in a second replay at Old Trafford.

Liverpool actually clinched promotion back to the top flight courtesy of a 2-0 victory over Southampton on April 21st, 1962. On a grey day with constant drizzle, 40,410 fans saw Kevin Lewis (in for the injured Ian St John) scramble the opener after 19 minutes, and after surviving a let-off they got the second 10 minutes later through Lewis again. The victory also clinched the championship with five games remaining and wiped away the misery of missing out on promotion in the previous two seasons.

The following details are gleaned from Michael Charters in the Liverpool Echo and Evening Express (28/04/62):

'The final whistle saw some 'youths' side-step their way past the police barrier and head to the players on the pitch. Southampton's players also formed a 'guard of honour' and clapped Liverpool's players off the pitch. The Kop chanted "We

**My dad Vic Gill (left) exchanging Shankly memories with the famous Melwood groundsman Eli Wass**

want the Reds" and chairman Tom Williams, over the PA, thanked the players and the crowd for helping to achieve one of the hardest things in football – winning the Second Division.

'Next came Shankly himself, who claimed that "this had been the happiest day of his football life." The rest of his words were drowned out as the crowd chanted for the players to return to do a lap of honour.

'This they did, having been changed. Out came the heroes eventually, led by Yeats and St John who did not play in the game. Immediately, the crowd swarmed on the pitch with a vengeance. Yeats and St John were submerged under the back-slapping, kissing, wildly enthusiastic mob. The

rest of the team, from the top step leading to the pitch, took one look and very wisely disappeared back to safety.

'The final word went to Shankly, who afterwards reflected thus: "We won the championship in the first month when we were fitter competitively than our rivals. We beat Sunderland and Newcastle twice in that spell and we never looked back. We have a great team and they're still young."'

### 1962/63

## Impressive cup run in a season of progress

Liverpool established themselves in Division One with a creditable eighth-place finish, which also saw the Reds go close to FA Cup success for the first time (Leicester City winning the semi-final 1-0 at Hillsborough).

Roger Hunt was the only ever-present, scoring 24 goals while St John found the net 19 times in 40 games.

Role model: Shanks and Nessie at a Dr Barnardo's event

He would often play a game of five-a-side with the kids on the playing fields at the end of the road.

Don't imagine that these were unwelcome intrusions into his private life. He would often get the boys' numbers and call them up on Sunday mornings to arrange a game, much to the amazement of many a mum and dad, who would look at the phone in utter disbelief when the caller

revealed himself to be *the* Bill Shankly and not some prankster playing a practical joke.

There's many a dad who, suddenly, after years of indifference to their son's football skills, turned up at the local playing fields in their best suits to proudly support the lads. It wasn't just the children though, who felt at home with him. The feeling was reciprocated.

> Changes to the side saw James Furnell displaced as first choice by Tommy Lawrence, having started the first 13 games of the season, while Tommy Leishman also lost his place to new £20,000 signing from Rangers Willie Stevenson in November. Despite not starting the campaign, Ian Callaghan displaced Kevin Lewis at No 7 in the fourth match of the season and rarely missed a game from then on, while Chris Lawler and Tommy Smith made their first-team debuts. It was Lewis's and Alan A'Court's final season.

## No deterioration in our relations—says chairman Mr T. V. Williams

**17 May 1963**

### We still get on well says chairman

A subject dominating the Press comment during Bill Shankly's early days was linked with his insistence of working without a contract. It was a topic of much debate in the close season of 1963. Having been offered a deal two months earlier, Shankly had decided not to sign.

He told the Liverpool Daily Post: "I considered the contract was totally unsuitable. That's why I have not signed it. I am not tied to Liverpool, of course."

This was a surprise

'RATHER THAN STAND AROUND AND CHIT CHAT WITH THE ADULTS (CHIT CHAT WAS NOT HIS SPECIALITY), MY GRANDDAD PREFERRED TO GRAB THE KIDS AND TAKE THEM OFF TO THE NEAREST ICE-CREAM PARLOUR'

development, for when it was revealed that a move was afoot to secure Mr Shankly's services for the next three years, it was hailed with great satisfaction by the supporters who already held the Scot in the highest esteem.'

Post reporter Horace Yates claimed: 'Mr. Shankly would have been happier had there been no revelation that a contract was even under discussion. Before arriving at his decision Mr Shankly took legal advice. His attitude runs true to form, for I remember him telling me when first he was appointed, that he had never had a contract and did not want one.'

Shankly's view was simple and straightforward. "If Liverpool don't like me they can sack me and if I don't like them I can go. That is the sort of freedom which suits me best."

Chairman Mr T.V. Williams said: "It is a matter entirely for Mr. Shankly. He has had a copy of the contract in his possession for some time now, and we believe it is what he asked for."

"The terms appeared satisfactory to us all, but when Mr Shankly saw the terms in black and white, he said he was not keen on signing anything.

"He had never wanted a contract before and when it came to the signing he decided he still did not like the idea. We have left it to him."

**20 May 1963**

## Shankly turns down new contract

The local Press seemed preoccupied by the manager's ongoing reluctance to sign a new deal. The Liverpool Echo reported:

'One wonders just how Mr Shankly's refusal to sign a contract at Liverpool may affect his career. It's a brave man who does not want contract security in 1963. The Liverpool manager is clearly content to be judged on results and to be in a position in which he can elect to leave if he

Often, on a family occasion for example, rather than stand around and chit chat with the adults (chit chat was not his speciality), my granddad preferred to grab the kids and take them off to the nearest ice-cream parlour to indulge them and himself in perhaps the only vice he had; Italian ice-cream!

He was also one of those adults who noticed children's moods and was concerned if they appeared to be upset or sad. He was no advocate of the maxim "children should be seen but not heard".

He wanted to listen if they had a problem. If it was in his power he would try to make them feel better.

Often, just his presence was enough to "soothe", as my sister Pauline and I once discovered for ourselves. I was 11 at the time and, in hot pursuit of my sister, had gone flying through the glass in the back door of our house in Yew Tree Lane. So now we were in the outpatients' department of Alder Hey Hospital; me with a chunk of skin hanging from my elbow and my prey, Pauline, requiring a couple of stitches in her head due to flying glass.

My granddad had been summoned to rush us to the hospital in his car, and was pacing up and down impatiently, cursing mildly. A little aside at this point to explain the mild

cursing: I'm sure you've probably read about or heard about his "inhumane" reactions when players got injured.

Players talk about him becoming annoyed or even ignoring them if they'd come a cropper on the field, well we knew exactly how it felt. He was not sympathetic in the face of injury.

Well, back to Alder Hey Hospital outpatients. As we were sitting waiting to be seen by the doctor, a young boy of about 12 or 13 was wheeled in on a stretcher, with a railing spike protruding from his stomach.

The boy was obviously in immense pain and understandably so; he had fallen from a tree right onto the spike. Nurses fussed around him trying to make him comfortable, but to no avail. As soon as his eyes rested on my granddad however, the change was unbelievable. His face lit up, all pain was instantly forgotten.

I'll never forget it. The boy just forgot about his gory injury, asked to be wheeled over to Mr Shankly and for the next half hour my granddad chatted and comforted the delighted little boy, who in his extreme misfortune felt like the luckiest boy in the world.

Inevitably, our trifling injuries were forgotten.

Kop heroes: With 'Sir' Roger Hunt at Anfield, 1972

# The songs that inspired Shanks going into battle

Music man: At Radio City in 1975

feels unhappy. There are some plum managerial jobs coming up within the next few weeks, and if some club does not try to tempt Mr Shankly to their aid then we shall be surprised.'

### 23 August 1963

### Why I signed up for five years at Anfield

Incredibly, it would be nearly four years before the contract issue was settled. The Liverpool Daily Post reported Shankly's reaction:

'I suppose it is the modern trend to have agreements such as this, and I have simply fallen into line.'

He revealed that the agreement was reached at a meeting of the directors, with the proviso that it should be left to him to decide the time to announce it. "I have said nothing before," added Mr. Shankly, "because there were several little points to be cleared up and now

Pledging his future: The Echo story

that everything is settled I don't mind anybody knowing I intend staying at Liverpool, which has become my second home.

"The atmosphere could not have been happier when we shook hands on the deal. During

M y granddad was a creature of habit. I suppose when you're putting all your energy into your work, things have to run smoothly and efficiently behind the scenes. No upheaval, no unpleasant surprises, just comforting familiarity. Every night he would go through the same ritual.

The last thing before he went to bed he would set the breakfast table in the front room, even pouring the orange juice, in readiness for the following morning. He couldn't wait to be up and out first thing. Holidays were always taken in the same place, the same hotel; The Norbreck Castle Hotel, Blackpool.

Of course for a man who lives and breathes football there was no

the last four or five months it would be idle to pretend that there had not been some uneasy moments, but all that is a thing of the past and we go forward now into a new era."

The Post added: 'We have reason to believe that only a few weeks ago the management of the Nottingham Forest club was Mr Shankly's for the taking, but Liverpool has become so much part of his life that he turned it down.'

The man himself said: "Deep down in my heart I never wanted to leave Liverpool. I have been completely captivated by the Anfield atmosphere without an equal anywhere in the country. We have the finest supporters and I always like to regard myself as just one of them. I share their feelings, hopes and ambitions.

"My relations with the players and a first-rate staff have always been of the best, and I look forward to spending the happiest years of my life on Merseyside.

"I believe that my job with Liverpool FC has only just started. A lot of work has been done, the spadework, but much more remains to be done. We have to build on the now very substantial foundation.

"I am convinced that they will be one of the truly great clubs of our time. I will never be truly content until Liverpool are undisputed champions of the land, a position I will strive to bring about in the shortest possible time.

"We are making giant strides in that direction and I am not at all unhappy with the prospects which now confront me."

**1963-64**

## To the summit – the First Division crown

Just two years after winning the Second Divison, Shankly led Liverpool to the First Division for the first time in 17 years.

The Reds hit the summit in late November following a win at Manchester United, courtesy of

sunning oneself on the sand, no relaxing walks along the promenade, oh no!

Thankfully the waiters were on hand though, to provide some light entertainment in the form of a game of five-a-side in the hotel car park.

There was no escape from football even on holiday, but then that was the last thing he wanted anyway.

What would he do, what would he talk about without football?

Before a big match he also had his little "rituals"; he would always play the same songs in exactly the same order. The order of the songs is no longer known, but the songs themselves were Jim Reeves "I Love You Because"; Tom Jones "The Green Green Grass Of Home"; Ray Charles "Take These Chains From My Heart"; Englebert Humperdink

"Please Release Me"; Peters and Lee "Welcome Home"; Judy Collins "Amazing Grace" and last, but not least, Gerry Marsden "You'll Never Walk Alone", which I'm certain was the song he listened to last.

This was his psychological preparation before an important match. Music was a very integral part of his life, it lifted him up, gave him the inspiration that he needed and reflected the passion that he felt.

It was very fitting therefore, that the rise of Liverpool Football Club should coincide with the meteoric rise to fame of the Merseyside Sound and even more fitting that inspiring football should be played for the first time at Anfield, against a backdrop of rousing contemporary chants.

It was a perfect combination and one that my granddad fully appreciated.

Kop idol: Cilla Black makes a hit with Bill Shankly at Melwood

Tuned in: The young Shanks listens to the radio

When people think of the song 'You'll Never Walk Alone' they can hear it booming out of the terraces or gathering momentum and bursting from the Kop.

For the supporters it's their anthem, it unites them.

For the players it's always a motivating force, a metaphorical pat on the back in times of victory, sometimes a consolatory one in times of defeat.

When I think of that song I can only ever hear it being sung in Liverpool Cathedral on Sunday November 22nd 1981, sung in a way it had never been sung before: a haunting tribute which filled that vast cathedral with passion and simplicity, the embodiment of my granddad.

I can never listen to that song without being swept back to that day.

I can hear Gerry Marsden's melancholic voice injecting those words with new meaning and remember how our hearts were ready to burst with sadness at the realisation that, at least literally speaking, we would be walking alone from now on.

> Ron Yeats' strike.
Having contested the leadership with Tottenham, United and Everton for the remainder of the campaign, a crushing 5-0 victory over Arsenal on April 18 – their seventh successive win – confirmed the title.
A winless final three games proved academic, with United finishing four points behind in second.
Legendary marksman 'Sir' Roger Hunt struck 31 of Liverpool's 92 league goals (60 of the total coming at Anfield) with six players, including Hunt, playing 40 or more games. Ian St John (21), Alf Arrowsmith (15) and Ian Callaghan (8) also contributed.
Arrowsmith, who had been given his bow in October 1961 by Shankly (having signed from Ashton United as a 17-year-old) had played only four times up until this season, but scored his goals in only 20 games.

Peter Thompson, in his first season, having joined for £37,000 from Preston in August 1963, played all 42 games – also making his international debut in May 1964.
The man they were to ultimately christen the 'Silent Knight' because of his attacking style from full-back, Chris Lawler, made only six appearances while Tommy Smith did not add to his one game from the previous season.
Jimmy Melia also made the last of his 268 league appearances, losing his place to Arrowsmith – with St John being brought back into midfield by Shankly.

'FOR THE SUPPORTERS IT'S THEIR ANTHEM, IT UNITES THEM. FOR THE PLAYERS IT'S ALWAYS A MOTIVATING FORCE, A METAPHORICAL PAT ON THE BACK IN TIMES OF VICTORY, SOMETIMES A CONSOLATORY ONE IN TIMES OF DEFEAT'

FA Cup success still eluded the Reds though, with Swansea Town causing a shock with a 2-1 quarter-final win at Anfield.

Although the title was sealed against Arsenal, the game before was the signal that here were the champions elect.

Tuesday, April 14th, 1964 saw the Reds make the short distance to Burnley. Backed by 20,000 fans in a crowd of 34,900, two goals from Alf Arrowsmith and one from Ian St John gave Liverpool a 3-0 win.

Afterwards Shankly claimed: "It was fantastic.

"We are elated beyond words. It seems that nothing short of an earthquake can stop us now.

"The pity of it is that we cannot transport Hampden Park to Anfield for Saturday for I am sure all Merseyside will want to be there.

"It is a matter for real regret that so many of our fervent fans will never get near enough to see this game.

"I don't know what time they will start queuing but knowing them nothing would surprise me.

"We aim to beat Arsenal and so win the title without relying on the successes or failures of others, but solely by our own efforts.

"If we win on Saturday, what are the odds against us finishing in a blaze of glory by winning all three away games as well?

"You can bet that will be our goal."

The 5-0 scoreline four days later in front of 48,263 at Anfield could have been different had George Eastham not seen a penalty brilliantly saved by Lawrence with Liverpool only leading 1-0 through St John's early goal at that stage.

As it was, Arrowsmith added a second before the break and Thompson (2) and Hunt on the hour made the final 30 minutes into a procession.

Ian Callaghan, the only forward not to have found the target, also saw a spot-kick stopped by Furnell – but it proved academic in the end.

'Pass to a red shirt!': Shanks kept his first-team meeting simple

# 'Your daughter is

The 1964-65 season was an extremely memorable one for my granddad. First Liverpool won the FA Cup for the first time ever and then, when the season ended, I was born! In 1965 my dad had been officially welcomed into the Shankly family, marrying my mum, Barbara Shankly.

It had been something of a rollercoaster relationship; they had been dating on and off since their mid-teens. At the time, Victor Gill was an aspiring footballer, who had played for the Liverpool Juniors from

1957 to 1962. He too was something of a football nut. He remembers Melwood training ground when it was just "a shed" and actually recalls his first auspicious meeting with the new boss, Bill Shankly, on 15th December 1959.

He had changed into his training gear and gone downstairs to the toilets to relieve himself, when he noticed a fit middle-aged man, decked out in a red tracksuit beside him.

"How old are you, son?" the man had asked.

### Wembley heroes win first FA Cup

Although the champions failed to match the previous season's league exertions, finishing seventh, there was at last success for the first time in the FA Cup. West Brom, Stockport, Bolton, Leicester and Chelsea were beaten, before Liverpool overcame Leeds United 2-1 after extra time at Wembley.

That triumph also came three days before the European Cup semi-final tie against Inter Milan – the club's first season in European football. Having despatched KR Reykjavik, Anderlecht, FC Cologne (on the toss of a coin after a third match on neutral ground in Rotterdam ended level), the Reds won 3-1 in the first leg at Anfield – only to go down 3-0 in Milan eight days later on May 12.

In terms of personnel, the Liverpool first team was generally unchanged. Gordon Wallace (for Melia) and Phil

Chisnall, a signing from Manchester United the previous April and in for the injured St John, started in the team that beat Arsenal 3-2 on August 22nd, 1964. The match was the highlight of the very first edition of the BBC's Match of the Day programme. Indeed, Wallace scored twice (adding to the two goals he scored in the club's first-ever European game against ▶

# pregnant, Shanks!'

"16, sir" came the reply

"Aye, yer a big lad for 16" quipped my granddad as he strode off, leaving my dad thinking to himself: "Bloody hell, they're signing some old players."

Back up on the field, they jogged off for a few laps of the ground, chatting as they went. By this time the rest of the lads had turned up to train and my dad had gone over to chat to them. At this point Eli had approached him and teasingly called him a "big suck!"

"Why?" my dad had asked.

"Sucking up to the new manager. That's the new boss, Bill Shankly."

The following week they were playing a midweek match at Bloomfield Road, Blackpool. The line up included Tommy Lawrence, Tommy Smith, Ian Callaghan, Willie Carlin, Frank Twist and a few other very good players.

While they were changing, Tom Bush, who was in charge of the team that night, said:

"The new boss is coming to watch and he's going to say a few words before you go out."

KR Reykjavik). He lost his place in late September and it proved his only season in the first team at the club. Likewise Chisnall found the target in Iceland.

Tommy Smith was given four games at centre-forward. He scored twice, having been brought in for Chisnall (who lasted only two league games – despite also playing in Iceland). Smith came back into the team in December, playing at centre-half, centre-forward and inside forward, clocking up 25 appearances and four goals.

Chris Lawler also established himself with 33 appearances, and £40,000 signing from Arsenal, utility man Geoff Strong, was given 13 games. Shankly used 22 players – handing debuts (and their only Liverpool first-team appearances) to goalkeeper Bill Molyneux, Tom Lowry, Alan Hignett and John Sealey (who scored the second goal) in the final League game of the season at Wolves, a 3-1 win.

This game also saw Ronnie Moran make his final appearance, having lost his place to Lawler while apart from Hunt (25 goals in 40 games), no Liverpool player made it into double figures.

Final mention must go to Bobby Graham, who two months before his 20th birthday, in September against Aston Villa,

scored a hat-trick on his debut in a 5-1 win. He would play little until the 1969/70 campaign.

Having been held to a 2-2 draw by West Ham in the Charity Shield on the Saturday, Liverpool travelled to Iceland to make their debut in European competition. The European Cup preliminary round, first-leg tie was played on the Monday night. Only 1,000 tickets had been sold on the Monday, according to Horace Yates in the Liverpool Echo and Evening Express, although the

Wedding day: My dad married mum with Grandy's blessing

## 'WHEN MY DAD HAD DISCOVERED THAT BARBARA WAS PREGNANT, IN THE DECEMBER OF 1964, HE WAS QUIVERING IN HIS BOOTS ABOUT BREAKING THE NEWS TO BILL'

This was a big surprise to the players, who in the previous years had rarely seen former boss Phil Taylor, let alone spoken to him.

The new man's words of wisdom that night had been: "OK lads, keep it simple and pass to a red shirt." They did, and won 3-2. That was of course their first taste of the famous Shankly philosophy.

As my dad says about that time: "I think it's safe to say that all the part time and amateur players on Liverpool's books at that time were more than a little surprised to have the boss run our training sessions and talk to us; it had never happened before. Now training sessions were enjoyable and there was lots of ball play. We could even talk to the boss now, just like the first teamers. It was a great boost to morale."

My dad was struck by many things about his prospective father-in-law. First was his complete dedication to his art. Even important family occasions, like a wedding for example, came second.

Grandy's own wedding had been carefully engineered to take place at the end of June so as not to clash with the football season. My mum and dad's wedding took place on January 23rd, 1965 at 10 o'clock in the morning. "Why so early in the morning?" I hear you ask. People don't usually get married at that time of the morning, do they?

Well, not unless you're Bill Shankly's daughter. You see it's quite simple; Liverpool were playing Everton at Goodison that day and one guest in particular had no intention of missing the match.

I was also present on that day, but a well concealed presence. That had been difficult news to break to the boss! When my dad had discovered that Barbara was pregnant, in the December of 1964, he was quivering in his boots about breaking the news to Bill.

Liverpool had been playing Stoke City in an away game and my dad was waiting at Bellefield Avenue to welcome Mr Shankly with the news. My dad remembers that the first thing Bill had done when he walked through the door had been to give him two big loaves of bread. You see there was a bread strike on in Liverpool at the time and you couldn't get a loaf for love nor money.

My dad remembers thinking, 'What a nice man. To think of my family when he must have a million things on his mind. But how the f*** am I going to tell him about the pregnancy now?'

Anyway, not feeling up to the task ahead of him, Ness had stepped in to deliver the news. There was an ominous silence as Mr Shankly paced up and down behind the settee my dad was sitting on. My dad had braced himself for a punch in the back of the head or at least, having the bread snatched back off him! But my granddad just said: "It happens to the best of families," simple, just like his approach to football.

A month later at the wedding reception my dad was warmly

> prices of £1 for seating and 3s (15p) for children meant the home side would be boosted by around £5,000 in time for the return at Anfield. An Icelandic official summed up their expectations thus:

"This is the end of the road into Europe for us, but with such opponents it will all have been worthwhile. We could not have

chosen more desirable opposition. We expect to receive a football lesson."

Shankly had admitted beforehand that he had not seen the amateur side play (it was also their first venture into European competition), although he had talked to people who had played against them. Of the party of 21, 14 were players while Alf Arrowsmith was left out due to injury (as was Ian St John, who was recovering from an appendix operation).

The 5-0 defeat was felt something of a moral victory for the home side, who even at four goals behind, retained their rigid ploy of keeping 10 or 11 men behind the ball. That said, the Daily Post's Horace Yates noted in his summing up on the Tuesday that 'the North Wales enthusiast at the match may have put the issue in proper perspective when he asked: "Do you think Borough United could have held this team?"'

It was also noted that 'Liverpool were sportingly labelled "one of the three best teams to visit Iceland", being ranked with the West German national side and Moscow Dynamo.' Indeed, some of the

**Holding court: Shanks with fans at the Vines pub in Lime Street**

players thought the Reds were the best team they had ever faced.

Peter Thompson was singled out as the man-of-the-match, with Wallace (2), Hunt (2) – his second a 35-yarder - and Chisnall the scorers in front of 10,000 fans.

With the build-up to the FA Cup final, it was easy to forget that following the final on Saturday, May 1st, Liverpool had the small matter of a European Cup semi-final first leg to contest against Inter Milan at Anfield on the Tuesday.

The preview by Leslie Edwards in the Liverpool Echo and Evening Express the Thursday before referred to Inter's ruthless defensive tactics – and the threat of No 10 Luis Suarez. It was to be a busy few days for the club, with the final on Saturday and homecoming on Sunday – plus Chris Lawler's wedding on the Monday morning ahead of Tuesday night's match against the Italians (a Cup replay would also have been played on the Thursday).

The message relayed from the team ahead of the final was: 'We're going to bring the Cup back to Liverpool.' Despite intensive treatment, Gordon Milne missed out due to a knee injury with Geoff Strong coming in

although reporter Michael Charters did relay reports of a defeat for Shankly before the final:

'I acted as referee and timekeeper for a four-a-side session with the four reserves – Arrowsmith, Chisnall, Moran and Molyneux – facing the executive

Manager of the Month: But Shanks was not one for extravagant rewards

welcomed into the family and in my granddad's short speech he claimed that it was "the best transfer deal I've ever done!"

Bill Shankly's loyalty was another thing that made a big impression on his new son-in-law. Often Sunday afternoons were spent round at the Shankly household for Sunday lunch. After lunch the men would sit around talking football and drinking tea.

One particular Sunday, towards the end of the 65-66 season, Liverpool had played Arsenal at Anfield the day before. With about 10 minutes to go and with Liverpool 3-1 up, Tommy Lawrence suddenly made a terrible mistake and Arsenal scored to make it 3-2. My dad had brought the matter up in the after-lunch conversation and my granddad

had snarled: "Aye son, if I'd had a sniper's rifle I'd have shot the bastard!" (meaning Tommy Lawrence one would assume).

Just then the telephone had rung and Bill answered it. The person on the other end was Colin Wood from one of the national papers, presumably broaching the same subject my dad had only minutes before. My dad was more than a little surprised by the strident response, "Nah, nah Colin, Tommy's the finest goalkeeper in the worrrld!!" He might have been seething within, but he wasn't going to bad mouth one of his players or allow anyone from the Press to do so.

If anyone asked me to add to my granddad's list of qualities, I'd have to mention his generosity. It's one of

department of Bill Shankly, Reuben Bennett, Bob Paisley and Joe Fagan.

'This was really a light-hearted frolic, but they put a good deal into it and the score, for the record, was a win for the Arrowsmith boys by a hotly-disputed 3-1 margin.'

An additional aside ahead of the Wembley final was the failure of a police motorcycle escort to meet the team en route to the stadium. As a result, Shankly ordered the coach to carry on and after meeting heavy traffic, a sole police motor-cyclist was spotted, with trainer Bob Paisley leaving the coach to ask him to help them to the stadium – the team arriving just on 2 o'clock.

The 2-1 extra-time victory has been well documented, as has the bravery of Gerry Byrne, who damaged his collar bone after a collision with Bobby Collins after only five minutes – but carried on to play his part. The win was deserved, with the Reds playing the better football.

Sunday saw the victorious homecoming, with an estimated 250,000 packing the city centre. Shankly said: "There has never been a reception like this in the whole history of the game. This has been fantastic – there is no other word for it. I have been in football all my life and had my ups and downs and played in Cup finals both losing and winning. This, without doubt, is the happiest moment of my life. I am not happy just for myself but for my players and club. No manager had a greater bunch of players."

The Tuesday night was declared to be the greatest triumph of the season by Michael Charters – despite the Cup win days earlier. The European Cup semi-final first leg against Inter Milan at Anfield saw Liverpool

'HIS REWARD WAS SEEING THE TEAM HE LOVED AND HAD BUILT UP, FINALLY REACHING THE POSITION THEY DESERVED. HIS REWARD WAS THE LOVE AND RESPECT OF THE PEOPLE AROUND HIM. HE WOULD HAVE VERY HAPPILY DONE HIS JOB FOR FREE'

the things that stood out about him. My granddad never made millions like the managers of today and to be quite honest he didn't see money as the reward for what he did. His reward was seeing the team he loved and had built up, finally reaching the

position they deserved. His reward was the love and respect of the people around him. He would have very happily done his job for free.

Of course in comparison with other professions at the time, he earned a very respectable wage.

claim a deserved 3-1 win – it could have been 6-1 according to the report – against the Italians who at that time were world club and European champions.

The 54,082 crowd saw the Italians take to the pitch first before the injured Gordon Milne and Gerry Byrne entered the pitch with the FA Cup.

For the record Roger Hunt (4), Ian Callaghan (34) and Ian St John (75) were the scorers, with Mazzola (10) netting an away goal. Chris Lawler also saw a goal chalked off at 2-1, having scored with a left-foot shot following a 40-yard run – Austrian referee Karl Keiner making the decision that a Liverpool player standing near the penalty spot was offside (the linesman did not flag).

Missed chances and the goal being disallowed would prove key in the second leg, played on Wednesday, 12th May. A rowdy welcome came from some local fans, although the main problem for Shankly proved to be a local church clock that even he couldn't manage to get stopped throughout the night before the vital second-leg tie.

Unfortunately, the Reds went down to a 3-0 defeat in front of 90,000 fans. Weak refereeing from Spaniard Orziz de Mendeselle was cited a factor in Michael Charters' report, apparently allowing one debatable goal while generally

**Milan: Controversy**

favouring the home side. Inter were given 20 free-kicks for fouls, Liverpool were given three (within eight minutes Liverpool had been penalised six times). From one of them (awarded when it appeared the ball had been won), Corso

Posing for a summertime snap in the garden - mum holds baby Emma. Seated next to her is her sister Jeanette. That's me (left) with my sister Pauline (right). Looking on with Grandy and nan are David Parry and Geoff Carline

Let's not exaggerate and make him out to be a pauper. But money for him was a tool with which to help other people who were less fortunate than himself. He was always giving money away or giving people things he thought they might need. I'm sure there are enough "ticket stories" to fill this book.

Whenever he used to come and pick my sister and I up from school, he would always stuff £10 notes into our hands, saying "Get yerselves a wee something with that" (£10 was a small fortune to a young teenager in the late 1970's). If you ever mentioned that you liked something he had, chances are you'd end up getting it.

I'll never forget a chic, black leather, three-piece suite which adorned the Shankly living room for many a year.

It had been an expensive buy, a rare concession to luxury, but it was getting old and starting to crack in places. The right-hand armrest on the arm chair was very worn and ready to drop off.

That was the chair my granddad

would always sit in to watch the TV and the arm was used to rest on, while he religiously filled in his football coupons every week.

One day a great family friend of ours and my godfather, Colin Taylor, made some admiring comments about the suite.

A few days later when he returned home from work, Colin was startled to find two suites crowding his living room.

My granddad had sent him the leather one. I was talking to Colin recently on the phone and he informed me that up until six months ago the suite had been in the possession of his son, Michael, who had had it all repaired except for the loose armrest.

While we were chatting on the phone Colin told me another story which brought a smile to my face.

One Sunday afternoon in the mid 1970s, Colin and his sons walked into the kitchen of Bellefield Avenue to be confronted with an extraordinary sight.

There was none other than Bill Shankly, wearing an apron and yellow rubber gloves. What a sight to behold.

He was cleaning the Shankly silverware which consisted of shields, cups and various other "trinkets". Michael, the son, stood admiring one of the shields on the work top (It was the 1964-65 FA Cup winners shield).

"Take it son; it'll save me having to clean it!"

Needless to say, Michael still has the shield in his possession.

opened the scoring.

A minute later came the goal that so incensed the Reds.

'Peiro chased a through ball which was too fast for him and Lawrence came out to the edge of the penalty area to intercept.

'Lawrence actually put one foot outside the line while he was holding the ball, but the referee ignored it and the goalkeeper moved along the line, bouncing the ball.

'Peiro, who had gone yards past him, came from behind to challenge, kicked the ball out of Lawrence's grasp and then cracked it into the empty net from the edge of the area.

'The Liverpool players protested as they did so often during the game, and indicated to the referee that the linesman had flagged offside against Peiro.

'As I saw it Peiro was not only offside, but had also fouled Lawrence.'

Afterwards Shankly said of the incident: "Above all things in Continental football you expect to get protection for the goalkeeper.

"The referee never protected Lawrence in this case and Peiro kicked him on the arm to get possession of the ball.

"The goal was a disgrace."

The third and decisive goal, scored by left-back Facchetti after 62 minutes, proved too much for off-form Liverpool to deal with.

It had been their 17th cup tie of the season – and it was only the first occasion they had ended on the losing side.

Afterwards Shankly also told reporters: "There was a lot at stake and neither team had a good game.

"The second goal was the decisive one. The referee should not have allowed it. Centre-forward Peiro was clearly in an offside position when he scored.

"He was behind goalie Lawrence when he snatched the ball from him and turned about to kick it in.

"Peiro also hit Lawrence on his arm as he shot at the ball the goalie was then holding."

**All for one: Shanks (left) as a young boy. People in the mining communities like Glenbuck pulled together**

## ◢ 1965/66

### Second title in the space of three years

The previous season's League disappointment was swept aside as Liverpool secured their seventh championship title for the second time in three years, finishing six points ahead of Leeds United with the best defensive record in the division (the 34 goals conceded was their best since 1923).

Again consistency of selection proved key, with only 14 players used – reflected in the fact that nine of the squad played 40 games or more (this included Tommy Smith, mainly in the No 10 shirt). Roger Hunt (29 goals), Ian St John (10 goals) and Gordon Milne (7 goals) took most of the goalscoring burden, while the other 'squad' players used were Geoff Strong (22 appearances), Alf Arrowsmith (5) and Bobby Graham (1).

The Reds also reached their first European final in the European Cup Winners' Cup. Juventus, Standard Liege, Honved and Celtic were beaten but Borussia Dortmund proved a step too far, as despite Roger Hunt's goal, the Reds went down 2-1 after extra time in Glasgow.

Incidentally, the FA Cup defence was ended at the first hurdle at the hands of Chelsea.

It was to be a revenge victory over Chelsea that would secure a second First Division title for Shankly. The match, a 2-1 win on Saturday 30th April, had almost been won before the start, with the Anfield visitors lining up in two rows to clap the Liverpool players onto the pitch (Liverpool needed only a point to make sure).

A goalless first half saw Hunt hit the post, but he soon made

# Once upon a time . . . my thumb was hanging off!

My granddad's generosity and kindness was obviously a trait he had inherited from his mother, my great grandmother, Barbara Shankly. She was famous in Glenbuck for her open-handedness and willingness to help. It was a kind of necessity borne of growing up in adverse conditions.

People in the mining communities pulled together and shared things. You gave help to someone one day because the next day you might be in need of help yourself. You shared things in order to survive the hardships; you looked out for each other and worked as a team.

What better training for a footballer? These were the tenets which were to stand him in good stead for his career. These were the

**Young genius: Portrait of Shanks**

tenets he was to live by for the rest of his life. Glenbuck, the lifestyle there and its people were instrumental in moulding Bill Shankly's character. We have them to thank.

Growing up in a small mining village wasn't all hardship and misery, of course. The Shankly children were a lively bunch (all 10 of them), especially the girls, who were always sneaking out to dances while the boys were made to keep watch at home. It was usually their sister Liz's loud laugh, however, that would give the girls away as they crept, giggling, back into the house.

The brothers and sisters were pranksters too. One time they painted spots on my granddad while he was asleep to make him think he'd caught the Measles. You can imagine there would have been some mild cursing when he found out what they'd done. Or there was the time they popped some laxatives into a friend's drink. All good clean fun!

As we know times were hard then and money was difficult to come by, but Bill would always manage to put some of his wages from the pit away, in a box set aside especially for that purpose. The box soon filled up with half crowns and one day he decided to open it up to see what meagre sum he had managed to collect.

To his chagrin, he found that the half crowns had been cunningly replaced with shillings, which weighed more but were obviously worth much less. Again the air would have been tinged a slight shade of blue.

Shanks' old school and Glenbuck neighbour Mary Graham

He had warm memories of those years and he loved to tell us about them. Whenever my sister Pauline and I would spend the night at my nan and granddad's, that's what we looked forward to most . . . the bedtime stories about Glenbuck.

After he'd tucked us up in bed he'd regale us with accounts of trips through the rain and snow on foot to see his favourite Jimmy Cagney film in Muirkirk or tell us about the cycling accident he'd had after hurtling down a hill at breakneck speed.

There was the one about the accident down the pit, when his thumb had got caught between the carts that carried the coal, and he'd had to rush to hospital with his thumb half hanging off.

However many times we heard this one, our faces would always wrinkle up with a mixture of wonderment and disgust as we stared at the scar on the disfigured thumb in question. Just after the stories and the ritual switching off of lights, but before we closed our eyes to dream of bleeding thumbs, Bill would creep back into the room with an old wooden stick used for lifting the loft cover and frighten the life out of us.

He managed every time. Then we would drift off to sleep, dreaming of the old cottage on The Monkey Row with the key always dangling from the front door, of massive stolen bunches of bananas that took five people to carry and of illegal card games going on down in the woods of Glenbuck.

amends three minutes after the break courtesy of a slight deflection off Dunn. Murray levelled on 62 and Chelsea started to look more menacing – before Hunt struck again seven minutes later to ensure Liverpool achieved their goal in front of 53,754 fans.

The celebrations that followed revolved around a replica trophy, as the Football League would only 'release' the real thing when the title was decided. The celebrations encouraged Blues boss Tommy Docherty to hail the Anfield faithful: "Liverpool are a great side. Their record over the past four years speaks for itself and their support is the best in the world."

Unfortunately there was heartache at Hampden Park the following Thursday. Favourites to beat Borussia Dortmund in the European Cup Winners' Cup final, Michael Charters' report declared that Liverpool had lost to a 'flukey goal' in extra time, with Liverpool doing most of the attacking. Hunt fluffed a one-on-one chance near the end of normal time with the score at 1-1.

Held had given the Germans the lead, finishing off an incisive attack just after the hour mark before Hunt (who was suffering with an ankle injury) levelled on 68. But from their only attack in extra time, Dortmund won it two minutes into the second half of extra time. With Held racing through Lawrence came out to block bravely. The ball fell to Libuda 40 yards out, who lobbed it goalwards. Yeats, racing back to block, was unfortunate that the ball hit the inside of an upright and then bounced onto him and into the net.

Shankly later said: "We were beaten by a team of frightened men. It was obviously their plan from the start simply to keep us in subjection. They had no real attacking plan, but they won and I am quite sincere when I say they are the worst team we met in the competition this season.

"Standard Liege, for instance, are a much better team than

'WHENEVER MY SISTER PAULINE AND I WOULD SPEND THE NIGHT AT MY NAN AND GRANDDAD'S, THAT'S WHAT WE LOOKED FORWARD TO MOST . . . THE BEDTIME STORIES ABOUT GLENBUCK'

Borussia.

"If Tommy Smith and Roger Hunt had been fully fit we would have won easily."

## 1966/67

### Fairs Cup consolation for league slide

Liverpool finished nine points behind champions Manchester United, a distant fifth in the table – winning only one of their last 5 League games which included a 3-1 Anfield defeat to rock-bottom Blackpool on the final day (one of only two at home that season).

However, Liverpool did qualify for the European Fairs Cup as a result.

There was also disappointment in the cup competitions.

Ajax proved too strong in the European Cup, with Liverpool going out 7-3 on aggregate in round one (which included a 5-1 humiliation in Amsterdam) while local rivals Everton knocked the Reds out 1-0 in the FA Cup fifth round – watched by over 100,000 people (which included over 40,000 watching on big screens at Anfield).

Nine players made 39 League appearances or more, although Gerry Byrne, an ever present the previous season, made only nine appearances.

Goals were shared around more, with Roger Hunt (14), Geoff Strong (11), Peter Thompson (10) and Ian St John (9) top scorers while Ian Ross, David Wilson (his only appearance) and Emlyn Hughes were given debuts.

Indeed, Hughes, who started out for the Reds as a midfielder following his £65,000 move from Blackpool the previous month, played 10 games during that campaign.

It was in the fifth of those, a 3-1 home victory over Newcastle United, that he earned the nickname 'Crazy Horse' after he rugby-tackled the Magpies' Albert Bennett, who was slipping through his grasp.

'GREAT GRANDDAD JOHN SHANKLY'S INFLUENCE ON HIS SON CANNOT BE UNDERESTIMATED. AS YOU MAY ALREADY KNOW HIS FATHER WAS A TAILOR OF SOME REPUTE AND SET GREAT STORE BY APPEARANCE'

My great grandmother Barbara Blyth Shankly was an extremely house-proud woman. Everything in the Auchenstilloch cottage was spick and span. Nothing out of place. Bill Shankly was to inherit this quality and in turn pass it down to the next generations. You have already heard of the famous scrubbing of the oven and polishing of the silverware but you have yet to hear of the infamous picking up of fluff from the carpet.

No, seriously, this habit reached almost pathological proportions. When he was supposed to be relaxing at home, he was in fact engaged in a vicious never ending battle with . . . dirt! He would spend a major part of his time at home bending down to pick up offending pieces of fluff or

Appearance matters: Shanks was always well groomed as a young man

### 11 May 1967

## Shankly to live here for good

In May 1967, Daily Post correspondent Horace Yates spoke to Bill Shankly when news broke that he was to sign a new five-year contract, despite his present deal still having 12 months to run.

The Reds' boss said: "Come what may, whether or not I am still associated with Liverpool Football Club after that time it would seem that my wife and I will spend the rest of our days in Liverpool. We have been made to feel at home here. We like the place and can see no reason for going elsewhere.

"I am not playing with words when I say we have the most loyal supporters in the world. That is a challenge – to look after them. If they are happy, the players are happy, the club are successful and that is the sort of dividend I seek for my labours. I have never cheated the fans. Nor do I intend to do. They deserve the best and no man can strive harder to give them just that than I am seeking to do."

### 1967/68

## Prolific Hunt helps Reds close the gap

There was an improvement in the League, with the Reds finishing in third, just three points behind champions Manchester City and a point behind runners-up Manchester United. Along with Everton, Liverpool had the best defensive record in the division while Roger Hunt was again top scorer, with 25 goals in 40 games.

In terms of the squad for that season, Tony Hateley was the main change, being signed for a club record £96,000 from Chelsea in the summer of 1967 – he contributed 16 goals, 27 in all competitions.

Another summer addition was

any other undesirable object in his path.

Of course the house was spotless. He himself had probably just given the carpet a vigorous (and vigorous is the operative word) vacuum. He wanted nothing less than absolute cleanliness. (As an aside, both of his daughters, Barbara and Jean had and still have the imaginary fluff picking

habit and if the truth be known I'm rather partial to it myself). You can now see why standards were hastily raised at both Anfield and Melwood. He would simply not abide unhygienic conditions.

Of course great granddad John Shankly's influence on his son cannot be overlooked or underestimated. As you may already know his father was

goalkeeper Ray Clemence, who joined from Scunthorpe United – although it would be January 1970 before he made his League debut.

The season saw debuts for Doug Livermore, who came up through the junior ranks (one of only 18 games for the club) and Peter Wall (signed from Wrexham in October 1966), while Willie Stevenson made his final appearance before moving onto Stoke City in December 1967.

In the cups there was defeat in the League Cup (having returned to the competition after seven years) to Bolton in round two and to Ferencvaros in the third round of the Fairs Cup – while eventual winners West Brom shocked the Reds in the FA Cup semi-final replay at Maine Road.

## 1968/69

### Rock-solid defence as Reds finish second

Liverpool edged a step closer to a third championship success under Shankly, finishing second to Don Revie's Leeds (six points behind). Liverpool again had the best defence in Division One, conceding just 24 goals aided by the ever-present run of full-back Chris Lawler and central defender Tommy Smith.

A further six players made 38 appearances or more, while Alun Evans came into the team, scoring on his debut in a 4-0 defeat of Leicester City (all four goals being scored in the first 12 minutes). Shankly paid Wolves £100,000 for the 19-year-old, having sold Tony Hateley almost immediately.

Gerry Byrne made the last of his 274 League appearances while Brian Hall made the first of

a tailor of some repute and set great store by appearance.

The whole family was always well turned out even if money was hard to come by. Photographs taken of him when he was a boy show a waist-coated, well-dressed and well-groomed lad. Forever after, wherever he went, except when he was kitted out in his red tracksuit, he was always impeccably dressed.

His suits were all tailor made of the finest quality fabric. Neither was he averse to making a fashion statement, often combining a brightly coloured shirt with a jazzy tie for example.

The outfit was always set off with a pair of the best quality Italian leather shoes, so well polished that you could definitely see your reflection in them. He always did the polishing himself; nobody else could get it quite right.

This obsession with perfection was often carried to extremes. Once, my aunty Jean had bought a pair of shiny patent leather shoes.

They were her pride and joy, but not for long.

Bill decided they needed a good polish and proceeded to polish them so vigorously there was no shine left

on them. Needless to say after that we kept all of our shoes well hidden just in case!

Another quirk of his directly handed down from his father John was that buttons always had to be well secured on shirts, coats and the like.

He would spend a lot of time, armed with his needle and thread tightly sewing buttons onto his own and the family's clothes.

Jean will never forget a great new coat of hers that had had the buttons so tightly sewn on, it was impossible for her to fasten and she had spent a cold winter night out with her friends shivering to death. (Unfortunately this flair for needlework was never passed down to my mum or me.

I spent many a needlework class unpicking items that had inadvertently been sewn onto my skirt and once, I made a hideous brown skirt for nanny Ness, which though she graciously accepted, she had the good sense never to wear).

Despite his unquestionable ability in all matters concerning football it was a totally different ball game when it came to domestic affairs.

Other epithets spring to mind when we describe Shanks "the handy man".

**Fastidious: Shanks with a cap and medals at home**

Grandy's girls – me and sister Pauline in the garden at Bellefield Avenue, but Grandy was no keen gardener!

# Why Bill and DIY never went hand in hand

When my Grandy wielded a paintbrush everyone would run for cover. Once he took it upon himself to paint the landing ceiling and the loft cover, a day to be remembered as much for the mild cursing as for the white paint which not only adorned the ceiling but the carpet, the stairs and of course, Bill himself.

The paint pot had upturned while he was precariously perched on the ladder covering everything in a sticky, white blanket of stubborn gloss paint which refused to be removed with ease and tiny spots of which stuck to his hair, ears, eyebrows, etcetera for a long time to come. He smelt of turps for quite a while afterwards and the carpet was never quite the same again.

If my memory serves me well, the professionals were always called in after that to undertake any paint jobs

his 155 towards the end of the season. Top scorer Roger Hunt (13 League goals) also broke Gordon Hodgson's club scoring record in January 1969.

The cups saw a fifth-round defeat to Leicester City in the FA Cup, a fourth-round loss to Arsenal in the League Cup, while the toss of a coin saw the Reds bow out to Athletic Bilbao in the first round of the Fairs Cup.

## 1969/70

### All change and Hunting for a new striker

There was a 15-point gap between champions Everton and Liverpool in fifth. Shankly began to make more changes to his team, introducing Ray Clemence for Tommy Lawrence in goal, while Roger Hunt left in December to join Bolton.

Phil Boersma made his debut, although he was one of many strikers who failed to convince following Hunt's departure. Alec Lindsay (signed from Bury for £67,000 in March 1969), Ian Ross, Stephen Peplow, and Doug Livermore were also all tried in the No 8 shirt. That season, it was Bobby Graham who filled Hunt's boots, finishing as top scorer with 13 goals from 42 games – having played only 10 matches in the previous three seasons. Chris Lawler also bagged 10 in 42 games.

Again cup success also eluded Shankly, with the quarter-finals of the FA Cup being the furthest they reached – before a shock defeat at Watford, a result seen as a watershed for Shankly's team of the 60s. Defeats also came to Vitoria Setubal in round two of the Fairs Cup and to Manchester City in round three of the League Cup.

## 1970/71

### Wembley heartbreak against champions

This was another season of 'what ❯

could have been' for Shankly. In the League Liverpool fell short again, finishing fifth although they were unbeaten at home and again had the best defensive record in the division, conceding only 24. It is at the other end where the Reds struggled, scoring only 42 goals (the lowest of the top nine and also lower than third-bottom West Ham).

It could be deemed as another season of transition in terms of personnel also, with Shankly chopping and changing.

Larry Lloyd had been bought from Bristol Rovers in April 1969 after only one season with the lower league club – and replaced Ron Yeats, who himself still managed 12 League appearances at left-back, which proved a problem position (Alec Lindsay played the most games here that season). Kirkby boy John McLaughlin came through to become a regular, making 33 appearances in midfield, having made his debut at the end of the previous season.

Ian St John and Roy Evans did not play again for the Reds after this season while Brian Hall took over as the regular No 11 from Peter Thompson. There were also

**Wembley '71: Not to be**

debuts for Steve Heighway (signed from Skelmersdale United) and John Toshack (a £110,000 signing from Cardiff City in November). Alun Evans was the only player to reach double figures with 10 goals.

Despite these changes, the club did come close to some silverware in the cup competitions. Although there was a third-round exit to Division Two side Swindon Town in the League

RSVP: Shanks took time to reply to fans' letters on his trusty typewriter

that needed doing. Some people probably find DIY very relaxing as it takes their mind off things. My granddad never had that harmonious communion with inanimate objects.

They offered no solace but were in fact, more often than not, the cause for vexation and mild to not so mild cursing. I've read in many books and newspapers about Bill at home, "pottering around in the garden, his second favourite hobby after football" and it always brings a smile to my face. Let's get this straight: he didn't have any other favourite pastimes.

If flowers could express emotion, then I can truly say, without fear of contradiction, that they would have been trembling in their "roots" whenever Bill made his appearance in the garden.

You see he often mistook them for weeds and dealt with them accordingly; that is to say, they were firmly and unceremoniously uprooted unless Nessy was at hand to intervene on their behalf.

To be fair though, he had a flair for mowing the lawn and when he

was through with it, it could compare with the pitch at Anfield. Once upon a time at Bellefield Avenue, pilgrims would trample their way through the front garden to reach their destination and naturally enough this took its toll on the grass.

One day after months of Ness complaining about the fact, Grandy reassured her that he would take care of the matter while she was out shopping. My grandmother was expecting to return and find that new grass had been planted, maybe a few colourful rose bushes thrown in for aesthetic effect. No such nonsense.

The whole front garden had been paved over with flagstones. Much more practical and easier for the fans to negotiate.

One thing that he did enjoy doing when he was at home was replying to fan mail, which there was always an abundance of. He could often be seen at the window in the front room, hammering away (and 'hammering' is the operative word) at his old faithful typewriter.

Since I started writing about my granddad I have been contacted by people who still have letters that they received from him and they all strongly feel that there are not many busy football managers who would take the time to sit down and reply to their fans in person. He has even been known to make a phone call if circumstances required.

I recently received an email from a lady called Jackie Bristow telling me about the time in 1974 when she wrote a letter to my granddad cheekily asking for some tickets for a London game. In her letter she informed Bill that her great granddad Dr. D. Barbour had actually been the doctor responsible for delivering him into the world on September 2nd, 1913 in the "Miner's Row" cottage.

She was amazed to receive a prompt reply and also to learn that her great grandfather had also had a hand in delivering the other nine Shankly siblings.

When you read the reply, you realise just how much he really admired and appreciated his mum.

What has impressed people who came into contact with him the most is Bill Shankly's genuine warmth and humility. These qualities of his were indeed something to be admired.

*These are the qualities I miss most about you, and even though you're no longer here to set an example, I've drawn a lot of inspiration from the memory of you. Having all these people tell me their stories has been such a bitter sweet experience. I now realise just how special you really were but have to suffer the pain of losing you all over again.*

Family values: At home with mum, dad and one of his brothers

'PEOPLE WERE OF THE UTMOST IMPORTANCE TO MY GRANDFATHER. THE FACT THAT A QUARTER OF A CENTURY AFTER HIS DEATH, PEOPLE OF ALL AGES STILL TALK ABOUT HIM WITH SUCH PASSION AND RESPECT IS TRUE TESTIMONY TO HIS GREATNESS'

Cup, Liverpool reached Wembley to face new League champions Arsenal in the FA Cup final, having beaten Everton in the semi-final at Old Trafford.

The same side lined up that had beaten the Toffees, with Alun Evans preferred to Peter Thompson at No 8. The team: Clemence, Lawler, Lindsay, Smith, Lloyd, Hughes, Callaghan, Evans, Heighway, Toshack, Hall.

The team was confirmed by the Wednesday, after five of his players had been picked in Sir Alf Ramsey's latest England squad, with Chris Lawler and Tommy Smith earning long overdue call-ups. It meant that of the Wembley side, only two had yet to receive call-ups for their country at full international level – Alec Lindsay and Brian Hall.

To this Bill Shankly added: "Now England have added a touch of class to the side. And you can take it from me the only defender who hasn't been included, Alec Lindsay, has also got a bit of class.

"Everything Chris and Alec do is right. Every ball they deliver is a pass. They know what they are going to do with the ball before they get it – and that is the essence of class!"

Shankly was pleased with the wet weather on the eve of the game, as it would "soften the pitch up" while he believed "most of these boys are young enough and good enough to come back here once or twice more." He wasn't wrong.

However, on the day it proved a step too far though, with the Gunners clinching their first Double thanks to a Charlie George winner in extra time – the 90 minutes having ended 0-0. Steve Heighway had opened the scoring only 65 seconds into the extra period, before the Reds were stunned by two goals in nine minutes from George Graham (103) and George (112) to clinch only the second Double of the 20th century.

Shankly said afterwards: "The Cup was there for the winning. I thought a break would win it –

and Arsenal got a break for the equaliser. One goal in extra time is enough to win any game. You don't give away goals like that equaliser. Ray Clemence was coming for the ball thinking Tommy Smith was leaving it and Tommy deflected it past him. It hit Graham on the leg and bounced in."

Back in the city on the Sunday, Shankly told the 100,000 crowd at St George's Hall:

"Yesterday at Wembley we lost the Cup. But you the people have won everything."

Europe would also prove a close-run thing with the Reds' Fairs Cup stint ending at the hands of Leeds in the semi-final, 1-0 on aggregate having put out Ferencvaros, Dinamo Bucharest, Hibernian and Bayern Munich in the previous rounds.

**1 May 1971**

### Simplicity – the Shankly recipe for success

In a lengthy article done with the Liverpool Echo's Anfield reporter Chris James in the summer of 1971, Shankly's philosophy for success was highlighted.

He said: "Football is a simple game. To be a player you've got to be able to give a pass and take one. You must have skill. Skill is the ability plus strength."

On diet he said that "a little, but often was his motto when it comes to feeding his players, mostly with steak, toast and honey and jam, and tea."

Simplicity—the Shankly recipe for success

'Skill is the ability to give and take a pass'

Shanks' old driving licence: But he often avoided going behind the wheel

# The prankster and the Inter Milan imposter

Another of his qualities that people found appealing was his childlike enthusiasm and innocence. He was also something of a prankster.

Once, Kenny Quayle, a good friend and neighbour who was often commissioned to drive my granddad around (he himself had a real aversion to driving) recalls that he had received a phone call from Bill asking him if he could drive him to the opening of a Sayers' shop, where he was to be the guest of honour.

Ken, who had just returned from a holiday in Portugal, agreed and off they went. As they were driving along Bill commented on the great tan that Ken had acquired on holiday and then started to giggle to himself.

"When we get there Kenny son, don't say a single word. If anyone speaks to you just make some grunting noises and we'll have some great fun. OK?"

Then he continued to chuckle to himself for the remainder of the journey.

After the official opening rituals, Grandy was invited to make a short speech to the large crowd which had gathered. Towards the end of his speech he made a slight change to the script.

"Ladies and gentlemen, we are extremely honoured to have with us

Fanfare: Popular with the ladies – a bit like 'Traverto' of Inter Milan!

> "Five-a-side is good. You do everything in five-a-side that you do in a proper game so if you can play that well it is only a question of transferring it into a full-scale match. That was the key to Tottenham's success."

James added: 'For Shankly, changes in routine are out. He frowns on golf as a relaxation and criticises clubs who use cross-country runs as a means of building up fitness. The manager was quoted as saying: "You're trying to train footballers to play football not be marathon runners. Football is a game in which you jog for a spell and then sprint. It's all stop-start, stop-start.

"Men who can run a mile probably couldn't last a game of football. Equally, a lot of footballers couldn't run a mile. Each sport has its own training routine and it's wrong to mix them up."

### 3 May 1971

## The arrival of a superstar

The signing of Kevin Keegan was confirmed, with the player himself admitting his surprise that Liverpool had come in for him. After clinching a £35,000

deal with Scunthorpe United, Shankly said: "We've watched him for about nine months. We are pleased. He's our type of player. He's a sturdy little player, quick and strong. He knows the game."

He was to join the squad for their Cup final preparations, and was the third player to sign from the club in recent years after Dick White and Ray Clemence.

today, one of the greatest European footballers alive, 'Traverto of Inter Milan fame'" and he promptly turned to indicate the stunned figure of Kenny Quayle, humble friend and neighbour of Bill Shankly.

Kenny remembers how he spent a good part of the afternoon signing autographs and having his photo taken by some swooning females and making grunting noises!

When the event was over, they were given 12 huge cream sponge cakes to take home.

After wondering how on earth they were going to consume so many cakes, Bill decided the best thing to do was to give them away, so they duly stopped off at 12 different houses on the way home and gave the flabbergasted householders a sponge cake for their tea.

# Flying the flag . . .

## 10 May 1971

### Shanks happy to sign a new contract

Daily Post writer Horace Yates reported that Shankly, still with around 18 months left on his current deal, would be offered a new deal in the near future.

Yates revealed that club chairman Eric Roberts had said: "I have had preliminary talks with Mr Shankly and we hope he will continue with us for a long time. He said he is quite happy to go on working here, and that contracts don't matter, but I hope that if we put a new contract before him he will sign it."

Mr Shankly said: "The happiest and hardest years of my life have been spent here. Only Celtic and Rangers in their pomp could begin to compare with Liverpool, but I don't think I'll be going back to Scotland. I see no reason why I should even think of going to another club."

## 26 June 1971

### Shankly – why I came to Liverpool

Talking to Chris James in the Echo, Shankly said the following:

"It was in the autumn of 1959 that I was given the opportunity of taking over another Second Division club – Liverpool. Financially, there was not much more money in it but what attracted me was the potential of the support.

"For me, the support given to Rangers and Celtic has always been unequalled. But at Anfield I felt that there was potential support to rival even those. And I think the fans have proved it over the last dozen years.

"I felt a challenge to wake up the support that was lying dormant. Here was fanatical support. They only needed a good team to make them the finest supporters in the country.

"That was one of the main reasons I took the job."

Cars were among the inanimate objects with which my granddad had a very special love/hate relationship.

He fully appreciated their usefulness and of course in his line of work they were an absolute necessity but he was just very heavy handed and he detested driving. It was something he avoided at all costs and Kenny Quayle often took on this unpleasant responsibility.

Kenny, now 71 years old, remembers those days with fondness and when we reminisced about the halcyon days at Bellefield Avenue, it was touching to hear the warmth and respect in his voice, even after all these years.

There was something else though, that made an impression on me as we chatted, and that was the pure pleasure and joy that accompanied Kenny's memories. Certain reminiscences caused him to break into a fit of uncontrollable giggles.

He recalls with fondness, the time the gear stick was roughly handled and how it took its revenge by coming off in Bill's hand, ditto the hand brake (on more than one

occasion). Or the time when, en route to see Nessy in hospital, Bill slammed on the brakes so hard at the traffic lights that my mum, Barbara, who was at one point safely ensconced on the back seat, shot out of the back door landing heavily in the middle of the road.

Then to add insult to injury, she was left scratching her head as the unwitting Bill shot off as the lights turned green. My aunt Jean recalls how on that day, my granddad visited Ness on one floor of the hospital, while my mum was treated for her cuts and bruises on the floor below.

Despite his anathema for automobiles, he would trade them in every five years for a newer model (I used to think this was one of his little extravagances, but now realise that it was out of pure necessity, having thoroughly destroyed the previous model). Cars and him just didn't go together and they somehow managed to get him into sticky, embarrassing situations.

There's many an innocent driver out there who's felt the angry lash of Shankly's tongue, or been on the receiving end of a good telling off for

Driven mad by Shanks: Kenny Quayle was there to help

# a pair of knickers

violating some non-existent traffic regulation or other.

Sometimes he'd come home ranting and raving about some absolute idiot who had almost killed him and should not be allowed out on the roads, and somehow or other, we would always learn about the same "idiot" proudly boasting that *he'd* nearly been crashed into by Mr Bill Shankly.

As it was not uncommon for fans to select some part of the car as a souvenir, another tedious chore that Grandy had to carry out regularly was navigating the car up the front path and into the garage.

As you've probably gathered by now, this was not your common or garden garage filled with DIY equipment and pots of paint. It was, in fact, a rather empty little garage boasting a solitary

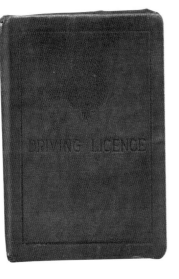

washing line where Ness would hang the laundry in the winter.

One chilly winter morn, Bill drove out of the garage down the path, along Bellefield Avenue as per norm. He did a left at Eaton Road, then a sharp right, stopping at the lights on Town Row, before continuing along Melwood Drive and onto the training ground.

A normal day like any other, you might think, but with one small difference.

On this occasion, he had travelled the whole distance from house to training ground with a pair of his daughter Jean's knickers flying from the car aerial!

(He had unwittingly, sequestered them from the washing line in the garage.)

Shankly preferred being behind the camera rather than the wheel for this picture he took of his friend Albert Bragg during his days as Workington FC boss in 1959. Nessie and daughter Jeanette look on from the doorway

> **9 July 1971**

### We're 'Pro-Liverpool and Anti-Nobody'

In the wake of signing a new three-year deal, the Echo's Chris James reported the following:

'As he left a Press conference, at which the Anfield staff changes were announced, he vowed: "Now, we are going for the big stuff. The League, the European Cup and the FA Cup will do for a start."'

James added that Shankly would have a further option on his contract when the new one expires in May, 1974.

'He was offered a five-year contract, but decided to settle for three. But there is an agreement between Shankly and the Liverpool directors that the job is his as long as he wants it.'

Bill Shankly to-day praises the Anfield training staff —Joe Fagan, Bob Paisley and Reuben Bennett.

The reported changes were the promotion of Bob Paisley from senior trainer to assistant; Joe Fagan, formerly reserve-team trainer, was promoted to the first team; subsequently Ronnie Moran was asked to look after the reserves, having been in charge of the junior teams; while responsibility for the club's youth policy and junior teams went to Tom Saunders. There was a final mention of first-team coach Reuben Bennett, whose new role would mean 'special duties in conjunction with the manager' (assessing opponents and checking recommended players).

Shankly said: "We are trying to build a fortress at Anfield – an impregnable fortress – and we

are nearly there. The Liverpool fans are worthy of that.

"Last season with a team of mere boys we had the greatest average attendance in the League. That is the greatest tribute to those supporters.

"When I first came here, we were in the doldrums. No stone was left unturned. Groundwise, we are now developing and soon it will be worthy of the name.

"We will live on strength not weaknesses. There is nothing for anybody who does not give 100 per cent. We have too many good players around. Our motto is pro-Liverpool, anti-nobody."

**29 July, 1971**

### I will stay manager while I'm fit

Bill Shankly was talking to the Press about his future. He said: "Retirement is something I rarely consider. For me, football is my life, provided I still do my job satisfactorily, and as long as I feel able to carry on.

"It often seems silly to me to say you are such and such an age and therefore you are too old to carry on working and must retire.

"It's that old motto – you're as young as you feel. And that will be one of my yardsticks whenever I come round to thinking about retirement. I will base my decision on two things: (1) my means, and (2) how I feel.

"Basically, any man must go on working until he has earned enough to live independently.

"A lot of publicity is given to the high salaries to be earned in football, not only by players but by managers. But there is not a lot said about the vast tax that has to be paid.

"The higher a person's income, the more severely taxed, with surtax and then supertax following the normal levels of income tax. These taxes mean that someone earning £100 per week, in fact, receives little more than £50 in his pay packet.

"As a result, it is only when you reach the age when you begin to

# Leaving the dog to mind the baby

Anything with four wheels then, was an object of disdain. So too, any four-legged creatures which also seemed to be intent on getting him into trouble.

Nessy had always had a soft spot for the canine species and the young couple owned a dog from the start. After my mum was born (in the same bed as my nan, incidentally) they remained in Glasgow for a while; my granddad was still in the RAF,

stationed at the Bishopbriggs Base.

One day my nan had to go out for a while and left my mum, a mere babe in arms, in the care of my granddad. He was ordered not to leave the baby alone and strict instructions were issued in case of an emergency.

When Ness returned she was appalled to find Bill missing and the baby unattended.

When he eventually returned (he'd been out to put a bet on!) Ness was

consider retirement that you realise the benefit and value of the pension schemes and the like that have been introduced into football in the last 10 years.

"There are not many men in soccer today who can say they have made enough money to retire. So much for means. As far as feeling one's age is concerned, I'm feeling perfectly fit and ready to go on for years yet.

"I train every day and do nothing that is likely to jeopardise

**I will stay manager while I'm fit**

my health. I don't smoke. The only time I drink is for medicinal purposes, when a drop of Scotch will keep out the cold and do me good. As a result, I feel fit and much younger than most people of my age.

"I am well able to continue as manager of Liverpool as long as they are willing to have me.

"Football management can be a soul-destroying profession but I think I am about to achieve what I set out to do when I took over almost 12 years ago. At the beginning of next season, the new main stand will be open.

"It will be a place fit for a king. I will be proud to take anyone into it. It will mean that three sides of the ground have been completely rebuilt, and on the fourth side, the Kop – which must never be rebuilt – we have made improvements.

"When I arrived I aimed to get Liverpool out of the Second Division and win respect for the club at home and abroad in the

**Me as a baby: In the Bellefield Avenue garden with Grandy, Nessie – and the dog!**

quite rightly outraged.

"I thought I specifically told you, not to leave the baby on its own," she yelled. Bill responded in a puzzled voice: "But, she wasn't on her own, the dog was here."

At Bellefield Avenue, my aunty Jean had a woolly black poodle called Scamp. Sadly, he caught a disease which required him to have all his teeth removed and thereafter was unable to eat any solid food. Everybody was upset about it including my granddad. As he put it, "What's the point of living if you can't ever enjoy a plate of solid food?"

After a few weeks the poor dog was a shadow of its former self and Ness was distraught. "What are we going to do Bill?" she asked. "It's

okay, I'll take care of it," he volunteered.

Off he went with Scamp tucked under his arm. I think my nan naively thought he was going to get Scamp some dentures fitted, because she didn't seem unduly concerned when he returned an hour later, empty-handed.

"So where is he then?" she asked. "I had to put him down," he replied, "he's better off. It was the only humane thing to do."

Needless to say it was a few weeks before anyone spoke to him again. He was in the dog house, so to speak. (He actually adored that dog and often took him for a walk along to Everton's training ground, where he would let him run loose around the ground, amongst other things!)

First Division.

"Next was the ground and, after that, another team. I think the end is now in sight.

"But for me the end is not in sight yet. Retirement is something I have not yet considered. While I still feel as fit and able as I do now, I shall go on as manager of Liverpool."

## 1971/72

### Reds edged out in thrilling title finale

One of the tightest top-flight finishes ever ends with a 1-0 defeat at Derby County, and a subsequent final-day 0-0 draw at Arsenal proves decisive.

The Rams surprisingly take the title by a point, with Leeds United, Liverpool and Manchester City all finishing a point behind.

The Reds in third again have the best defensive record, and significantly boost their goals for column with John Toshack (13 goals) and new signing Kevin Keegan (nine goals) establishing a fruitful partnership in attack, while Emlyn Hughes, yet to win silverware in a red shirt, contributed six from midfield.

Eight players made 35 appearances or more while Peter Thompson, John McLaughlin, Ian Ross, Bobby Graham and Alun Evans made their last appearances in a red shirt – while Tommy Lawrence moved on to Tranmere. There was a mid-season cameo from striker Jack Whitham, who scored 6 times in 9 games although injuries would end his career prematurely in 1974 (he had been signed from Sheffield Wednesday in 1970), while there was a first-team debut for Phil Thompson at Manchester United on Easter Monday – a 3-0 win.

The cups would again prove a disappointment, with defeats in the FA Cup (to Leeds United in round four), League Cup (to West Ham in round four) and European Cup Winners' Cup (to Bayern Munich in round two).

Fine young man: An early portrait of Shanks

# How Nessie fell

A certain naive responsibility shines through these stories, which I think was the downside of that precious childlike quality that Bill Shankly possessed.

It was that very quality which allowed him "to find glory in a boy's game" (Hugh McIlvanney).

It was at the very heart of his personality, the source of all his tireless enthusiasm and motivation. Bill Shankly was a boy at heart.

This fact in combination with a streak of stubborn determination meant that he found it very difficult to give up until he got what he wanted.

It is a well-recorded fact that my grandmother was not enthralled by my granddad when she first set eyes on him at Bishopbriggs. In fact, as she would tell us in a conspiratorial whisper, she thought he was a "bloody idiot!"

Apparently, he would turn up out of the blue wherever she was and persistently ask her out on a date, which my nan, equally persistently, refused. One day when she went home, she was met at the door by her dad.

"Someone called Bill is here for you," he informed her.

Lo and behold, there he was, sitting comfortably in her front room, having a cup of tea and chatting away to her mum.

He had decided that if she wasn't going to agree to a date, he might have more luck by going over her head and getting permission from her mum and dad first.

Early days: Shanks does his duty with the RAF (middle row, far right)

## for a 'bloody idiot!'

Beat the goalie! At a summer fete with colleagues in August, 1952

He asked them if he could take her out, they agreed and she was obliged to go the pictures with him that evening.

She still remembered the film they went to see, "Stormy Weather" starring Lena Horne.

The rest is history, as they say.

### 15 January 1972

#### Coventry joke is lost on Shankly

In January, 1972, Daily Post correspondent Bob Whiting revealed that Shanks was short and to the point regarding a possible move to the Midlands and Coventry City after Noel Cantwell was fired by the Sky Blues. The story indicated that Coventry could afford the best in the world.

"I've no time for jokes. Goodnight," was the Liverpool manager's sharp retort to a call made to him mid-evening.

### 1972/73

#### Reds secure Shanks' third league title

After a seven-year wait, Shankly finally secured his third First Division title, holding off the challenge of runners-up Arsenal by three points.

The 2-0 defeat of Leeds United in the penultimate game virtually wrapped up the title while only Arsenal won at Anfield that season. The Reds failed to score in only four of their 42 games, had the best goals for and meanest defensive records, while there was also a first success on the continent in the guise of the UEFA Cup (a 3-2 aggregate win over Borussia Moenchengladbach) – the first time the club had won two major trophies in a season.

In the league John Toshack was joint top scorer with 13 goals in only 22 games alongside Keegan (from 41 games), while goals were also shared around between Peter Cormack (a £110,000 signing from Nottingham Forest), Hughes, Boersma and Heighway. Phil Thompson was also given a run in the side while there were debuts for reserve keeper Frank Lane and utility man Trevor Storton – although only 16 players were used in the league.

Incidentally, Jimmy Case was bought for just £500 from South Liverpool in May 1973 – although he had to wait nearly two years for his debut.

The domestic cups saw Manchester City in the FA Cup (in round four) and Tottenham in the League Cup (in round five) end

**Anfield erupts as their Super Reds make it eigh**

by HORACE YATES

the Reds' interest, while the UEFA Cup triumph saw Liverpool account for Eintracht Frankfurt, AEK Athens, Dynamo Berlin, Dynamo Dresden and Tottenham – before the victory over the then West German side.

### I take my hat off to Shankly – Catterick

Everton manager Harry Catterick paid homage to his great rival in the Liverpool Echo.

He said: "I take my hat off to him for the way he has kept his club at the top."

"For my money, Shankly must rank as one of the greatest managers in the history of British soccer."

**13 July, 1972**

### Why not the Bill Shankly Gates?

We all pay homage at the Shankly Gates these days, but when was the idea first suggested to honour the great man in this way?

Certainly, veteran Liverpool Daily Post correspondent Horace Yates was on the case.

A life together: Treasured wedding mementos kept by Bill and Nessie

'A surprise is in store for Liverpool fans when they travel to Anfield for the opening game against Manchester City on August 12,' he wrote.

## Why not the Bill Shankly Gates?

A SURPRISE is in store for Liverpool fans when they travel to Anfield for the opening game against Manchester City on August 12, writes Horace Yates.

Gone will be the r painted wooden gates a fencing that barred way to the club's n entrance and car p Instead they will be f with wrought n fencing with a pa of elegant gates, in ich will be incorporate the club's emblem, the iver bird.

The gates, I ar told, will be very sim r to those at the Lord's cricket ground, which have been named he "W. G. Grace Gat s" to commemorate one of the world's most famous cricketers.

Surely, here is the spark of an idea for Liverpool.

Why not name theirs the "W. Shankly Gates" to perpetuate the name of the manager who pulled Liverpool out of the doldrums

'Gone will be the red painted wooden gates and fencing that barred the way to the club's main entrance and car park. Instead they will be faced with wrought iron fencing with a pair of elegant gates, in which will be incorporated the club's emblem, the Liver bird.

'The gates, I am told, will be very similar to those at the Lord's cricket ground, which have been named the 'W.G. Grace Gates' to commemorate one of the world's most famous cricketers.

'Surely, here is the spark of an idea for Liverpool. Why not name theirs the 'W. Shankly Gates' to perpetuate the name of the man who pulled Liverpool out of the doldrums and led them to the finest phase of their history?

'For years Anfield and Shankly have been synonymous.

Happy couple: Bill and Nessie on their wedding day – a match made in heaven

EXTRACT OF AN ENTRY IN A REGISTER of **MARRIAGES**, of 17° & 18° VICTORIÆ, kept in the undermentioned PARISH Cap. 80, §§ 56 & 58.

| No. | When, Where, and How Married. | Name (in full) of Parties, with Signature. Rank or Profession, and whether Bachelor, Spinster, Widower, Widow, or Divorced. | Age. | Usual Residence. | Name, Surname, and Rank or Profession of Father. Name, and Maiden Surname of Mother. | If a Regular tion of Offic Signatures. If an Irre Declaratio |
|---|---|---|---|---|---|---|
| 128 | 1944 On the Twenty-ninth day of June at Wellpark Church, Glasgow. After Banns; According to the Forms of the Church of Scotland. | William Shankly (Signature) W. Shankly Professional Footballer, (Leading Aircraftman, Royal Air Force).(Bachelor) (Name in full) Agnes Wren Stewart Fisher (Signature) A. Fisher. Slater's Clerkess,(Aircraft-woman;Women's Auxiliary Air Force).(Spinster) | 30 23 | 6, New Houses, Glenbuck. (Now engaged in War Service) 128, Dunchattan Street, Glasgow. (Now engaged in War Service). | John Shankly, Tailor (Deceased) Barbara Shankly M.S. Blyth James Fisher Garage Proprietor Annie Fisher M.S. Michael | (Signed) Hugh Minist Churc (Sign John D Counc Glenb elenor 650, A Glasg |

EXTRACTED from the REGISTER BOOK OF MARRIAGES for the DISTRICT of TOWNHEAD in the BURGH of GLASGOW, this 3rd day of July 1944.

In terms of the 58th Section of the Act 17 & 18 Vict. c. 80, every Extract of an Entry in the Register Books kept by a Registrar under the provis and Marriages (Scotland) Acts, duly authenticated and signed by the Registrar, is admissible as evidence in all parts of His Majesty's dominions without any

Any person who falsifies any of the particulars on this Extract or makes use of such falsified Extract as true, knowing it to be false, is liable to prosec

'Why not preserve the connection for all time? This, I am certain, would be a step warmly endorsed by the club's vast following.'

## 11 January 1973

### Spotlight on one of soccer's magic men

In January 1973 Bill Shankly featured on the famous "This Is Your Life" television show, presented by Eamonn Andrews.

A newspaper review of the programme said: 'All the stories about him stressed his dedication to football and made the famous yarn of how he took his wife to see a Third Division match on their wedding anniversary rise above the routine guff.

'Some of Shankly's dry wit also came over when he told of his transfer from Carlisle to Preston for £500 and quipped dourly: "It costs more than that in rail fares now."'

## 29 January 1973

### I do everything for the people – we're one big happy family

Stories about Bill Shankly's remarkable football appetite and how it affected his wife Nessie are legendary.

The Liverpool Daily Post added to the folklore when it reported: 'There is a famous story of the night that Bill – no chaser of the bright lights – announced that he was taking Nessie out for a birthday treat.

'They ended up in Birkenhead for a Tranmere game. Nessie was not altogether pleased. She stayed in the car while her husband watched the game, "but she forgave me afterwards," chuckled Shankly.'

Talking about his marriage, he said: "I think it is better that only one member of the family should be involved in sport, but don't run away with the wrong idea. Despite all I have said I think Nessie gets

Winning team: Bill and Nessie with daughter Barbara carrying sister Jeanette

# The odd couple together as one

They were a bit of an odd couple, poles apart in many ways, but there were strong bonds between my nan and granddad. When Grandy died, my Nan fell apart.

She propelled herself onwards for some years, continuing his charity work, pushing pennies over for the blind and turning up for various openings but her health deteriorated rapidly after the death of her daughter, my mum Barbara, in 1991.

At the end, when Ness was really ill and could barely breathe she would often say she could see Bill and Barbara standing close by, waiting for her and this brought some comfort to us; at least they would be reunited.

One thing that Bill and Ness had in common was their humility and respect for the people of Liverpool. Neither my nan nor my granddad would ever have taken advantage of

the adoration the fans felt for them.

When Ness went to pay her respects to the victims of the Hillsborough disaster, she queued up outside Anfield like everyone else and apparently waited for quite some time before she got inside the stadium.

She could have taken advantage of the fact that she was Bill Shankly's wife and gone straight to the reception but she wouldn't have felt that it was right, especially when people around her, relatives and friends of the victims, were suffering so much.

It would have been petty and mean spirited to want to get to the front of the queue so as not to suffer the discomfort of waiting. If my granddad had been alive then, he would have chosen to stand in that queue too. He would have wanted to share his grief and sadness with the people who really mattered to him the most.

through about 50 fags every time we play a match.

"Our marriage has been an incalculable help to me. It is no good if there are distractions at home. There are enough troubles in this game without running into another crop at home.

"I don't take my wife out to pictures, theatres or meals. You can't find time. She doesn't hold it against me. It is hard lines for

her but she never moans. Maybe she doesn't want to gallivant. At least she doesn't complain.

"Sometimes I do take football problems home with me but not often. Occasionally, if there is something irking me, I have to disclose what it is.

"Nessie is very knowledgeable. She'll talk about the transfer of a player or about buying one. She doesn't say much but what she says makes sense. She says if a club is willing to let him go there is something wrong.

"And make no mistake, results do make a difference to her. They make a difference to all of us."

On keeping busy at home, he said: "I do my chores in the house regularly. Many times when I am silent I am bubbling inside. I have to do something. I can't sit still. I cut the lawn. I clip the trees and clean all the windows and I wash the kitchen walls – they get dirty quicker than anywhere else."

On his favourite other sport, boxing, he enthused: "It's a great sport. We didn't get much chance as kids living out in the country but I do think that in different circumstances I might have taken up boxing as a middleweight.

"I did some boxing during the war. I did it mostly to keep myself fit, but as a member of the boxing team we used to get extra food,

**Doing the people proud: Nessie with Jessie Paisley**

# A new generation

and that wasn't bad.

"I was in an Army team that won a cup in a competition between 10 camps. I won five or six of my fights and lost one – but he was a professional."

Bill was once introduced to two Americans at a hotel who knew little about football:

"They tell me you are better known than the Prime Minister," said one.

"Aye", cracked back Bill, "and a hell of a sight more popular."

He was once playing in a testimonial match after his playing career was over when Tommy Finney happened to say to him: "It's true, Bill, isn't it that you never conceded an own goal in your entire career?"

"Aye, that's right," said Bill, and thought no more about it.

Three minutes after the kick-off he gently passed the ball back to former Manchester City goalkeeper Bert Trautmann, and diving in the opposite direction, Bert laughed his head off as the ball trickled over the line.

"Now brag about that one," quipped Bert.

Prior to Liverpool's European Cup semi-final at Inter Milan, Shankly was relaxing near Lake Como. The only problem was that the quiet was ruined by the clock on the village church, which chimed every quarter of an hour.

"You will have to stop that clock chiming," Bill told a startled Italian priest!

On being seen as Liverpool's biggest favourite, Shanks declared: "I don't know that, that is debatable. The players are there all the time on the field, active, working and entertaining. I never try to steal any thunder. That's not in my nature.

"Anything I do for Liverpool Football Club is mainly for the crowd. I am a crowd's man. If the players are successful, the club is successful and the crowd's happy. And I am successful, too, so that we are one big happy family.

"I am outspokenly in favour of the crowd. How could I be otherwise with such a following? I don't court their favour.

When I started reading and talking to people about my Granddad, trying to find out more about the real Shankly, I began to realise how important the fans were to him.

The stories and letters that were received about him confirmed that the appreciation and respect was mutual. However, it was only when we started our journey of discovery by looking through boxes of my granddad's belongings that I realised just how deep this attachment really was.

Letters, scarves, and gifts of all descriptions which had been sent to him by fans had been kept and cherished.

Everyone is familiar with the story of how Bill "rescued" some supporters' scarves from being irreverently trampled upon by a policeman in front of the Kop as another championship celebration unfolded.

Bill Shankly Testimonial Souvenir

LIVERPOOL v. DON REVIE SELECT   10p

Tuesday, 29 April, 1975          Kick-off 7.30 p.m.

I knew about this story and I liked the sentiments that it displayed, but suspected it might have been a bit of a "show" for the cameras.

When I discovered that he had kept these very scarves and many others beside, I was deeply moved by his genuineness and sincerity.

He physically could not throw any of these things away. They were tokens of the supporters' admiration and were treated accordingly. Everything received on his testimonial night in 1975 had been kept.

That night was, as he said himself, "the greatest thing that happened to me in all my life."

The greetings card, with more than a thousand signatures in red, the magnificent Road to Glory plaque, a complete record of his 15 years at Anfield and the silver tankard, engraved "To Shanks, with thanks, from a fan" had been kept.

> 'EVERYTHING RECEIVED ON HIS TESTIMONIAL NIGHT IN 1975 HAD BEEN KEPT. THAT NIGHT WAS, AS HE SAID HIMSELF, 'THE GREATEST THING THAT HAPPENED TO ME IN ALL MY LIFE''

# caught on camera

The next generation: The great grandchildren recreate that famous snap

When he said: "I'll treasure these presents for the rest of my life because they came from people who mean everything to me," that's exactly what he meant.

A month after his testimonial, in May 1975, the then three grandchildren had our photograph taken with Grandy and the card, at our house in Yew Tree Lane.

Recently, we decided it would be a nice idea to have all six of Bill Shankly's great grandchildren reconstruct the pose of that day.

He would be very proud if he could see that photo.

"Our crowd are fanatics. I'm used to crowds. I was brought up in a crowd at home. There were 10 of us, five boys and five girls.

"Any popularity I have achieved has come about through the players. Don't let anybody forget that. They are the men who make the image for the manager.

"Let us say that I am very content with the relationship that has existed for so long between the Liverpool following and myself. I hope it will always stay that way. They know that anything I can do through the team is not only my duty, but my pleasure.

"I would never want to leave. My work, my home, and my heart are here. There will never be another club for me. We have achieved much, but I hope there is far more still to be done."

**30 January 1973**

## Bill Shankly – An Insight Into A Great Man of Soccer

An in-depth article by the prolific Horace Yates took a fascinating look back on Shankly's life to date, covering an array of issues.

It touched on Shankly's first interest in football as a child in Glenbuck, and briefly documented his step into the professional game. Having then been given his first step on the managerial ladder at Carlisle, he applied for the Liverpool job in 1951. Yates reported:

'Selected for interview, he arrived at Anfield to find his old friends Andy Beattie and Scott Symon were the other candidates. The man who got the job – Don Welsh, who had played wartime football with Liverpool – was not even there.

"Both Andy and I knew the job was not for us, because of what went on at that meeting. I wouldn't want to disclose what happened at a private meeting.

"I didn't think then that the opportunity to return successfully later would come. Anfield, I thought, had passed me by.

"But in 1959, I got the message. By then I had had managerial experience with Carlisle, Grimsby, Workington Town and Huddersfield Town.

"It didn't take long after that for the move I always felt was the one to transform my future.

"West Bromwich Albion and Middlesbrough had both sounded me out. They didn't have to sell Liverpool to me. I had been there before, heard the noise and seen the enthusiasm of their fans. It's a big city and I knew there was room for two big clubs, not just Everton, who were Merseyside's only First Division team then.

"I came really because I knew there are people like me here, working class people, people with ambition. I couldn't have been more right."

On the secret of his success, Shankly said: "The will to live, natural enthusiasm, to

**Code of living:
A hand-written sheet from
the Shankly era detailing
a strict diet**

be ambitious for every minute of every day. If you have no natural enthusiasm you have nothing.

"Natural enthusiasm means living for the family and for football. I never give less than 100 per cent to any job I tackle and that is what I expect of everybody else. Even if I was playing in a three-a-side match at the back of a stand I'd still want to win 10-0.

"I'll tell you this. If I was shovelling coal instead of playing football I would want to shovel

**Surprise: The moment Shanks was 'caught' for the famous TV show**

# Liverpool team plays up to save Shankly's 'Life

Liverpool's soccer stars played for time last night — and saved Bill Shankly's "life."

A seating blunder on a Liverpool-London express almost spoiled the season's most surprise tactics — the appearance of the Liverpool manager no the This Is Your Life TV programme.

For Eamonn Andrews and his programme crew were almost caught off-side when the Liverpool party were in the wrong carriage when their train arrived in London.

The panic of platform 3 at London's Euston terminal began over two hours earlier as the Liverpool party, on their way to to-day's game at Westham, were ushered into the front coach of the Liverpool Pullman.

But as the express nosed into Euston, the cameras and spotlights were trained on the third coach — and almost a year's research and planning by the programme crew was lost.

The players and officials who had been in on the secret came to the rescue, however, as they played for time before getting off the train when the cameras and lights had focussed on the right carriage.

When he eventually stepped into the limelight Bill Shankly was stunned and speechless, as Eamonn Andrews emerged from behind a pillar to present him with the "red" book.

Within seconds, Mr. Shankly was being chauffeured away to the television studios, where the programme was recorded for showing sometime within the next few

**The dramatic story of how Eamonn Andrews nearly missed Shanks**

The man with Bill Shankly's life in his hands—Eamonn Andrews hides behind a pillar at Euston Station waiting for the Liverpool train.

**Take it as Red: With sister Pauline holding the 'big book'**

Delving into the boxes and bags of his things brought many memories flooding back.

One of the most vivid memories for me was awakened when I saw the red leather bound "This Is Your Life" book replete with photographs of the night.

Preparations for that big night in 1973 had been kept a very well guarded secret.

The only piece of information we were given was that we were going on a surprise journey and we weren't to say a thing about it to anyone.

It was all very mysterious and exciting for an eight-year-old.

The whole family travelled to London by train and we were put up in a very luxurious hotel. My granddad was on another train headed for Euston Station, as Liverpool were to play Arsenal at Highbury.

I remember rehearsals at the LWT studio when we had to pretend that one man was my granddad. Over and over again we had to walk over to him and give him a kiss – very unpleasant!

There was a big party later and I remember that me and my sister Pauline must have sat on every Liverpool player's knee!

We also tried to talk to some of the other famous people there and realised for the first time that not all celebrities were as warm and genuine as our granddad.

It was a wonderful night and we felt really proud of him.

It was something he deserved and I know that he thoroughly enjoyed having everybody he loved and respected gathered together in his honour.

> more coal that the next man.

"I once did a stint shovelling sand and although I shifted so much that I began to think I was shifting the Sahara Desert, I kept going. That's it, that's the secret, you've got to keep going."

Talking of some of the fiercest battles he had known, one brave journalist asked: "Bill, is it a fact that when you were playing, you would have kicked your own grandmother if she had got in your way?"

Quick as a flash, with the repartee for which he is famous, Shankly replied: "Don't be silly, man. My grandmother would have had enough sense to keep out of my way."

On being asked whether he was a 'Sergeant Major Manager', Shankly responded: "There's no sergeant major stuff about me. There's discipline in life and sergeant majors used forced discipline.

"There's no forced discipline at Anfield.

"There is a code of living which has been preached by me ever since I came here and the players all understand what it means.

"I set them an example. I preach the gospel that strength and fitness plus ability can make them into players.

"So there is no sergeant major nonsense. But I have no time for slackers. They rile me and anybody who is lazy or slack, I show them what is what.

"I am modelling my players now on what I did, the way I approached football in my playing days. I trained like a slave and I played like a slave.

"I gave every minute of every day when I was playing.

"The trainers didn't need to watch me. I want such players here and I want them to get it into their heads that even if nobody is watching they've still got to train.

"Players who start slacking as soon as the trainers turn their back are no good.

"They are no good to me. They are no good to anybody.

"They are no good to themselves."

In an honest interview, he went on to reveal his thoughts on a range of issues . . .

## On retiring when he is still fit and well:

"I think that would be pointless. As long as I think I am capable of doing the job I am doing now, I am going to keep working.

"In any case, a man can only retire if he is independent. How many jobs are there with pensions at 60 in this country? You have to wait until you are 65.

"Who's going to be a football manager until he is 65? Me, I hope. There is a lot still to be done in this game. It is going through a phase when there is a lot of pessimism. They say we are going downhill and all this kind of trash. I have heard this sort of talk from time immemorial. In life there has always been recession and slump. I have heard this all my life. That's what feeds me up when I hear people saying everything is black. I don't believe these things. It's just like playing back a record. I still hear them but we are still alive."

## On staying at Liverpool until retirement:

"I don't want to go anywhere else. That would be pointless."

## On the stresses and strains of the game:

"Some of the things that happen sometimes sicken you a little bit. Not everybody in this game is honest. Quite frankly sometimes you do begin to ask yourself, is it all worth while?

"But after all, if you do your job honestly, let people think what they like. That's their business, but it will only land them in trouble at the finish."

## On being caught by 'This Is Your Life':

"I didn't suspect a thing until I

A picture from This Is Your Life with Pauline and me among the many guests who also included Cilla Black and Tommy Smith

# Newspaper cutting that filled him with pride

As we were rooting through the boxes I found a newspaper cutting from May 3, 1965, which my granddad had kept. The newspaper writes of an event that I know was particularly special to him.

It was, of course, the tumultuous reception that Liverpool had received the day before, on bringing back the FA Cup. The headline in the Liverpool Daily Post that day was: '250,000 make the Beatles reception look like a vicarage tea party.' The team were greeted by a red and white mass, roaring "L-I-V-E-R-P-O-O-L" over and over again.

I know my granddad was overawed by the welcome because my dad was at Bellefield Avenue when Bill returned and he could talk of nothing else.

He described the homecoming thus: "The reception in the city centre was unbelievable. The emotion was tremendous. When we came out of the station, we couldn't see anything but buildings and faces. People were climbing up the walls of shops and banks and hoardings to get a better view. They were in dangerous places. But their name was on the cup at last and that was all that mattered."

And people were indeed in dangerous places. Apparently there were around 600 casualties, a lot of which were fractured arms and legs as people fell from buildings. (Afterwards the police gathered a huge pile of footwear, mainly teenage girls' shoes. A lot of people must have gone home in stockinged feet that night!)

Despite the casualties, for him the

saw Eamonn (Andrews) coming towards me. Then I knew just what they were all up to. I had never imagined that one day I would be featured on this programme. The thought had never crossed my mind.

"I was stunned a little bit and baffled. A million different things flooded through my mind. The

SHANKLY granddaughter number one, Karen . . .

first thing was that my wife had been up remarkably early that morning. I said to her 'What are you doing up at this time?'"

On apparently being close to tears during the programme, he added: "Not at all. I think that was just appreciation at seeing the people. I am not one of those actors. I have seen them on TV crying, with men kissing men and that sort of rubbish.

"I might have been absorbed a bit, but you can believe me there were no tears. I enjoyed it when I had an idea about who was going to be there. When they showed the village on the screen I knew brother Jimmy was going to be there. That was good for I had not seen Jimmy for a long time.

"The thought of my two little granddaughters being there too. That flashed through my mind and I looked forward to that."

### On the birth of his first child or grandchild:

"That's a different kind of emotion. I was pleased at that but that's more pride than anything.

"I don't think there have been any really emotional things. The only emotional thing you get in

Our name is on the Cup: The fans gather in May, 1965

'PEOPLE WERE INDEED IN DANGEROUS PLACES... AFTERWARDS THE POLICE GATHERED A HUGE PILE OF FOOTWEAR, MAINLY TEENAGE GIRLS' SHOES. A LOT OF PEOPLE MUST HAVE GONE HOME IN STOCKINGED FEET THAT NIGHT!'

life is when somebody close to you dies. Like my mother (below), for example. Even though she was only a month off being 80 years of age you still feel it. That's what I call emotion."

## On answering fans' requests to have the ashes of loved ones scattered or buried at the Kop end:

"I know how they felt. These chaps' greatest love outside their family was Liverpool Football Club. They lived as Liverpool fans all their lives. Who could refuse a last request to stay near their favourite spot for all time?"

## On being able to relive a part of his life:

"There are a lot of things, but that night when Liverpool thrashed Inter Milan in the European Cup semi-final at Anfield was unforgettable. Liverpool at that time were the greatest team in the world.

"Considering Inter Milan at that time were well nigh unbeatable, any team in the world could have played them and lost, then this was possibly Liverpool's greatest display of all time."

## On Liverpool's celebrity fans:

"Tarbuck, Doddy, (Johnny) Hackett and the rest of the Liverpool clan are all football mad. They are all members of the family now. It's possibly because

'FOR HIM THE RECEPTION "WAS THE MOST FANTASTIC I'VE EVER SEEN, PROBABLY GREATER THAN ANY OTHER SPORTING SALUTE. I WOULDN'T HAVE BEEN SURPRISED IF THE LADS HAD LIFTED THE COACH OFF THE GROUND AND CARRIED US TO THE TOWN HALL"'

they have come round to our training ground at Melwood and are so often at our games. Tarbuck has trained with us from time to time and Kenny Dodd has stripped off as well.

"Jimmy has heard most of the patter that goes on. Sometimes this is humourous to get the players in a good mood and that's where Jimmy comes in very useful.

"But even Jimmy doesn't hear the final quarter of an hour before kick-off. Nobody is ever in there when we are ready to give the axes out."

## 1 February 1973

Yates' article ran through into the following day's paper. By now this was a day when Bill Shankly was talking about the greatest footballer he had ever seen . . .

"Tom Finney, the Preston plumber. The greatest Englishman of them all was Finney. I had the good fortune to play with him.

"Luckily for me I didn't have to play against him.

"If I'd had to oppose him I would have been 10 years older. Or at least he would have made me feel ten years older.

"Peter Doherty is probably the greatest Irish-born player of my experience despite George Best.

"There were many more who could play a bit as well, like Stan Matthews, Raich Carter, Tommy Lawton, Bill Dean, Billy Liddell, Alec James, Hughie Gallacher, Jimmy Hagen, geniuses of men.

"Finney had everything. You name the qualities you demand in a star and Finney had them all.

"I think he had eyes in the back of his head as well.

"For calculated coolness, the ability to change his mind and fox you he was incomparable.

"He could score goals as well, and there was no fault to find with his tackling. Brilliant is an overworked word in football reporting these days, but it was a word that never did full justice to this most elusive man."

reception "was the most fantastic I've ever seen, probably greater than any other sporting salute. I wouldn't have been surprised if the lads had lifted the coach off the ground and carried us all to the Town Hall."

Such a massive display of support was something that would always live on in his heart. It was an occasion to savour.

I think it also brought home to him that together with the people of Liverpool he had finally managed to "create an institution, something more than a football club, something alive and vibrant, warm and successful."

This was the huge family that he would always talk about with such warmth and love.

Amazingly enough, I was sent some spectacular photographs of that event taken by fan Joe Neary from a policeman's box on Lime Street.

They really do conjure up the atmosphere of the day completely.

### On signing his own star players:

"If I thought the player was good enough I would gladly dole out £300,000.

"There is a player in this country now that I would pay that money for. I tried to sign him this season.

"I approached their manager and he said: 'Yes, you can have him - we'll take Kevin Keegan,' and that was the end of that little conversation."

### On missing out on the signing of Lou Macari, who opted for Manchester United instead:

"Lou Macari never had the chance to turn down Anfield.

"At no time did he give the impression he was interested in anywhere but Manchester United, although he never said so in so many words.

"I rang Celtic's manager Jock Stein, while Macari was on his way home and told him we had no further interest in the player."

### On being turned down by Bob McNab (who chose Arsenal instead):

"The man could never play anyway."

### On his finest signing:

"Keegan came out of the smaller leagues. That meant it is more difficult for him, but he has come forward quicker than most. He is still very young with a lot of football skill ahead of him, but it is an impossible job to name my greatest signing.

"Emlyn Hughes has been simply immense in all positions. He is the most adaptable and most versatile player in England probably. He can play in four or five different positions and still look a star.

"St John and Yeats both come

Liverpool fan Joe Neary's snapshots highlight the incredible excitement in Lime Street in 1965

# Taking the dog for a walk – in enemy territory

Packed away with the other things were some really interesting telegrams from various close friends and admirers.

One was from the Beatles wishing Bill the best of luck, just before the 1965 Cup final, another from The Merseybeats wishing the same, and another I really like from Don Revie, the defeated Leeds United boss and his wife Elsie, congratulating him on his win that day.

I love this one because it shows the true respect that existed between the two managers and bore testimony to something he said himself: "Football club managers are a very small group, very tightly knit, very close to each other."

Bill had also kept a telegram from Billy Bingham sent at the time my granddad resigned, along with photos of himself in the Everton Directors' Box and Everton season tickets (used for spying missions across the Park) and these are testimony to the friendship that existed outside the 90 minutes, twice a season, when they played against each other.

My granddad would always take my sister and I around to the Everton training ground and we were allowed to run free among the trees that edged the ground.

He would often go for a sauna there or play a game of five-a-side with some neighbours and the Everton club doctor or, of course, take the dog for a walk there!

to mind. Peter Cormack has been an object lesson. At last he has found a job to do and now he is doing it.

"Ray Clemence and Larry Lloyd have been great signings, too, both men from lower leagues. Geoff Strong and Gordon Milne would have gladdened anybody's heart. Look at Peter Thompson, too. There were times when he seemed like sheer magic.

"Roger Hunt was here when I came, and from the moment I first saw him I knew he could play. You didn't have to be a genius to recognise that.

"I would rather not try to put my finger on any one man. It is an intriguing subject and I would prefer to leave the question with the public. Let them decide. And the best of luck to them."

**On striker Frank Worthington, who failed a medical and missed out on a big Anfield move:**

"We knew he was a great player and experience has proved that, but the specialist told us: 'You can't sign him,' and so we couldn't. He had the ability to be a Liverpool player, but the medical men decided he was not for us.

**On those legendary five-a-sides:**

Shanks was quick to tell the story of a game against the players

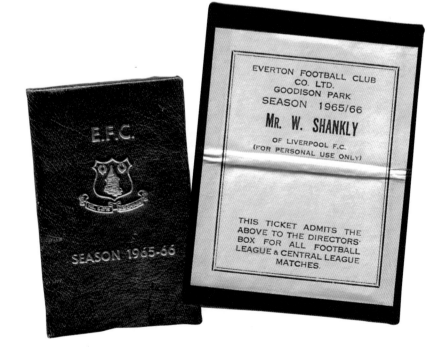

when they claimed they had won. The ball passed through the makeshift goals, without a bar, for what was to have been the goal to save Shankly's side.

"No goal, boss, it was over the bar," yelled the players.

"Nonsense", roared Shankly. "It was as fair a goal as ever I have seen." As a last throw Shankly turned to the quiet man of Anfield, Chris Lawler.

"You are an honest man, Chris", said Shankly in his most persuasive style. "Now you tell us Chris, wasn't that a goal?"

"No, boss", said Chris as usual entirely without emotion. "It was no goal."

Shankly exploded: "It's the first time you have spoken since I came to Anfield and now you have told a ******* lie."

Eighteen months into the job, Shankly had realised that some of the household names like Billy Liddell, Dave Hickson and skipper Dick White all had to go. He revealed what had been behind this clear-out.

"The fact that I was dealing with big names did not worry me. I don't like to do anybody any harm if I can avoid it, but this was a different story. I was working for half the population of this city. They are the ones that mattered. These names had been very good players but I felt that possibly they had seen their best days. The real turning point in my reconstruction formula was Ron Yeats and Ian St John. Callaghan and Byrne were brilliant boys, of course, and so was Milne, but the cornerstones were the two Scots.

"With them in the side we could have won the Second Division without a keeper. Yeats was so brilliant. In that class he could have played on one leg. They could have cut the other one off. He would still have been a giant among men.

"While he was doing such great stuff in defence, St John was just as effective up front. Newcastle nearly pipped us for St John. This was probably one of the most vital fights we ever won.

"I said after we won the

# Oh, how he hated to lose a game!

Most Sundays neighbours and friends would play a game of five-a-side in the playing fields at the end of Bellefield Avenue (one of the resident players was Harry Scott, the middleweight boxing champion from Bootle who my granddad had taken a shine to).

It was not uncommon for them to play for up to four hours. They would use coats as goalposts, nothing fancy! Whenever his opponents scored a goal and took the lead, my granddad could be heard to shout: "That one hit the post and came out!" Oh how he hated to lose.

One day Kenny drove my granddad to Old Trafford. It was about the time the newspapers had got hold of the story of Tommy Docherty and Mary Brown.

As they walked into the ground, Bill grunted: "We'll have to have a word with Tommy." After grabbing a cup of tea from his favourite tealady he found Tommy and took him into a side room.

"The Press is full of you, son. Is it true?" my granddad asked. There was a bit of a pause before Tommy replied in the affirmative. "Good God Tom, you're doing so well here. You're sitting on a goldmine. You could have any woman you wanted."

"I know Bill, but I love her," came the reply. There followed a pregnant pause. "Aye, I suppose so son. But what the f...... hell does she see in you?" Needless to say, they all burst into fits of laughter.

**Man down: Paisley's on the deck but Shanks plays on at Melwood!**

Fighting game: Retired local 'pro' boxer Gordon Ashun is presented with an award. Shankly was an enthusiastic boxing fan

Second Division that very soon we would win the First Division as well. To some it may have sounded like a Shankly daydream, but I knew what I was talking about.

"In 1963-64 we swept through to win the championship. It was heady stuff, but even then I knew we were only at the beginning. The only disaster in that season was defeat by Swansea Town in the FA Cup at Anfield.

"Everybody was moaning and Anfield was hardly like a holiday camp after that match. I said to the players: 'If you play for the rest of the season as you have played today, you will win the League.' It wasn't just a reflex comment or balm for the wounds. I meant what I said and it all came true."

## On the Liverpool fans, he just smiled:

"They are more than just supporters, they are the most knowledgeable and fairest crowd of them all. Nobody can kid that crowd. They know their football and they know fair play. They know weak referees and all. But it riles me to hear silly managers talking about them swaying referees.

"The Kop has 20,000 fans at every game. And I say of them that with their enthusiasm and fairness they can't be beaten. You have fanatical support in Scotland but they are neither as fair-minded or knowledgeable. The crowd come to Anfield to see a good game, to applaud the opposition and their good players if they are fair and nobody in the land can hold a candle to them."

## On the 1965 FA Cup final:

"This was our finest hour. There must have been 60,000 Liverpool fans among Wembley's 100,000 that day. Don't ask me how they got their tickets, but they were there all right.

"I went to them after the game

while the players were collecting their medals and they were the first to know that Gerry Byrne had played almost throughout the match with a broken collar bone. That was the most fantastic, heroic thing I have ever known.

"To play for two hours with such an injury was heroism beyond any call of duty. At half-time the broken bone was protruding. It was just padded up by the doctor and Byrne insisted on going back.

"We didn't want to reveal our hand, to let them know we had a cripple. We hoped we wouldn't get too much pressure on him and this proved to be the case. If we had moved him to another place we would have merely advertised his plight.

"He not only played his part but had a hand in the winning goal. For me, Gerry Byrne is one of the greatest competitors who ever played football. Nobody else in the world could have done for Liverpool what he did that day.

"The reception we were given was almost unbelievable. Our supporters were everywhere. They knelt in the road and bowed to the coach as it passed them by. When we arrived back in Liverpool with the Cup the following night we were just staggered and so very proud of the way we were greeted."

### 'If I was offered a free ticket and meal at Watford I would say no'

On the shock defeat to Watford in the FA Cup in 1970, Shanks was blunt in his appraisal of the Reds' conquerors: "I could have played against Watford. They were possibly the worst team that ever beat us.

"Swansea were a much better side than Watford, who were at that time possibly the most negative team I have ever seen in my life.

"If I had lived at Watford and been offered a free ticket and a meal after the match every Saturday I wouldn't have gone and watched them."

Trophy time: Prayers are answered with the 1973 title

# Proving football is like a religion

Another manager who we often heard my granddad speak of with the utmost admiration was, of course, Sir Matt Busby, a fellow Scot. Kenny Quayle would often drive my granddad over to Old Trafford, where Bill and Matt would dine together and then watch a match from the Directors' Box.

One day Kenny recalls that my granddad, Tommy Docherty and himself were walking past Matt's office. They could see a top dignitary from the Catholic Church in the office, holding out his hand to Matt, who was on his knees and kissing the proffered hand.

Apparently, my granddad turned to Tommy Docherty, who was a catholic too and knew about these things, to ask him what was going on. Tommy

explained that in the presence of a church dignitary, it was normal procedure to kiss his ring.

"What!" barked Bill. "It should be him on his knees, kissing Matt's ring!" A typical Shankly wise crack.

Kenny remembers one story that sums up Bill Shankly for him. One day they went off to Stoke to watch a match. Kenny was driving as usual.

It was a windy, cold and wet day as Kenny remembers and having parked the car they made their way towards the main entrance of the ground. Just ahead of them was a little old man, well into his 80s, slightly stooped, bandy legs just like an old footballer. All of a sudden Bill exclaimed: "Good Lord, that's Samuel Weaver, the great England half-back" (apparently they had even

Manager of the Year: With a sense of humour to match!

'TOMMY EXPLAINED THAT IN THE
PRESENCE OF A CHURCH DIGNITARY,
IT WAS NORMAL PROCEDURE TO KISS
HIS RING. 'WHAT!' BARKED BILL.
'IT SHOULD BE HIM ON HIS KNEES,
KISSING MATT'S RING!"

## 24 April, 1973

### Shankly hails the Liverpool faithful

With the Reds heading for an almost certain title success after beating Leeds United 2-0 at Anfield, Shankly talked to the Echo's Chris James about the fans. The Liverpool boss said:

"They excelled themselves. They gave the lads all the encouragement they needed. It was only Liverpool that mattered to them, the club and the colour of the jersey. Who was wearing the jerseys didn't matter, it was Liverpool they were cheering.

"There were fantastic scenes at the finish. I've never seen such a sea of colour. There were no dressing room celebrations, just the usual handshakes and backslapping."

James added: 'The champagne stayed on ice as the Orangeade Champions toasted their triumph with bottles of pop and cups of tea.'

## 30 April 1973

### Anfield erupts as super Reds make it eight

A last-day draw at home to Leicester, with the title in the bag, left Bill Shankly ecstatic.

He described it as: "The happiest day of my life.

"I have known nothing like it as player or manager.

"This title gave me greater pleasure than the previous two, simply because here we had a re-built side, some of them only two or three seasons in first-team football and they stayed the course like veterans. I am pleased for my wife, too.

"She could hardly speak and will have been biting her nails.

"I didn't realise she was so involved.

"Our crowd are champions, too. I am happy for them.

"I wanted that title more than at any time in my life. That's why it is such a relief."

> ### 3 May, 1973

### Cheers! Now for Manager of the Year

Shankly was confirmed as having scooped the manager of the month award for April. The award carried a £100 cheque and a gallon bottle of Scotch whisky.

However, the drink was hardly likely to be fully appreciated, according to Mrs Nessie Shankly, who said: "If it was left to Bill and I we would have this stuff in the house for years. We take out the bottle for some of our friends from time to time, but that is all.

"During the cold winter months Bill does have a couple of spoonsful, with sugar, before going to bed, but it would take him a long time to get through a bottle. I don't like the stuff at all. I think it is appalling."

### 19 May, 1973

### They all agree with the Kop: Shankly is king

Shankly paid the following tributes having been named Manager of the Year (scooping £1000 in the process):

"Money doesn't really matter. This is a club honour. But as it is the manager who gets the kicks when things are going wrong, it is perhaps acceptable to collect the bouquets when things go well.

"I don't know if there is a secret of success. I try to keep a core of experienced players and spot how you can change a player's role as he gets older.

"You've got to be looking to the future all the time. We have just won the Central League with a very young side and that is almost as important for the club as winning the League title.

"This was a day I shall never

played against each other when Samuel was at the end of his career and my granddad played for Preston).

They caught up with him and introduced themselves.

"What are you doing here, Samuel?" asked my granddad.

It turned out he was scouting for a Third Division team.

"Got a seat?" was the next question.

"I usually go to the stands", Samuel replied.

"Well, not today. Come with us" came the response and off they went to the main foyer, where my granddad asked for George Eastham, the manager of Stoke.

As George was coming down the stairs, Bill shouted: "You're honoured George. Today we have with us the legendary Samuel Weaver.

"Played for England. When he took a throw-in he would throw the ball from one side of the pitch to the other. Samuel Weaver is one of the great masters."

You could tell by the look on poor old George's face that he didn't have a clue who Samuel Weaver was, but to his credit he didn't let on.

"Ah, yes, yes.

"We're really honoured to have you here" George replied, shaking Samuel's hand.

"Bring him a cup of tea, bring him some sandwiches, he'll be sitting with us", my granddad said and they marched him off to the directors' box, where he soon had all the directors fussing round the old man.

Samuel Weaver may well have felt a little embarrassed that day at such a fuss being made, but to be treated with such respect must have been very touching too, and maybe for a while at least he felt some of the old pride welling up inside him.

**Human touch: Shanks never forgot a face from his playing days**

# 'Christ Ken, the girl's a genius!'

Kenny Quayle knew my granddad as well as anyone and I never tire of talking to him. One Saturday morning Bill went round to Kenny's house, which was just a few doors down from his own house. They were going off to a game as usual.

Kenny's 15-year-old daughter Linda was sitting engrossed in a book. "What's that you're reading lass?" my granddad asked. She showed him the cover of the book. There was a gasp from my granddad.

"Christ Ken, you've sired a bloody genius!" Linda was reading "Great Scottish Inside Forwards."

On a different subject, my granddad's dislike of the 'blazer-brigade' as he used to call the directors, is well documented.

After he had retired, they had gone to watch a match at Arsenal. They were having a cup of tea just before the match, when a chairman of Arsenal walked past. As Ken describes him, "he had a double barrelled name and spoke as if he had plums in his mouth!"

"Tell me, Mr Shankly, what's it like being retired?" he enquired. My granddad put on his best Scottish accent. "You don't retire until you're in your box sir!" When the chairman had walked away my granddad said to Kenny: "That shut him up!"

forget and I'm naturally delighted. I think you can say this has been Liverpool's greatest season. All we need now is the UEFA Cup and we must have a very good chance of that.

"This season we have had record gates, we have taken more money than ever before, including the greatest gate receipts for one match, and we have done the double for first and reserve teams. No manager can really ask for more.

"Everton's Harry Catterick should have had this in 1970. It was a shame he didn't get it."

Horace Yates returned to a theme in the Daily Post, with more ideas on how the club should salute the greatest manager in the game. He wrote: 'If they were to decide to perpetuate Shankly's connection with the club by giving his name a place of honour among Anfield's fabrics, I suggest it would be no more than he deserves.

'We could have as an example, "Shankly's Kop" or maybe "The Shankly Stand" or even "The Bill Shankly Gates" at the main entrance to the ground.' The latter was something Yates had touched on before and clearly the club were taking notice.

### 25 May 1973

The Liverpool Echo added their support for Shankly with a special series under the header:

## 'The story of Bill Shankly, the man and his achievements. Mr Liverpool and his clan'

The series majored on the magnificent double success of 1973 championship and UEFA Cup.

When Liverpool's plane from Moenchengladbach landed at 2.30am at Speke with the UEFA Cup on board, Shankly was asked by the Echo what he expected to do with the rest of the day.

**Signing Emlyn: But Grandy mistrusted some club directors**

# Tears as we heard

He said: "Aye, well, I think I'll go to my garage to get a service done. Not on the car but on myself."

The Echo talked to a host of people about the great man in a series which was hugely popular. They sought Tom Finney's recollections of Shankly, the player:

"Bill was a very good player as enthusiastic then as he is about the game today. He was a very intelligent player, a strong type of player and very quick. He was also a good passer of the ball. And a player you wouldn't want to be up against – you'd far rather Bill Shankly was in your team than playing for the opposition.

"Bill never gave you a moment's rest, and he never knew what it was to be beaten. He had the same sort of competitive spirit in him as Alan Ball - he hated losing.

"I remember playing in one game with Bill, and we were losing 4-1 with only two or three minutes to go.

"But Bill still had his sleeves rolled up, egging us on.

"He didn't concede that it was hopeless - and he didn't expect anyone else to give up, either.

"In the dressing room he was a wonderful character - when he was halfway through getting changed, he'd take some cotton wool and make a moustache out of it, and he'd be going round saying his piece and giving us all a good laugh. He was a scream!

"And when it came to talking about the opposition, he was just the same as he is now.

"You might mention that so-and-so was a good player, and Bill would rap back: 'Don't you worry aboot him, son. He'll no get a kick of the ball today.'

"He was a tremendous fellow to play in front of, and I learned a great deal from him about many aspects of the game. It stood me in good stead for the future.

"Bill and I have always had a high regard for each other, and whenever I go to Anfield I make a point of nipping in to have a word

Not all of the items in Grandy's boxes stirred up happy memories. As we were searching through we came across a programme from the memorial service held at Liverpool Cathedral in November, 1981.

That was perhaps the most sorrowful day of my life. Thousands of people had come from all over to honour him and their sorrow was all too evidently etched on their faces. I remember I was crying so much that I could hardly see.

Everything was just a blur. I kept my head down and eyes on the ground. I thought that if I could see the other people's grief-stricken faces, I might not be able to stand the pain of it and felt as if I may actually collapse.

All I know is, the biggest

# that famous song

LIVERPOOL CATHEDRAL

✝

A SERVICE OF THANKSGIVING
FOR THE LIFE OF
BILL SHANKLY

Sunday, November 22nd 1981 at 3.00 p.m.

'I KEPT MY HEAD DOWN AND EYES ON THE GROUND. I THOUGHT THAT IF I COULD SEE THE OTHER PEOPLE'S GRIEF-STRICKEN FACES, I MIGHT NOT BE ABLE TO STAND THE PAIN AND FELT I MAY ACTUALLY COLLAPSE'

with him.

"So far as I'm concerned, his only interest in life has been sport - he talks about nowt else but football, or maybe boxing.

"But he's a real family man, and he has so many good points - he's always been a good-living person, from an athlete's point of view, and he has always expected players to do the same.

"He's no time for players who don't work at keeping themselves fit.'

### 30 May 1973

### Bill Shankly and the big names have mutual respect

The Echo's salute continued with a chat with Ian St John who had been a key star for Bill in the 1960s. The Saint said:

"You cannot work with a man like that and not have it rub off on to you. Bill Shankly doesn't sit in his office, he runs the show, and his voice is a dominant voice in the club. Everything I learned in English football I learned at Liverpool through Shanks and the staff."

On the subject of Denis Law, whom Shankly managed as a teenager at Huddersfield Town, someone who has known Shankly for many years – and used to play against him – observed: "Bill was the fellow who put the devil into Denis."

### 31 May 1973

### Shankly an expert in man management

From across the Park came a special tribute from Everton's playing giant Brian Labone, who said:

"Bill did me a great favour by volunteering to bring Liverpool's first team to Goodison for my testimonial - especially with the pressures on Liverpool, who had played so many games and were in for two trophies.

"He would have been forgiven for crying off, for talking about a postponement, or for fielding a side well below full strength. But he kept his word. He did me a great personal favour, and I shall never forget it.

"But apart from my testimonial game, I have long admired Bill as a manager who can motivate players to do great things. Good players have gone to Anfield, and he seems to be able to make them twice the size they were, people with a great belief, people who appear to be operating at 110 per cent.

"He proffers a kind word . . . then he's going on about his own great team. He loves all footballers, those who are ready to work and give the game all they've got – but he loves his own team more than anything."

**2 June 1973**

## Iron Man with his heart in the right place

Leicester referee Gordon Hill noted the following of Shankly: "He has always been fair to me – he is one of the fairest and most honest men in the game. He is not frustrating, not undemonstrative. I call him the Iron Man – he seems to have icy control at all times.

"He was always the first to congratulate you when a game had gone well, in spite of the fact that Liverpool may have suffered. When he knows you have made a mistake, he doesn't speak, but it shows in his face as he walks past, and you know he knows."

**19 June 1973**

## The professionals' tribute to Shankly

Amongst the attendees at a Bill Shankly Tribute Event organised by the local branch of the Variety Club of Great Britain in aid of Merseyside's underprivileged children (which raised £13,050), were Jock Stein,

Silver lining: With Ian Callaghan, those fanatical Greek fans and the curator of the Liverpool FC museum Stephen Done (far left)

cathedral in Britain was full and even more people were waiting in the freezing cold outside.

I know there were soccer players past and present there, there were councillors, mayors and other officials, but I saw no one.

I could hear though. I could hear the soaring voices of the choir as we entered. They were singing, rather aptly, "Be Strong And Of Good Courage", followed by one of my granddad's favourite hymns, "The Lord's my Shepherd."

I could hear the simple but moving service which was based on the three distinctive features of my granddad's life; integrity, enthusiasm and inspiration.

I could hear Kevin Keegan talking about the integrity that characterises all true, effective leaders, Sir Tom Finney telling us to enter into life with zest and enthusiasm, never to make do with second best and Bob Paisley talking about how Bill Shankly inspired many people, not

only within football but in so many other areas of life.

It was all so apt and fitting. When the soulful sound of "Amazing Grace" was played by a solitary piper, it stuck me how different it sounded this time, compared to the hundreds of other times I had heard it on my grandfather's old gramophone player.

Every line seemed full of new meaning. But it was the emotion-filled voice of Gerry Marsden singing "You'll Never Walk Alone" which just transported everyone to a deeper level of grief.

It seemed to epitomise so well everything we felt at that moment. (Even now I can simply not listen to that song without tears flowing down my face and recently my 10-year-old son was mortified when we went to watch our first ever match at Anfield and I promptly blubbered for about 10 minutes after the match had started and the fans had sung their anthem.)

Willie Waddell (Rangers), Joe Mercer, Gordon Milne, Ron Saunders, John Harris (Sheffield United), Bobby Charlton, Billy Bingham and Jaap Van Praag.

The latter, who was president of then European champions Ajax, mislaid his suitcase and had to borrow a dinner jacket. Liverpool secretary Peter Robinson revealed: 'I rang up all the friends I could think of. In the end he had six dinner jackets to choose from and a number of dress shirts. He turned out to be the best dressed man there!

Jock Stein paid his own salute on the night.

He said: "There is no one who would have brought me all the way from Glasgow other than Bill Shankly.

"We hear all about coaching, all about systems but Bill Shankly appreciates that the main thing in football is the people on the terraces."

It was 11.29pm before the main event - the presentation to

Shankly of a bust of himself by local sculptor Arthur Dooley.

A generous Liverpool boss said: "It's more like me than me. This year has been an amazing one for me.

"Each one of the things that has happened has been greater than the one before and this one has been greater than the others because it comes from the people of Liverpool, which is where I work."

**Life couldn't have been better as Shankly and Liverpool prepared for what would be another successful season in the summer of 1973. Little did his beloved Kop know what would happen just after that season had drawn to a close . . .**

The whole service was everything my granddad would have wanted.

The personal items in those souvenir boxes are a living tribute to Bill Shankly's life.

Driving licences, passports, player's tickets from his days at Carlisle and Preston, RAF pictures, wedding photos, professional contracts, training programmes, they all tell the story of his life from beginning to end.

As Stephen Done, curator of the LFC Museum expresses it: "The boxes of personal items belonging to Bill Shankly brought into the museum by the Shankly family are an incredible and personal insight into a great man, a true legend of the club.

"It is a privilege to even hold these items, and they also bring greater insight into the life of a footballing genius."

Man in the spotlight: Bill
Shankly stunned the
world when he announced
his resignation from
Liverpool after another
successful season in 1974

# The LEAVING
## of Liverpool

THE SUMMER OF 1974 WAS A MOMENTOUS
ONE FOR BILL SHANKLY AND LIVERPOOL.
REVEALING INTERVIEWS FROM
BEFORE AND AFTER THE REDS' FA CUP
TRIUMPH OVER NEWCASTLE SHOW A
MAN WRESTLING WITH THE HARDEST
DECISION OF HIS LIFE — WALKING AWAY
FROM THE CLUB HE LOVED

**As Liverpool looked forward to another FA Cup final, everything was rosy in the Anfield garden. Behind the scenes, however, Bill Shankly was privately coming to terms with the biggest decision of his life – leaving the Kop behind. Here's how the story unfolded from the Wembley build-up to the tributes that poured in after the soccer bombshell was dropped on a fateful July day in 1974 . . .**

# They're not fans –

As the final approached, Bill declared: 'Before the Cup semi-finals I suggested Red Rum and Liverpool for a Merseyside double. Red Rum showed his class to leave no doubt about his pedigree, and I have great hopes that the second leg of that double is in very good hands.

'These people are not simply fans. They are more like members of a tremendous family. As long as I live I shall never forget the joy we were able to bring to them with victory over Leeds United in 1965, when the Cup came to Liverpool for the first time.

'They swept the road in front of our coach with their jackets and knelt as if in prayers of thankfulness. I have seen it suggested that I once said football was not just a case of life and death, that it was far more serious. It is fans such as those we saw on that day that almost makes logic of such a statement.

'I don't know how long it will take, but I intend to send a personal reply to every one of those supporters who have written making pleas for (FA Cup final) tickets. They will not find a ticket in the envelope, just an expression of my great regret I can do nothing for them.

'I would quite willingly give them all tickets without charge if only I could do so, but there's no chance. Wembley doesn't have elastic sides.'

## He loves the fans more than the team

Bill Shankly's famous goalkeeper Tommy Lawrence, affectionately dubbed the Flying Pig gave an unusual insight into Bill Shankly in a Daily Post interview.

Tommy said: 'There's not much what you might call affection between him and the players, more respect, schoolmaster-pupils.

'You wouldn't let him see you laughing at him unless at an airport when he's putting 'furriners' in their places. If you like, this is his one failing.

'He can't open out to anyone, or any of the players at least. Against that though, he won't let anyone call you, the Press or anyone. He'll bawl you out behind closed doors, but nothing in public. The players appreciate that.

'I'd say he has more regard for the supporters than for the team. On coach trips away he'd point at them out the window and say: 'Those people have travelled miles to see you. You should go out and die for them.'

'We'd never heard anything like it. I've seen him give the fans tickets, give fivers to some to help them home.

# they're our family

With his people (left) and alone with his thoughts on the Wembley pitch before Liverpool took on Newcastle in the final

'I'LL GET MY TRACKSUIT AND SWEATER OUT AND JOG AROUND. PEOPLE WILL LAUGH AT ME AND THINK I'M MAD. BUT SOME OF THEM WILL DROP DEAD THE NEXT DAY. I'LL HAVE THE LAST LAUGH, AND I'LL DIE A HEALTHY MAN'

## 15 February 1974

### Shanks has got 'a job for life!'

In February 1974 Liverpool chairman John Smith told the Daily Post's Erlend Clouston: "I would be happy if he would stay with us for life – but that decision is not for us to make. We are completely at Mr. Shankly's disposal, however."

> **Shanks has got 'a job for life . . .'**
> by ERLEND CLOUSTON
> 15 FEB 1974
> LIVERPOOL have made it clear, Bill Shankly is the best manager in the business—and as far as the board are concerned he's got a job for life.

In response, Shankly commented: "Staggered. It may be another year, or two, or three. But, one day I'll decide that that's enough and leave straight away. My career as a manager must have an abrupt end."

Asked about his eventual retirement, he made the following comment:

"I'll get my tracksuit and sweater out and jog around. People will laugh at me and think I'm mad. But some of them will drop dead the next day. I'll have the last laugh, and I'll die a healthy man."

The fans might have wondered what this was all about and Shanks' comments, while referring obliquely to his health, seemed to brush aside any thoughts of retirement.

But the words were still extremely significant.

Clearly, thoughts about his health and the future were going through his mind at this time. What we didn't know was that an explosive statement of intent would follow in the summer of 1974.

For now, Bill was concentrating on driving Liverpool towards Wembley with another FA Cup final in his sights.

## Reds box clever to see off Newcastle

The footballing world was still reverberating to the news that Sir Alf Ramsey had been sacked by the FA as England boss just days earlier as Liverpool prepared for their May 4th clash with Newcastle at Wembley.

Shankly had a couple of additional engagements in London, representing Ian Callaghan at a player-of-the-year presentation - and meeting with boxing legend Jack Dempsey. "I never saw him fight but he was possibly the greatest of all time. He was indestructible. I'll enjoy having a few words with him."

Shanks' message from Melwood before he left for the capital was simple: "The players know what is expected of them. Big games are routine to us."

After a relatively even but goalless first half, Liverpool's class shone through.

With youngster Phil Thompson snuffing out the threat of Malcolm Macdonald and full-backs Alec Lindsay and Tommy Smith virtually wingers, the breakthrough came on 57 minutes, with Kevin Keegan netting the first of his two goals.

Steve Heighway latched onto a John Toshack header to hit the second 15 minutes from time, before a superb team goal saw Keegan hit a late third.

Scouse power: Fans throng the streets to welcome the FA Cup heroes home

### 6 May 1974

The Liverpool Echo's Michael Charters recorded the thoughts of the man himself on the Monday after Liverpool's glorious triumph:

'I went to the barber's shop first thing this morning before going to Anfield. I wanted a trim to start the day right because I had been in London since last Wednesday and I felt as though I had been away for months.

'The mail and telegrams were piled high on my desk. They contained congratulations from people all over the country. And this was apart from those which people sent to Wembley before the game. There must have been just as many.

'The reception yesterday was just incredible. It was better than 1965. I want to thank them all for welcoming the players as they did.

'They are the best fans in the world and we try to win something every season because that's what they deserve.

## Cup success is just the start says Shanks

The comprehensive 3-0 victory - and the manner of the success – delighted Shankly: "What pleased me most was the way we won the Cup.

"It was done in style. I think now that this team can go on to become even better than the mid-sixties side. The prospects are endless.

"The old team won the League-Cup-League in successive years. We'll win the League next year."

At Picton Library, at 4pm on the Sunday, Shankly was able to address the huge crowd – some of whom had been there since midday.

"We have had many great memories at Liverpool Football Club during the last few seasons. I think today I felt prouder than I have ever done before.

"We have a great team here and I said we would go back to Wembley three years ago.

"They went back yesterday and not only did they win the Cup but they gave an exhibition of football. But above all we are pleased for you. It is you we play for. It is you who pay our wages."

He added: "Now we look to the future.

"That's always got to be done. We have our last game of the season at Tottenham on Wednesday so I've given the lads a day off today!

"They won at Wembley with great football.

"They can go on from there because we've been building up to this for three years, during which we have been the best team in the country.

"There's no end to it.

"This is basically a young side, capable of winning the League next year.

"We're good enough to win the League each season if we didn't have to play 60 or 70 games each year.

"We're the best team in the land and our consistency over the last three years proves that.

"It is all genuine ability.

"We played pure football at Wembley, stringing together a dozen passes to score goals."

## 15 June 1974

## Shankly OBE
## – take a bow!

The whole of Merseyside was delighted to see Bill Shankly given an OBE in the Honours List although most would have preferred him to have been knighted.

In the Liverpool Echo, he typically turned the praise to the club and the fans when he said:

"Naturally I'm very honoured that I am to get this medal, but I regard it as an honour for Liverpool Football Club and for the people who pay to come through the Anfield turnstiles.

"They should be getting an OBE – the Anfield crowd.

"Anfield was a very ordinary place in 1959 when I came. It was nothing like Goodison where men of vision had built a fine ground years earlier.

"But the money we have made with our successes on the field has been put to good use and Anfield is top class now.

"That is possibly what pleases me most, that the ground is worthy of a first-class club.

"So far as the honour is concerned, I would like to say that I haven't received it through any flannelling of dignitaries in the city or in football.

"I'm delighted that the honour has come to Liverpool.

"That is how I look at it – not a personal thing, but something which has been awarded through me to the Liverpool supporters."

# The soccer world is left in shock . . .

There are days in history that you never forget. Just like John F. Kennedy's assassination, the first moon landing, July 12, 1974 was a day, in a soccer sense, that will never be forgotten in the city of Liverpool.

It was the day Bill Shankly, a football god to Liverpudlians, stunned the world of football by announcing his retirement.

He had threatened it before, although not for public consumption. This time he went through with his threat and the fact that the Reds had just won the FA Cup and Shankly himself had received the OBE added to the shock.

Those words, spoken just a few months earlier about when and how it might happen with his health the number one priority suddenly hit home.

Bill Shankly always looked in control, the supreme master. But getting Liverpool to the top and keeping them there had come at a massive personal price. His life had revolved around football, football and more football. Now, for the first time ever, he had taken a decision for himself, his wife Nessie and his family.

It still left the whole of the football world reeling. His great pal

Joe Mercer said: "That's impossible. I can't accept that. That doesn't ring true. I hope not. I prefer not to believe it."

Tommy Smith, the Anfield Iron, spoke for the players.

"I just can't believe it.

"It's all very nostalgic. Retire?

"The close season's always been too long for Shanks, never mind retirement."

## Tributes pour in for 'one in a lifetime'

As the news filtered through, the tributes for Shankly began pouring in. Ian Callaghan said: "I can't believe it. He's been the biggest influence on my career."

Former Everton boss Harry Catterick declared: "He is quite a remarkable man. I thoroughly enjoyed the rivalry we had as managers when both clubs gained championship and FA Cup success."

David Russell (Tranmere general manager and a friend for nearly 40 years) said: "I can only say good of him. We were on courses in the Air Force together. In all that time I don't think he's changed. He was a wholehearted player and he's still a wonderful club man."

Blues manager Billy Bingham said: "This is a real surprise. I recall that about a year ago he did say that if he ever left Liverpool he would sever all connections so I'm not surprised about the way he's done it. I've nothing but admiration for Bill Shankly. He's getting out on top."

His old centre half and Colossus Ron Yeats revealed: "I was talking to him not that long ago. He still seemed as chirpy, as strong as ever. I think it's probably the best time for him to go. I would not like to see him on the downgrade. It's a bad day for football, for Liverpool and for me. He's one in a lifetime."

Momentous decision: Shankly breaks the news at a press conference

**13 July 1974**

## Day the news hit town

Experienced Liverpool Echo journalist Alf Green revealed how the city received the news. He said: 'An announcement broadcast over the public address system in St John's Market, stopped shoppers in mid-stride. "What was that?" said one woman. "If it's true my old fella will be in mourning for a week. Maybe longer."

The Echo then painted the picture of how the press conference unfolded that announced his retirement:

'Shankly picked up a cup of tea and helped himself to a brown bread sandwich.

As if he didn't want to get to THAT moment, he said "The World Cup was very disappointing, wasn't it?

"If some of the stuff played in Germany had been played out there" – indicating the Anfield pitch – "the teams would have been hooted off the park."

'The banter went back and forth. Not a word was mentioned about the reason for us all being present.

"I told you before the World Cup that Yugoslavia wouldn't do any good.

"They play for fun, not for keeps. They play cards for money and then give you your money back. Too sweet to be wholesome."

'One of the TV crews switched on his portable sunlight, bringing Mr Shankly to his feet with the comment: "Hold it a minute. John Wayne has not arrived yet!"

'The laughter was stifled by Mr Smith (chairman John Smith), as he made the formal announcement that the King of Anfield had decided to abdicate.

'It was true then. The tension of waiting was over. Our worst fears had been confirmed. But at least we knew for sure.'

'AN ANNOUNCEMENT BROADCAST OVER THE PUBLIC ADDRESS SYSTEM IN ST JOHN'S MARKET STOPPED SHOPPERS IN MID-STRIDE'

Shanks tries to explain why he is calling it a day . . .

## I was the best manager in Britain because I never cheated anyone

Daily Post writer Erlend Clouston captured more comments from Shanks at the press conference:

"Holland? If they started at Anfield like they started the World Cup final, they'd have been hooted off the park. Muller? A good player, but he had three bad games out of four against us.'

Then finally he spoke about himself and his legacy:

"I was the best manager in Britain, because I was never devious or cheated anyone. I'd break my wife's leg if I played against her, but I wouldn't cheat her."

## They made me offers Paul Getty wouldn't have refused

Did he have any unfulfilled ambitions? That was one question posed to the great man as he announced his retirement.

"Well, it would have been good to have won the European Cup.'

Highlights?

"Winning the Cup in 1965 – it was an affront that a club like Liverpool had never won that. And my recent dealings with the directors.

"I like knowing what makes people tick and I've seen them in their true light in the past few days.

"They made me offers Paul Getty wouldn't have refused."

LIVERPOOL DAILY POST
GIVES ALL THE LOCAL, NATIONAL & WORLD NEWS IN THE MORNING
RELIABLE NEWS • COMMERCIAL NEWS • SPORT • FEATURES

Liverpool Echo

MARI MARKET
FOR FAST RESULTS —
Tel: 051-227 3030

Spotlight is on Shankly—and out come the words that stunned Merseyside

# DAY THE NEWS HIT TOWN

By Alfred Green

## That's bad news says Wilson

Even the Prime Minister of the day, whose constituency was Huyton in Liverpool, couldn't believe it. A newspaper reported: 'Prime Minister, Mr Harold Wilson, told of the good news and the bad when addressing a rally at Bangor last night.

"I was hacking on the ticker machine at Downing Street this morning whether the news that the building society interest rates were to remain unchanged had been announced. The news came through and that was the good news.

"Then came the bad – that Bill Shankly was to retire. There will be much weeping in the hills and dales of my constituency tonight – except among Everton fans."'

## Nessie: 'I smoked 20 a game worrying for him'

Nessie Shankly told the Liverpool Echo: "No-one can go on forever and the last few years have taken a big toll. The strain on Bill has been tremendous. He's come through it. He's fine, but I've not had very good health this last year.

"It's stupid for a grown woman to admit, but I'm so anxious for him on a Saturday afternoon that I smoke 20 cigarettes just while the match is on."

## The debt to Shankly

In a leader article, the Liverpool Daily Post declared: 'It is only a few weeks ago that Merseyside was congratulating Bill Shankly on his OBE and not much earlier than that, the city was echoing to the cheers for his team as they returned with the FA Cup.

'Now alas the Shankly era has suddenly ended, and the city will never be quite the same again.

'The Scot has done his adopted city proud. He has boosted morale; he has been worth countless millions in upholding the image of the city throughout Britain and the world.'

Silver service: Nessie spoke honestly about Bill retiring

Both the Post and Echo carried an avalanche of tributes:

Brian Hall: "I told him he was mad. I didn't believe it.

"But I phoned up to check and they told me it was true. It's a great loss to the club. No matter who they get, they'll never get anyone quite like him.

"I can't imagine anyone ever again standing on the top of the steps of St George's Hall asking 250,000 to please be quiet and getting the kind of silence in which you could hear a pin drop."

John Fallon (39, of Cantril Farm): "Shankly couldn't retire . . . could he? And if he really has, who can take his place?"

As Mr Fallon spoke, in one of the most famous 'Liverpool' pubs in the city, a news broadcast announced Shankly's retirement. One man near him, who had been arguing vociferously Shankly would never go, burst into tears.

No one laughed as he pulled out a hankie then took a large swig of his beer. One of the stunned drinkers, Mr Alan Dugdale, 41, of Bootle said: "He's only showing how we all feel.

"This is a tragedy for the club and the city. Liverpool will never be the same again."

'BILL FIRST TOLD ME HE WAS GOING TO GIVE IT UP WHILE WE WERE WATCHING TELEVISION ONE NIGHT – THOUGH I HAD ASKED HIM TO RETIRE 12 MONTHS AGO. I WAS VERY UPSET WHEN HE REFUSED'

End of an era: Shankly with Brian Clough in his last match in charge – the Charity Shield against Leeds in August, 1974

It can be lonely when your husband is a local hero like Bill – Nessie

Daily Post journalist Diana Pulson conducted a fascinating interview with Nessie Shankly who told her:

"I'm also glad that the news is out. We've been discussing it for five weeks and since the decision was made it's been like sitting on a time bomb.

"Bill first told me he was going to give it up while we were watching television one night – though I had asked him to retire 12 months ago.

"I was very upset when he refused then so when I heard of this decision it was a great relief.

"Mind you, I realise what a wrench it is for him. When he says it was like walking to the electric chair, he means it.

"Football is his whole life, he eats, drinks and sleeps it.

"You'd be battering your head against a brick wall if you asked him to forget it, so I'm not deluding myself that though he's leaving Liverpool, he's also leaving the game. Nor would I ask him to – it would be too cruel.

"It has been lonely.

"There are tremendous stresses and strains involved when your husband is the sort of local hero Bill is.

"I don't begrudge him anything and any sacrifices he has made have been with my blessing – but it will be nice to have him home more often, not to have him going off for away matches.

"He's always been considerate, ringing me every evening. He had this funny habit of not telling me where he was going, when he was on the lookout for a good footballer.

"So I'd just get a phone call from goodness knows where – that's Bill.

"If he's got something to say to you, then he'll say it.

"He's like that with his family and that was how he treated the girls when they were growing up. I don't say that he's a hard man, but he's not sentimental.

"He doesn't go in for any sloppy presents, or anything like that."

# BILL SHANKLY

## Best Wishes

## FROM THE LIVERPOOL KOP

# THE KOP SAYS IT ALL!

## You'll never walk alone..

30 APR 1975

The final farewell—Bill Shankly salutes the Kop.

BILL SHANKLY and the Kop dominated the Anfield scene for 15 years. And they put on a memorable double act once again last night.

As the great Shanks bid an emotional farewell to the Liverpool fans, just nine months after he retired as manager, the Kop reassured him in full voice that " You'll always be our king."

It is with these adoring supporters that Bill Shankly has established a relationship unique in the history of the game. No manager has become so close to his club's fans, and Mr. Shankly, more moved than at any time I have known him, told them what their support had meant to him.

Before the real mechan-

## Touching farewell was always on the cards from Shankly's adoring Kop family

The Anfield messiah holds aloft a trophy for the final time in front of his beloved disciples. Only it's not the league championship, the UEFA Cup or the FA Cup – but it means just as much to him. Shankly is pictured (above) in a Liverpool Echo cutting from April 1975 at his farewell testimonial just nine months after he retired. He is holding a giant 'best wishes' card that had been passed around the Kop and signed by Kopites. A simple, personal gesture from the masses that touched the great man. He treasured those signatures like a fan with his autograph. A symbol of a special bond and still a prized possession of the Shankly family today.

# HAPPY

TO SHANKLY, MEMBERS OF THE LIVERPOOL
KOP WERE JUST AN EXTENDED FAMILY.
HERE ARE JUST SOME OF THE MANY
REMARKABLE STORIES FROM THE FANS
LUCKY ENOUGH TO HAVE KNOWN HIM

**With the world told of his shock decision to stand down, Shanks could plan ahead to his retirement after the Reds' Charity Shield date with Brian Clough's Leeds in August, 1974. He was to find out, however, that life after Liverpool was a very different game . . .**

## 15 July 1974

### Good days in the bad years

The Echo's Charles Lambert captured the essence of why Shankly was so down to earth. Bill was one of ten children of John Shankly – five boys and five girls. The man himself said: 'They were 100 per cent honest. They didn't have much themselves, but they were always willing to help others as much as they could.

'My mother was a very kind woman, and something she used to say still sticks in my mind. It was: "If I have enough I have plenty, and I don't want any more."

'That is a really great philosophy, and I've always tried to bear it in mind.

'I'm not greedy, and I don't want anything to which I'm not entitled. My father would always rather give than take.'

On his early life going down the local pits, Shanks said: 'All I used to live for was finishing each shift and tearing off to the nearest pitch for a game.

'When I had the money I used to pay 1s 6d return rail fare to Glasgow. I would come away fired with the idea of playing like Charlie Napier, of Celtic, or David Meiklejohn, of Rangers, depending on which team was playing at home that particular week. You see, I was always a wing-half.'

## Shankly on the Kop – and a chat on the phone

*From Chris Rafferty, Liverpool*

Bill Shankly always had this remarkable affinity with the Kop; its passion, its humour and its dedication to all things Liverpool. It was still a major surprise when he turned up on the Kop one day unannounced.

I was 13 when I decided to contact Shankly after a chance meeting on the Kop. It is a meeting I will never forget.

The date was 22nd November, 1975. Shankly had left the club a year earlier but on this day, for a home game against Coventry City, he decided to come back. Only this time it was different.

I can't remember too much about the game. It was 1-1, but I'll never forget the occasion. We always stood in the same place, as people did back then. So there we are waiting for the game to kick-off when at about a quarter to three Bill Shankly walks onto the Kop. He walked right past us and into the middle, so we followed him.

I remember my mate gave him a Wrigley's (chewing gum) and Shankly gave me a red Murray mint. I kept it for years but it dissolved in the end! Everybody was astonished to see him among us on the Kop. We just couldn't believe it. It was incredible.

He stayed for the whole game and had to get a police escort off at the end. They took him out down by the Paddock because he was getting mobbed. Everyone was trying to give him their scarves and we were all singing "Shankly is a Kopite" and all that. It was magnificent.

It wasn't long after this that I wrote to him.

I sent the letter on the Monday and got a reply on the Friday.

There was a campaign led by the fans at the time to get Shankly on the club's board and I recall him telling the fans thanks, but no thanks. He felt it might have hindered

**Personal message: Still treasured by fan Chris Rafferty**

# 'BILL SHANKLY WAS LIVERPOOL FOOTBALL CLUB'

Liverpool's season and he didn't want to cause any distractions. That's the way he was, but I still put in my letter that I thought he should be on the board. I couldn't believe it when he phoned me up later that night. At first I thought it was somebody messing about but then we just started talking about football.

Liverpool had a game the next day and we were talking about what we thought was going to happen, until my dad took the phone off me and he was on to Shankly for ages.

He spoke to my dad again on the phone. My old fella used to run the kids footy back then and had tried to get Shankly to come down and do something for them. Shanks had called back to apologise that he couldn't make it as he was due on telly the same night.

He didn't have to call back but he did. That's the type of man he was. The thing with Shankly was that he was respected. Evertonians probably won't admit it now but even they liked him.

He was a working class Protestant from Scotland but crossed all sorts of cultural boundaries.

Shankly had a respect for people who earned it. It doesn't happen nowadays but Shankly was bigger than the players.

Bob Paisley, Rafa and Kenny Dalglish, even Gerard Houllier to a certain extent, have all been heroes, but Shankly was everything to us. He was the embodiment of the club. Bill Shankly was Liverpool.

---

> **16 July 1974**

### From player to manager – with success

It was now a time for memories and Bill recalled his arrival at Workington in January 1954: 'I remember when I arrived. It was dark and I went through the door and felt round for the light switch. Someone asked me what I was looking for and I said the light. He said: "You won't find one here – there's no electricity."

**17 July 1974**

### The 'miracle man' moves to Anfield

The Echo's Charles Lambert now penned a nostalgic series painting an overview of Shankly's time with Liverpool, beginning where it all began. 'We reorganised the whole training system,' he quoted Shankly.

'Every day we conferred and discussed training, and before we left for the training ground every phase and detail was planned so that we could move swiftly from one function to another.'

In came group training, with players being divided into separate groups according to their needs.

In came the "Shankly sweat-box" – an idea which had been tried out at Huddersfield.

Melwood was immediately earmarked for special attention. It was a bit of a wilderness and the ground was bumpy, but Shankly saw its possibilities.

'I remember remarking to someone when I arrived – here was where Liverpool could be made great.'

The supporters could have been forgiven for remaining sceptical.

At the end of the first week under the new regime Liverpool played Cardiff at Anfield – and lost 4-0.

Liverpool lost the next match too – at Charlton, on Boxing Day.

---

MR & MRS W. SHANKLY,
30, BELLEFIELD AVENUE,
LIVERPOOL L12 1LS.

Chris Rafferty Esq.,
3,Henry Hickman Close,
Netherton,
Bootle.IO

Oct 28th I976.

Dear Chris,,

Received your letter,thanks very much indeed I really enjoyed your remarks about your loyalty to me,and of course your mates.I can assure you that what you say is more to me than all the money in the world.I knew before I came to Liverpool that deep down there were thousands of people like yourself who were dying to have a football team.So I worked hard to give you that.I can assure you it was no easy task.However,it worked in the end,and you have a team and a ground,and I am proud of all of you.

Give my regards to your Dad,he must be a busy man Chris,as football takes up all your life.

Remember me to the boys on the "KOP".I will come in again to see all of you.

"God Bless"

W.Shankly.

But then, two days later, they won 2-0 in the return match at Anfield.

It was their first win under Bill Shankly, and the last match of a decade of disappointment.

**18 July, 1974**

### Shankly: I'll be at Wembley

Bill Shankly now revealed that despite his announcement, he would still be with Liverpool for the pre-season Charity Shield clash at Wembley.

But not before former Manchester City coach Malcolm Allison claimed he had received an unofficial approach to take over from Shanks.

But Allison, manager of Third Division Crystal Palace at that point, said: "If there was an official approach I would still not be interested in the job.

"And the same goes for Leeds United."

He added: "The trouble is that both are too easy.

"Anyone reasonably good would be able to keep things ticking over at Anfield and Elland Road."

Clearly, the flamboyant Allison was living in his own dream world at this point.

**19 July 1974**

### Fighting spirit

Shankly opened up to the Echo's Charles Lambert with some intriguing thoughts:

'Obviously a cosmopolitan city like Liverpool produces some wildcats, people who are the nicest people in the world but who have hot tempers.

'They have a fighting spirit with fighting blood in their veins, but mixed with this is a tremendous kindness. They will take your life one minute and give you their last penny the next.

'I class myself as one of them. I'm a working class man. I used to work down the pit. I have no airs and graces. I might be better off now than some of them, but it

## Shanks' kindness ensured I never walked alone

*Jack Moran, Crosby, Liverpool*

It is not always what people do for you but for those close to you that leaves a lasting impression.

For me, it was Bill Shankly's helping hand to a good friend that prompted me to retrace the great Scotsman's steps, walking from Anfield to Glenbuck to raise money for charity.

I was more of a snooker man than football fan but my pal Harry Stratton lived and breathed Liverpool Football Club and worshipped the ground Shankly walked on.

Harry only missed two games in 33 years: the day his wife died and the day he buried her!

He would talk endlessly about Bill Shankly and how he would like to shake his hand. So I wrote to Shankly telling him about Harry. Sure enough, he replied a few days later saying how he would love to shake Harry's hand!

We were invited to Anfield to meet the manager. Harry got his wish and I met a man I would never forget.

I saw that day just how dedicated he was to his fans. He lived for them and they came before anything else. When we got there Gerald Sinstadt and the Kick Off team were waiting to see Shankly to interview him for their TV show.

But when Shankly came out of his office he looked at me and asked me and Harry into his office first and told the TV crew that they might have a long wait.

Two hours we were in there for, talking football with Bill Shankly. His enthusiasm was incredible.

As we came out it emerged that one of the cameramen had been onto the pitch trying to get some footage of the stadium. Needless to say, Shankly wasn't happy. Apparently nobody went on that pitch without

his say so. I've never heard a person swear so much. They never did get their interview but Harry got his handshake.

I recall him saying he would never wash that hand again!

I've never seen anyone as overjoyed as he was when he met Bill Shankly.

That was back in the early 1970s when Shankly's work toward building Liverpool into the 'bastion of invincibility' he spoke of was well underway.

It was some 25 years later that I returned to Anfield with that meeting in mind. At the age of 70, I had decided to raise money to help another friend, Father O'Leary at the Jospice in Thornton, and by making the 300-mile walk to Glenbuck I did so in memory of Bill Shankly.

They sent a piper down to Anfield from Glenbuck. "Amazing Grace" was one of Shankly's favourite songs. As the piper played it there was a tear in my eye as he walked towards the Kop.

I am not really a football fan but this was a marvellous moment.

My walk began from the centre spot in front of a full house against Manchester United in April 1997. A 3-1 defeat wasn't the best start but seven days later I arrived at my destination, tired but elated.

Among the 4000 strong welcoming party at Glenbuck were Ron Yeats and Ian St John.

A football match was arranged between a team from my hometown Crosby, the Shankly Reds, and an assembled Cherrypickers side. The Shankly Reds, captained by my grandson Shaun, ran out 5-1 winners.

The walk raised £15,000 and was timed to coincide with the last day of demolition of the old mining town where Shankly grew up.

There was still time, however, for me to visit the old family home and keep a brick as a reminder of the man who had made his good friend and countless more so happy. A small piece of history from the man who had defined that of Liverpool FC.

has not altered my outlook on life or how I feel.

'I like Liverpool and its people, and I'm glad I came here. They accepted me and I like to think that, with the success Liverpool FC has had since I joined them, I have repaid them for their loyalty.'

**20 July 1974**

### Fans pay their tribute to Bill Shankly in prose and verse

The Liverpool Post & Echo were both awash with tributes:

One fan wrote: 'Mr Shankly's greatest contribution to both game and personnel (player and supporter) has been his sincerity, honesty, wit and above all character. These virtues have extended beyond the boundaries of Anfield. So now we bid goodbye to a truly loveable man and I'm sure he will accept the royal truism that 'The King is dead! Long live the King!"
**J. McCarthy, Warwick Road, Banbury, Oxon.**

'He is worshipped by Liverpudlians throughout the globe. If the tragedy of his retirement becomes reality Liverpool FC will never reach the same heights as those reached during The King's reign. S.O.S. – Save Our Shanks.'
**D Quick, Cockshead Road, Woolton, Liverpool.**

**22 July 1974**

### 'Shankly Parade' plan under fire

There were reports of plans to change the name of Liverpool's city centre Bold Street to 'Shankly Parade'.

It was greeted with mixed emotions. Mr Louis Samson, who had built up his photographic business in Bold Street over 15 years, said: "I am writing to all the other traders asking them to support me in opposing any

change of name for the street, which is known nationally and internationally.

"I'm not against naming something after Mr Shankly. He has done a lot for the city. But I'm suggesting that instead of renaming Bold Street why don't they give his name to a youth club, a social centre, an underground station, or the St John's beacon."

The idea to dub the street Shankly Parade came from young Liberal Councillor David Alton, deputy chairman of the city's Highways and Environment Committee. He explained: "Bold Street has just been pedestrianised and, despite initial opposition, it is now working. Giving it this new name would help to transform it into an exciting, Continental-type piazza."

The street was never re-named.

### 24 July 1974

### Shankly's vision – another European trophy

As FA Cup holders, Liverpool were paired with Norwegian semi-professionals Stromsgodset in the opening round of the Cup Winners' Cup. The media still went to Shanks for a reaction. He said: "It's as good as a bye. Nobody could ask for anything better than that and Norway's a nice place into the bargain. We are starting off on the right foot without a doubt.

"I'll tell you something. Anybody who meets Liverpool will have a terribly difficult task on their hands. It's all taking shape. This lad Ray Kennedy (Shankly's last big signing, captured from Arsenal just days before his retirement announcement) is already looking a very dangerous player.

"He can play a bit, believe me, and I'll tell you something else – Liverpool could win a couple of cups this season. In all probability they will."

## Heavenly day I was 'adopted' by Shanks

From Lizzie Osborne,
Wenford, Exeter

**M**any years ago, like lots of us did, I used to keep scrapbooks from the "Pink Echo" treasuring reports and pictures of my beloved Liverpool.

At the end of the season, I would take the books into Liverpool's reception to ask if they could be autographed. I would collect them a few weeks later.

After the second season, the receptionist said I must wait as someone wanted to speak to me. I waited in the corridor, worried that I had done something wrong. I heard footsteps approaching and, on looking up, saw Bill Shankly coming towards me. He immediately gave me a bear hug, telling me he had wanted to meet the person who brought in the books. I was so overcome all I could do was burst into tears.

'HE LOOKED AFTER ME LIKE A SECOND DAD, ALWAYS SEEING THAT I WAS OKAY AND ALWAYS AT THE END OF A PHONE WHEN I NEEDED HIM'

### 24 July, 1974

### Letters bring tears to Bill's eyes

It was revealed that thousands of fans had written to Bill, pleading with him to stay. Shankly said: "I feel very touched. This makes me feel I have possibly achieved something at Liverpool."

Two young men arrived at Mr Shankly's home with a card signed by 200 customers from the Derby Arms Hotel wishing him well for the future.

Shanks said: "A couple of hundred signatures on the card were signed in red ink, but there were three signed in blue. It is amazing. Even Everton boys have said they are sorry to see me go.

"Everybody seems to be affected. I have had letters from Canada, New Zealand, Australia and Scotland as well as from Liverpool."

Commenting on Liberal Councillor David Alton's idea for changing the name of Bold Street to Shankly Parade, he said: "Anything that is in Liverpool that has my name to it I would be proud of.

"But I do not want anything to do with any controversy. I came to Liverpool to manage a football team."

### 27 July, 1974

### Paisley is king – and Bill goes in style

Horace Yates, reporting from the Liverpool shareholders' AGM, where Bob Paisley was confirmed as successor to Shankly, wrote: 'Mr Shankly's priceless humour prevented last night's handing over ceremony from becoming the tearful farewell it might have been.

'He recalled, for example, the day, more than 14 years ago, when president T.V. Williams visited Huddersfield Town's ground and asked him: "How would you like to manage the best club in England?"

He then invited me into the lounge to meet the players.

"Is this heaven?" I asked myself, not realising at the time that this would be the start of the friendship of my life. I had immediately been adopted! During the time that Bill was still manager I was constantly invited to have lunch with him at the ground.

Bill would even come to my flat for tea and, in return, would invite me to his house.

He looked after me like a second dad, always seeing that I was okay and always at the end of a phone when I needed him.

Our friendship continued until his death and there is not one day that goes by that I don't think of Bill and smile as I remember the pearls of wisdom he would relate to me.

I remember with love the legend, the genius, the man who was my confidante, my inspiration, my mentor and a wonderful, wonderful man who I feel so privileged to have been able to call my friend.

'Mr Shankly promptly replied: "You mean you want me to come and make them the best club in England!"

He added: 'The tributes, the letters, the Press comment, have meant more to me than money.

"If you think I don't want money, you would be wrong. But all I want is enough to live on. All I have done has been for the club and the people – for without the people there would be no club."

**29 July 1974**

### Make him Sir Bill plea by Reds' fans

Fans from Ormskirk near Liverpool petitioned the Queen to knight Shankly for his services to football and Liverpool in particular.

Shankly said: "It's all news to me. I don't ask for anything from anybody, but the fact that such an action has come from the ordinary man and woman in the street means more to me than money."

**1 August, 1974**

### I salute our fantastic football fans

Bill Shankly, talking to the Echo's Alex Goodman, remembered: 'Once, I recall going onto the Kop about an hour before a match just to talk to the fans and one of them thought I was going to watch the match from there. "Come and stand over here, Bill," he said. "You'll get a good view."

'Since I made my decision to retire, our front door has been besieged with people and I have received over 500 letters and telegrams. The tributes that were paid were wonderful, astonishing, emotional and touching.

'They came from people my wife and I know, and from people we don't know. And they came from people in high places right down to the rank and file, the working men, just like me, who go to Anfield.

## Furious Shanks told my mate he couldn't stay

**From Bernard Pentony, County Durham**

My memories of Bill Shankly relate to the early weeks of his Anfield career in 1959 when Liverpool were in the old Second Division. Dick White was the Liverpool captain and was coming up to my area with the team to play Middlesbrough. Dick had been in the Forces (National Service) with me and it was arranged that we would have a weekend in Darlington after the match.

Things didn't go very well in the game and Dick put through his own goal twice. In fact, he nearly made it a hat-trick with one hitting the post.

I met Dick outside Ayresome Park and was talking to him when Shankly came up. Dick asked if it was still alright to stay in Darlington. Shanks was furious. The game had finished 3-3 and in no uncertain terms he told Dick that he couldn't stay on as he was in for extra training on the Sunday. Gone was the reunion weekend. Shankly had demonstrated his determination to improve Liverpool in every way.

## Pilgrimage to the village where the legend was born

**Some contrasting memories from Chris Wood, Liverpool**

I went with some friends to see Liverpool play a pre-season friendly at Glasgow Celtic in August 1998 and on the way back we decided to call in at Glenbuck. We had heard about the plaque that had been placed there in the Spring of the previous year and it made sense to call in while we were in the area as it wasn't much of a detour from our route back to Merseyside. We found the plaque easily enough.

It was a lovely summer's evening and I parked my car right across the road from the plaque and we got out to inspect it closer. As we did so a couple, probably in their 60's, walked towards us with their dog and stopped to talk. The man said he lived a couple of miles away and he and others always came by to make sure the plaque was ok and to tend the area around it. At this stage we hadn't been to Glenbuck itself and the man said he would lead the way so we set off in a little two-car convoy up the road until we reached the village, or rather the site where the

Training day: Bill wanted everything right on the training ground

The lost village of Glenbuck where Shanks was brought up

'For me that was better than going round with the hat and collecting £100,000. The only money I want is what I have earned, and all these tributes from the fans mean far more to me than anything like that.

'I appreciate everyone who comes to Anfield. Now, perhaps in future days, I will have more time to talk to these wonderful fans; the fans who have meant so much to me during my time here.'

**2 August, 1974**

## Reflections on a great career

**I salute our fantastic football fans**

by Bill Shankly

Alex Goodman then went on to talk to Shankly – about Shankly: 'When Mr Shankly does bow out of the managerial chair he does not want to be judged on the number of trophies he has captured. He says: "I would like to be judged not really on what I did but on the fact that I never cheated, I was not dishonest and I was never careless with money or people. Basic honesty is the greatest thing any human being can possess. Some people cannot help being dishonest, but if everyone was honest there would be none of the tangles there are in the world today.

"I have never begged for anything and what I have received I have earned. And no matter what happens in the future the memory of that will never be erased.

"And it has all been done with just a basic knowledge of the game, of training and of people."

village had been. This man had lived in the village as a boy. It was years since the village had been inhabited. All that remained were shells of buildings and rocks where buildings had once stood. But this man could see something we could not see.

He could see the village as it used to be, with all its people, its close-knit community and its social life. He spread his arms wide and pointed at what to us looked like wilderness and explained how it had been before.

He brought it to life with his actions and words but all we could see were boulders, decaying properties (or what was left of them) and beautiful scenery in the distance. Then he stopped talking and I knew he was close to tears.

We were too. To see this man so upset at what had happened to a part of his life was upsetting for us too. But the village couldn't keep pace with modern life. It was too isolated and the mining industry that had kept it alive was long gone. We returned to our cars and went our separate ways.

We've all heard of the Glenbuck Cherrypickers. It has a mythical almost legendary name. And we stood near the spot where they used to play and it took us back in time too, but to a time we hadn't experienced ourselves. As we stood amongst the debris of a once-proud village with one of its former inhabitants, we probably shed a silent tear too for all the history that was destroyed when the village was emptied; except it never can be totally destroyed because it will always be there in someone's thoughts long after its last inhabitant has died.

A tiny village but what an impact it created. It wasn't just about Bill. He might have been the most well known of his siblings, but five Shankly boys played or managed in the professional game.

Glenbuck has gone forever from the face of the map but its name can't and nor should it. A beautiful plaque so thoughtfully chiselled and so tenderly cared for is a permanent reminder, not just of Bill Shankly's early life, but of all the men, women and children with whom he shared his childhood and adolescent existence.

> ### 13 August 1974

### The last goodbye – crowned with Celtic honour

In front of 60,000 at Parkhead for Billy McNeill's testimonial, Bill Shankly was given a rousing reception by the home crowd in what was his grand farewell from football.

It was Billy's testimonial night and when he walked out with Mr Shankly to join the players round the centre circle, the crowd erupted. 'Shankly, Shankly,' they chorused.

When Jock Stein joined them and embraced his friend Shankly, the enthusiasm knew no bounds.

"I never dreamt when I used to come to this ground as a schoolboy 50 years ago, that I would end my career here with a finale as memorable as this," said Shankly.'

### 14 August 1974

### Official retirement day one, but Shanklys take life as usual

In a personalised feature piece, written in the local press by Margaret Farrall, it was revealed that on day one of official retirement Nessie Shankly was at home looking after her two granddaughters, Karen, aged nine, and Pauline, aged eight, who were staying at their West Derby home (Bill was on his way back from Scotland after the friendly against Celtic).

"It will be just the same as any other day," said Mrs Shankly.

The feature reported that there were no special plans, apart from a decision to take a holiday.

"But we haven't even discussed that," answered Nessie, when asked where and when they were going.

"It will be a trial period. Retirement comes to everyone. We will just have to face it as it comes along," she said.

"I'm a Scrabble addict, but Bill

## The day Nessie paid her respects with the fans

I once wrote to Nessie Shankly in the 1990's and asked her if she would be willing to be interviewed by Liverpool's Norwegian Fan Club. Sadly, this lovely lady's health was declining but she took the trouble to ring me up and explain why she wasn't really up to it.

I felt bad about asking her then, but I didn't know she was unwell at the time. I would never have approached her otherwise. She was kind and gentle over the phone, despite her illness.

It started me thinking about her and reminded me of the day when she went to Anfield to pay her respects after Hillsborough. She could have gone straight to the reception and by-passed the queue, but she obviously didn't feel that was right. She queued up with everyone else for a long time before she got inside the stadium. And you know Bill wouldn't have gone to the reception either. He would have been in the queue with his beloved fans.

## How Shanks came to the rescue after hotel disaster

I had two Norwegian Liverpool fans stay with me over Christmas in 1977. I was living in London at the time and they were booked into some grotty hotel near Paddington Station. When I met them at their hotel on Christmas Day, I gave them their presents, personally signed photographs of Bill Shankly.

They were absolutely thrilled, but they left the photographs in their rooms because we were going straight to St Pancras station to catch a train to Nottingham where Liverpool were playing the following

**One of the people: Nessie signs an autograph at Bill's testimonial in 1975**

> ## 'I SPOKE TO MY MOTHER A FEW DAYS LATER AND SHE SAID: "OH, SOMEONE RANG FOR YOU THE OTHER NIGHT BUT THEY DIDN'T LEAVE THEIR NAME" AND WHEN I ASKED FOR MORE SHE SAID: "OH, I DON'T KNOW BUT HE WAS SCOTTISH'

afternoon. We didn't return to the hotel until the end of their week. To our horror their rooms had been completely cleared out and because they hadn't stayed in the hotel for more than one night, the staff assumed they had moved on.

I was absolutely furious. They had paid for those rooms for a week and everything should have been left untouched whether they were there or not. Those priceless signed pictures had been thrown out, but there was

nothing I could do about it. The boys were distraught, but I told them not to worry because I would sort it (without knowing how the hell I was going to do that!).

I got replacement photographs and sent them up to Shanks with a covering letter explaining what had happened. He returned them to my address in Lewisham, but the letter I had written was on the headed notepaper of where I had recently been living, at my mother and step-father's

› doesn't like it very much. He has tried it but maybe now he will have more patience and more time."

**15 August 1974**

### Boersma to sign contract today

Of course, life had to go on. Shankly did show up briefly at Anfield when he responded to an invitation from the members of the staff. With his particular brand of North East humour, Bob Paisley asked: "Have you got the time, Bill?"

"No," he replied.

"Well, put this on your wrist and find out," said Paisley, handing over a gold wristlet watch.

"And give this to Nessie too, with our good wishes," added Bob, with a similar gift for Mrs Shankly.

**10 September 1974**

### Shankly 'no' to Portsmouth offer

Bill Shankly revealed that he was "not interested" in managing Second Division Portsmouth, said to be prepared to offer £20,000 a year for the right man able to restore them to football's elite.

The Echo's Michael Charters quoted the ex-Reds' boss as saying: 'I don't know where the Portsmouth chairman found my number, but he managed to phone me yesterday.

'It is flattering to be asked but I'm not really interested in the Portsmouth offer. If I can help anyone in the game, I will do so – when I am ready.'

**16 November 1974**

### Shankly magic boosts Tranmere

Bill Shankly had been asked by Tranmere boss Ron Yeats to give his struggling side a team talk ahead of their game against Preston at Prenton Park. The

> **Personal touch: Shankly typed out this letter to fan Chris Wood**

result? A 3-1 win for the home side.

Said Yeats after the game: "Mr Shankly enjoyed being part of a club again. He said a few words to the boys before the kick-off. He told them the game was easy and that it was only managers and coaches who made it hard. He will be coming training with us all next week. I enjoyed having him here. He was a morale booster and he did me a great favour."

Said Mr Shankly, obviously impressed by Tranmere's display: "I'll help anyone. That's my aim in life. I'll be coming to Tranmere periodically if I can assist them."

**22 March 1975**

## Testimonial also tribute to fans

Bill Shankly continued to be saluted across Merseyside. On this occasion he was made a life member of Southport Football Club and his response was typically enthusiastic. 'I was involved in a very pleasant and happy occasion at Southport, where I was presented with a magnificent inscribed scroll on being elected a life member of their club. It means as much to me as anything I have received because they are only a little club and they had gone to a lot of trouble to organise it.'

**22 April 1975**

## Salute to a folk hero

Liverpool FC would never forget Shankly's role in laying the foundations for a world class club. Chairman Mr John Smith said: "Not many of us have become legends in our own lifetime, but Bill has. And what he has done for football will reverberate in the game for years to come."

Bob Paisley added: "Paying tribute to this man is difficult. His example has been one for all to follow. I spent 15 years working with him and it was a privilege and a pleasure to be with him in

Honest Bill: Shanks in happy mood at his beloved Melwood

Great Scots and great pals: Shanks and Jock Stein

flat in Highgate, north London.

I never dreamed for a moment Bill would ring me, but it seems that he did to confirm he had sent on the pictures. I spoke to my mother a few days later and she said: "Oh, someone rang for you the other night but they didn't leave their name." When I asked for more she said: "Oh, I don't know, but he was Scottish."

I knew then what I had missed! But that's the kind of guy he was. When it came to "us", nothing was too much trouble for him. I know of someone else who did what I did one day, found the courage to walk up his drive and knock on his front door.

Bill chatted to this guy for a while and obviously it didn't take long for football to enter the conversation! The young man said he was going to Glasgow at the weekend to watch a Rangers v Celtic match. It turned out that he didn't have a ticket. He was just going up on the off-chance that he might find one up there. I think it was a final actually.

Tickets would have been like gold-dust. Without being asked, Bill said that he would see what he could do. Then he rang his good friend Jock Stein, Celtic's manager at the time, who sorted a ticket out for this

young guy. I don't know whether it was waiting for him at the stadium or whether Jock posted it to Bill, but that isn't really relevant to the story because it is what Bill did that IS the story. He took the time and trouble to help out a perfect stranger. This is why we loved him so much because he always told it how it was and he was always honest.

I think he would have hated being a manager in the modern game with all the agents and sky-high wages and that sort of thing. He was right for the time. My godson Dominic is now 21. His younger brothers Luke (16) and Matthew (12) both support Liverpool too.

But they know all about Bill and what he did for the club they follow. It's wonderful that his good name continues like this a generation on from the day he left us. His family can all be so very proud of what he achieved because he did it with such humility. The Press loved Bill because of his honesty. Compare that to modern-day managers. No comparison is there?

That's why I think Bill and Bob Paisley too would have hated to manage today. They were right for their time and what a time it was!

all those years of success.

"The shock of his departure from Liverpool was the biggest understatement of all time. His doctrine was to look after the easy things and let the big things take care of themselves. This he did to perfection."'

### 26 April 1975

A Liverpool Echo special saluted the great man ahead of his testimonial. The front page carried a lengthy salute from Bob Paisley regaling famous, and not so famous, tales. The following extracts are taken from this.

'He was completely dedicated to fitness. He didn't drink or smoke; he lived like an athlete. So when he demanded these qualities from his players, they could see in front of them the living example of what he was preaching – a fitness fanatic who could play in five-a-side football at 60 as well as he could when he was a younger man.

'In fact, he is so fit that I think he believes that when he goes up there (pointing to the skies) he will step right into the five-a-side team – on merit.

'Fitness was everything in his football creed. He looked on the game as simple, based on movement and possession, with players fit enough to move around fluently. He would not have complicated ideas in training or playing.

'His personality was overwhelming. Even now, as I walk around Anfield and Melwood, I can feel his presence in the air. It is everywhere. You open a drawer, sit in a chair, work at a desk, walk down a corridor and he's there around us still.

'It was this terrific personality, his passion for the game, which enabled him to lift the players. He did it by personality, not by tactical talks.

'He didn't have tactical talks at Anfield as most people understand them.

'We had a tactical board which we used – in the oddest way.

'It was my job to lay out 22 counters which represented the two teams.

'I used to do this before we had a team talk. Notice, not a tactical talk.

'The players would be sitting around the board when he walked in.

'The first thing he did, every time, before every match, was to sweep up the five opposing forwards and put them in his pocket. "They can't play", he said – always.

'So our 11 men were faced with just six opponents and that was before he really started.

'And some of the 'forwards' he swept into his pocket included people like Cruyff, Charlton and company, some of the best in the world!

'But that was his method – your opponents couldn't play.

'His favourite word was 'rubbish'. He would tell the Liverpool players that their opponents were rubbish and they were the greatest.

'It may seem silly, but it worked with Bill Shankly because of his personality. He made his players believe.'

Paisley also regaled a story from Shankly's Carlisle days:

'When he was manager at Carlisle, his team came off at half-time, two goals down, having been played out of sight. Bill's first words to the captain: "Why did you play towards that goal in the first half?" Captain: "Because I lost the toss and had to play that way."

'Bill: "What did you call at the toss?" Captain: "Heads." Bill: "My God! You should never call heads!"'

Frank McNeill, a Liverpool fan for over 36 years since childhood, regaled a Shankly tale from his playing days with Preston.

'My first glimpse at the potential intimacy and humanity of an Anfield crowd came in an early war-time game. Liverpool were playing Preston and – strangely enough – the two great Scottish masters were in direct opposition.

## Postcards from Rome and the European dream team

You may remember in his autobiography Bill made comments about the way he felt he had been treated by the club after he had retired and that he felt "insulted" when after months of not being asked to accompany the team to matches as a guest ... or even be at home games ... he felt "insulted" (with justification) when he was placed in a different hotel from the official party for the UEFA Cup final in Bruges in 1976.

Well, it seems things had changed a year later because he was definitely in Rome for the club's first European Cup final in 1977. What follows is an exact transcript of the dialogue from BBC radio commentator Peter Jones as the final whistle went:

"That's the whistle and Liverpool have made history, the third British club to win the European Cup, the one they wanted more than anything ... and Emlyn Hughes runs across to the bench and all the Liverpool staff are there, Bob Paisley and Ronnie Moran and Joe Fagan, the men who plotted this for Liverpool ... some of them look as if they cannot believe it ... and below us the figure of Bill Shankly, Bill Shankly ... the man who made this Liverpool team ... Bill, just lean across this commentary-box ... down there is the side you helped to build. What about that, Bill? What a night for you."

"This is the greatest night in Liverpool's history and the result of planning and simplicity and how to play the game in a simple manner and I think the whole world now realises that this is the way to play."

"Bill Shankly there, the man who built it all for them, a remarkable manager and taken over by another remarkable manager Bob Paisley ..."

There was so much pride and emotion in his voice as he answered the question from Peter Jones. I know he was never, ever a bitter man.

But he was a disappointed man after the way he felt the club had ignored him since his retirement. I didn't know he was in Rome until I bought the LP. I was there myself so obviously I wasn't listening on the radio. I am glad he made it. It must have been a great thrill for him to

**The succession: Shanks built the foundations and saw the Bootroom Boys lift the big one at Rome in 1977**

Emotional send-off: Shanks with Billy McNeill at Celtic

'The 18-year-old Billy Liddell played a penetrating ball to his captain and mentor, Matt Busby, who ghosted through the defence as if it wasn't there – only to fall in agony with a purely accidental pulled muscle.

'Watching from the old Boys' Pen in Kemlyn Road, I was privileged to see the succeeding events in close-up.

'First, the genuine anxiety on the sweating face of Shankly – a face made familiar by cigarette cards of the day.

'Next, the delicate care with which he and Liddell escorted their fellow Scot to the wall behind the Anfield Road goal. Finally, and most important, the complete lack of fuss with which Shankly coaxed an overcoat from a postman at the front of the crowd, to drape round his injured opponent's shoulders as he sat awaiting attention.'

## 'I loved scoring – I got 14 in one game!'

Picking up on the theme, Shankly said on his approach to fitness: 'When I was manager at Huddersfield, there was a field behind my house.

'The neighbours, men and boys, used to get me out there every Sunday to play.

'It started as a simple five-a-side game we called Lads and Dads.

'Then, as word of it got round, people used to come up from the town and try to get a game.

'I used to love scoring goals – I got 14 in one match.

'And one Sunday I played three 90-minute games – before breakfast, between breakfast and dinner and then in the afternoon.

'The players were mostly neighbours and their children who came along.

'And when I left to take the Liverpool job, they gave me a very nice gift which has an honoured place in my home.

'The Sunday game in the field at the back became quite famous in our neighbourhood. I loved every minute of it.'

watch Liverpool win the biggest prize of all with so many of his boys in the winning XI.

I sent him a postcard from Rome actually! Well, three of us signed it ... me, Dave "kissing the shoes" (!) Brown and another friend called Jeff. I knew his address from my visit the year before and whether he had been in Rome or not I just wanted him to know that he needed to be remembered too.

I can still remember exactly what I wrote. It was "Liverpool champions of Europe at last. Thanks for the part you played in making this dream come true," then we all signed it. I guess the card would have been delivered a couple of days after he got back from Italy. I hope it made him smile!

Another personal memory doesn't involve Liverpool's supporters; it concerns Glasgow Celtic's. Two days after the Charity Shield match at Wembley when Bill was given the honour of leading out his men in red for one final time, I made the long journey up to Glasgow from London by train where Liverpool were playing at Celtic Park in a testimonial match for Billy McNeill, the man who had captained the Celts to their European Cup win seven years earlier.

Before the teams appeared Billy McNeill walked into the centre-circle to take the applause of his people and then he beckoned for Bill Shankly to come and join him. Everyone knew it was Bill's last match 'in charge' before the competitive season started five days later under Bob Paisley. It was McNeill's night but that amazing crowd of 60,000 stood as one and it seemed the whole stadium was chanting "Shankly, Shankly" and "Liv-er-pool, Liv-er-pool."

They didn't just clap and cheer. They roared. I have never seen or heard anything like it before or since, not a tribute like that to someone who had never worn their famous green-and-white hoops. It was breathtaking. Makes me shiver thinking about it even now.

## On looking back on his time as a player:

'My attitude was that when I had finished playing one game, I began to prepare for the next one. I loved training and playing.

'But, when I think back now, I think I missed some of the fun out of life. Perhaps I was too dedicated. The laughs were there with the players but I think in general, I was too serious.

'I lived the life of a monk and I carried it to extremes. I saw other players fall by the wayside through drink or women. I was determined never to follow their example, but there is a happy medium which I should have tried to find.

'Many of my playing mates enjoyed themselves. They went out with girls, had a drink or two, and they could still play well. This was because of their mental attitude. They didn't allow the fun side of their lives to affect their playing careers...and I can see now, so many years later, that I might have been like them a bit more.

'But being alive was fun in those days. I loved it all, all the training and the playing. I just couldn't play enough.

'Playing for Scotland was the proudest moment of my career. Little boys at school in Scotland are taught about Scottish national heroes, people like Robert the Bruce.

'So when a Scot plays football for his country, he imagines himself as a national hero as well. That is why Scottish teams play the way they do for their country – with everything they've got.

'It is drummed into them at school and they never forget it.

## Shanks on my shoulders and our son's godparent!

**From Richie Williams (landlord of the Fir and Feathers, West Derby)**

I met Bill at a social club in Anfield a week after getting married in October 1972. It was an unforgettable night. At one point I had Bill on my shoulders singing "You'll Never Walk Alone." The party was for a wedding but Mr Shankly cut the night short because Match of the Day was on and he wasn't going to miss it! We lads all felt the same

but none of us had the guts to get up and go! Anyway, I told him that I ran some children's football teams, so we exchanged phone numbers and a friendship was formed. Bill used to phone and chat for hours about football tactics! One time I asked him to come to one of the presentations for the kids. I knew how busy he was and didn't really expect him to turn up, but he did and all the kids were absolutely thrilled. He spent the whole time signing autographs and when people had run out of paper for him to sign, they started coming over with £1, £5 and £10 notes but Bill refused to sign them, saying: "You

A man of his word: The people took Shanks to their hearts

never know when you might need them, son."

I had always said that if I ever had a son I would call him after Bill Shankly. Well we didn't have to wait long, because in June 1973 Richard George Shankly Williams was born and though it seemed like a dream, Bill agreed to be a godparent. What an honour. Of course nobody believed me when I told them, I didn't really believe it myself to be honest. I told him to be at the church (Christ The King, Aigburth) at 1 o'clock and when I got there, not really expecting him to turn up, he was pacing up and down looking extremely annoyed. He

thought I had said 12 o'clock and had been waiting there for over an hour! I was impressed. Not only had he turned up but he'd waited too. He knew I felt bad and simply said "If everything went to plan life would be boring, son", immediately making it alright again. I'll never forget him standing at the font and sighing as his name was put into a new life. I'm sure many people have done the same so that the great man's name lives on.

Scotland were touting him when he was at Liverpool but he said he would die in Liverpool. A day I'll never forget because it was my birthday.

'But the greatest moment of elation in my playing career was when Preston won the FA Cup at Wembley.

'At the end of the game, when I realised we had won, I don't mind admitting that I looked up at the skies and said: 'Thanks, God.''

## Thoughts along the way . . .

With a little bit more lesiure at his disposal Shankly was able to reveal his thoughts in a number of interviews he gave to the Press, as highlighted in the Echo special . . .

## On the black Brazilian tea which he drinks:

'This will cure the gout, arthritis, rheumatism – anything. Drink this and you'll live forever.'

## On playing for Scotland:

'It's fantastic. You look down at your dark blue shirt and the wee lion looks up at you and says: 'Get out after those English bastards.'

## On the Kop fans:

'They've no time for brutality. They've only got time for sportsmanship – and they've got time for football.'

## On stamina:

'Aye – it's a ninety-minute game for sure. In fact I used to train for a 190-minute game – so that when the whistle blew at the end of the match, I could have played another ninety minutes.'

### 29 April 1975

## Take a bow, Bill!

On the eve of Shankly's testimonial, he said: "I am glad the day has come.
"The worst thing in football is

waiting for the match, but it's all right when it comes. It's been even greater for me than waiting for the Cup final.

'I feel easier now that the day has arrived. The build-up has been lengthy, there has been much hard work by the testimonial committee and now I'm simply looking forward to going to Anfield to see the people I worked for all those years, who mean so much to me."

## Thanks Shanks, all the very best!

The game naturally encouraged further tributes. Bob Paisley revealed how Bill would never concede they had lost to superior opponents.

'If Liverpool lost, it was never because their opponents had been a better team. Bill would blame the pitch, the weather, the referee, the players' boots, even the strip they were wearing – never that they had lost to a

A proud man: Shanks at the christening he waited for

'WHEN I GOT THERE, NOT REALLY EXPECTING HIM TO TURN UP, HE WAS PACING UP AND DOWN LOOKING EXTREMELY ANNOYED. HE THOUGHT I HAD SAID 12 O'CLOCK AND HAD BEEN WAITING THERE FOR OVER AN HOUR! I WAS IMPRESSED. NOT ONLY HAD HE TURNED UP BUT HE'D WAITED TOO'

better team on the day.

'That was his reaction immediately when the game was over. But about Tuesday of the following week, he would be telling his men what they had done wrong and how bad they had been the previous Saturday. It was his psychology never to criticise his players immediately after they had lost. He reserved that for days later.

'He knew that our opponents had deserved to win but he'd never say so. Not for days, anyway.'

Shankly picked up on the theme to talk about training at Melwood: 'I never kept the Liverpool training system a secret. Anybody was welcome to look at it and copy it if they wanted to.

'Over the years, we had many visits from the foreign coaches, including the famous Yugoslav, Milanic. They were always welcome at Melwood where they could study our methods, almost live with us. There were a couple of Romanians, who lived with us for weeks and they were so hard up for money that I used to buy them meals.'

## The tributes poured in as the testimonial game loomed:

JOCK STEIN – 'He is the best thing that ever left Scotland as regards football.

'But he never denied Scotland. Many people leave and climb up the ladder to success and forget their own country.

'But Bill was always very proud of being a Scot.'

DIXIE DEAN – 'He was more like a father to his players than a manager.

'I never heard anyone criticise him in any way. He seemed to bring out the best in his players. It's just as well he wasn't at Liverpool when I was playing, though. The Kop wouldn't have been singing so much – I would have quietened them!'

**Kop honours Shankly**

NEARLY 40,000 fans crowded into Anfield last night to pay tribute to Liverpool's former manager, Bill Shankly, in a testimonial game in which Don Revie's select XI were beaten 6-2.

"You'll always be our king," the crowd roared as Shankly did a pre-match lap of honour, and then again at the end of the match he stood on the rail of the stand, with a two-fisted acknowledgement of the salute.

The match is expected to raise about £25,000.

"It was fantastic that so many people should come here for me," Mr Shankly said.

"To a pre-match message I would like to thank you for your loyalty to Anfield, for the greatest part of my life."

no man could be more grateful and no man could have more friends.

When excitement flared in the first half the Kop took over to provide an impromptu entertainment with a never-ending series of chants. They made former Everton skipper Alan Ball, now of their captain, the butt of their humour and he responded equally light heartedly.

(Full story—Back Page)

`30 APR 1975`
`L04 16`

### 30 April 1975

### Emotion, humour and eight goals in emotional farewell

Of course, Shanks had to be a winner on his big tribute day.

The Daily Post's Horace Yates reported on a 6-2 victory over Don Revie Select X1.

'The Kop had apparently had their fill by half-time, or had exhausted their repertoire, and it was marked how much better the game suddenly became with the amateur comedians silenced.

'A dog and a cat on the pitch provided diversions and for a spell Keegan swapped positions with Emlyn Hughes.

'Alan Ball became an early target for the Kop and collected boos almost every time he made contact with the ball.'

' Without a competitive bite it was hard to sustain interest and then the Kop tried to stir things up by chanting 'England, England' and followed it with 'Liverpool are rubbish.'

### 17 May 1975

### King of Kop Shanks wraps up Mark's little problem

Four-year-old Mark Maloney from Fazakerley lost a Liverpool scarf – which had been in the family for years – at Shankly's testimonial. It had been the youngster's first match.

Shanks heard about it and gave the youngster one of his own treasured collection, saying: 'They were looking for a needle in

## Shanks signs in to pay his respects to a true Red

**From Peter Cook, Liverpool**

My story starts with the death of a true Red, Billy Bristo.

When Billy passed away, his sons thought that if they could get a mass card signed by Bill Shankly it would mean a great deal to Billy. So they thought they would be bold and knock at Bill's house and ask him to sign one, which he did. Away they went, very happy.

On the day of the funeral, in the middle of the service, my dad nudged me and told me to turn round. To my surprise there was Bill Shankly, trying not to look obvious at the back of the church. "F--- me! There's Bill Shankly" I said in an extremely loud voice. My dad nearly had a fit (not because I'd said the "F" word really loud in the middle of a funeral service, but because Bill Shankly was there). Of course, I wanted to get up and go over to him but my dad threatened to kill me if I moved. So after the service I was off like a shot to get his autograph, grabbing the first thing at hand which was in fact a mass card, and asked Bill to sign it. So there was me, proudly displaying Bill Shankly's autograph on a card which said "Deepest Condolences!!" I was dancing up and down outside the church shouting "F--- me I got Bill Shankly's autograph," with my dad looking on in horror. I know,

though, that Billy Bristo would have been smiling down on the scene, especially as it was him that had turned me into a fanatical Red.

That Bill Shankly should turn up at the funeral of a man he didn't even know says a lot about what kind of man he was. It's not the big deeds that made him great but the small ones.

That autograph was one of my most treasured possessions until it was placed in the coffin of another true Red and a good mate, Tommy.

RIP Bill Shankly, Billy Bristo and Tommy.

## The day the Gwladys Street stole the sleeping tablets!

**From Bryan Robinson, Liverpool**

I met Bill Shankly in the early 1970's at Everton's Bellefield training ground. I was getting treatment on my ankle when all of a sudden in walked Bill with Jim McGregor, Everton's physio at the time. Jim said to Bill: "Tell Bryan about when the Liverpool kit basket went missing during a trip to Aston Villa with all the different tablets for the players in it."

Bill replied: "Well son, we found the basket in the Gwladys Street end and all the sleeping tablets were missing!" I didn't know what to say. What a man.

> 'THAT BILL SHANKLY SHOULD TURN UP AT THE FUNERAL OF A MAN HE DIDN'T EVEN KNOW SAYS A LOT ABOUT WHAT KIND OF MAN HE WAS. IT'S NOT THE BIG DEEDS THAT MADE HIM GREAT BUT THE SMALL ONES'

## Lucky break that turned my agony to ecstasy

**From Christine Beyga,
West Derby, Liverpool**

I enclose a newspaper clipping and copy of a photograph (I have the original of both) of when I met Bill Shankly. A few days before my 16th birthday I fell and broke my arm badly and while lying in hospital awaiting an operation, already in agony, I heard that Shanks had announced his retirement. As a die-hard Red, this was devastating news and compounded my agony.

By the time my mum had arrived at the hospital I was inconsolable and she presumed the pain was so bad that this was causing my distress, I sobbed to her that I didn't care about that pain, but couldn't believe Shanks was going (I think she was tempted to break my other arm!).

The next day I went over to Melwood to watch the team train. This was a treat for my birthday and as I was off school because of my arm. There were a lot of Press and photographers about due to Bill's announcement, but when he arrived he ignored them all and made a beeline for me once he saw my arm was in a sling.

He asked what I had done and I told him all about it and how upset I had been to hear the news of his retirement.

He reassured me that the team would go on from strength to strength without him and I shouldn't worry!

He then sent someone to get a pen and signed my plaster cast, it was the first signature on there and I was delighted. In the meantime the photographers came over and took photos, although I was on cloud nine at the time and didn't realise.

The next day I returned to school and one of my teachers enquired as to why I had been absent the previous day. I told her about my arm and that was the reason I was off.

She smiled and said (tongue in cheek): "Well you must have been busy as you had time to get your photograph on the back page of the Daily Express!"

> a haystack, so I decided to give them one of my own scarves.'
(See letter, page 129)

**King of Kop Shanks wraps up Mark's little problem**

17 MAY 1975

**3 October 1975**

## Shankly: I'm not moving for anything

Linked with the vacant Scotland Under-23 coaching post, Shankly had this to say:

"I've not heard a word from the Scottish FA.

"Anyway, I don't want any job which would take me away from home. I'm not leaving here.

"I'm prepared to give advice to people.

**Shankly: I'm not moving for anything**

-3 OCT 1975

"I'll even work in an advisory role for anyone who wants me to check on players, or check on teams' tactics, and so on.

"I'll help anyone by going to a match for them – but nothing more than that."

**Treasured picture: Christine Beyga's photo of her meeting with Shanks**

### 18 October 1975

### Shankly's gospel

Liverpool, with Bob Paisley now in charge, finished their first season with Shanks in second place, but made little progress on the domestic Cup front and in Europe. As the 1975/76 season unfolded, people were debating who might win the title.

People wanted Shankly's views on a host of issues and he covered many of them in the Football Echo.

### On the title:

'At the moment any 10 or 12 clubs could do the job. But when I have picked out my two teams then I'll have a little bet.'

### On Manchester City hero Francis Lee:

'Francis should have been a Liverpool player. He is the kind of man the Kop love.'

### On management:

'It can be a soul-destroying job. You've got to impress directors at board meetings, obviously have a sound knowledge of the game, but most important you've got to have the natural ability to pick a player. If you have these attributes, can deal with people then you've got a chance."

Linked with the theme of money and power, he commented on the big-money award being offered at the time for the first player to reach 30 goals. 'All the money in the world will not make a man score goals. Goals will

Newspaper cuttings of the signed plaster cast and giant scarf stories

The class was in uproar and she made me come to the front of the class to tell everyone about it, and to be honest I have been 'dining out' on the story ever since!

As a post script to the story, when I eventually went to have the plaster cast removed at the hospital, I was determined to keep the piece with Shanks' autograph on forever, and I asked the technician to carefully cut this piece out .

It was right on the elbow joint and so it was very awkward to do.

To make things worse he was an Evertonian, but to his credit he did do it and I still have the piece of plaster cast to this day!

### Giant scarf that kind-hearted Shanks really warmed to

#### From David Brockway, The Crescent, Whiston

After reading your request for Bill Shankly stories, I decided to talk to my nan, Christine Brockway, about her memories of the great man. Her fondest memories are of going to Melwood with her daughter, Monica and her son, Stephen when the players were training.

Whenever they had any spare time they would walk to Melwood from their home in Dovecot to watch their heroes train. Her favourite player was Roger Hunt. They would stay all day until the players and coaching staff were ready to leave and they would take photographs and get autographs from the players.

My nan remembers how Bill Shankly would always stop and let the fans get photographs with him and get his autograph, no matter how long it would take. He always had time for the fans and "Made the people happy."

She tells me that she would often chat with Bill on her many visits to Melwood and would enjoy conversations about upcoming matches and players old and new. Bill sent her a letter which she has since given to me. She received this in reply to a letter from her inviting Bill to her daughter Monica's birthday.

My nan has always enjoyed knitting and she started to knit a red and white Liverpool scarf in the late 1960s. Eventually this scarf measured over 350 feet. She tells me that she took the scarf to Melwood on one occasion and Bill allowed her onto the field to take photographs with it.

A Daily Mirror reporter was at Melwood that day and the pictures appeared in the following Saturday's issue.

She took the scarf with her to many home and away matches and eventually donated it to the Hillsborough Disaster fund and helped raise over £16,000 at auction along with many other scarves and memorabilia donated by other fans.

I have enclosed a photograph of my nan, my two sisters, Joanne, Gemma and myself with her latest scarf, which we recently measured at 555 feet in length.

Also enclosed is a photograph of my nan in front of a picture of her hero in the Liverpool Football Club Museum on a recent trip to celebrate her 84th birthday.

Another of my nan's fond memories of the great Bill Shankly is of going to the many matches at Anfield and joining in with the crowd shouting "Shankly, Shankly, Shankly".

She, her husband Louis and her daughter Monica would stand in the Anfield Road end and her sons Louis, Ron, Victor and Stephen would stand in the Kop.

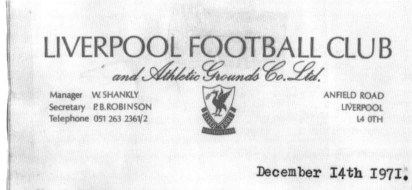

LIVERPOOL FOOTBALL CLUB
and Athletic Grounds Co. Ltd.

Manager   W. SHANKLY
Secretary  P.B. ROBINSON
Telephone  051 263 2361/2

ANFIELD ROAD
LIVERPOOL
L4 0TH

December 14th 1971.

Mr & Mrs. Brockway,
36, Churchdown Road,
Dovecot,
Liverpool, 14

Dear People,
            Received your letter along with the newspaper photographs, thanks very much indeed. Also thanks for the invitation to Monica's birthday party on the 31st, which is the night before we play Leeds United.
            In actual fact the players, the trainers and myself will be in special preperation for this vital game. I am sure you will all understand how important it is, especially your four sons, who are members of the greatest place on earth "THE KOP".
            We all wish Monica the best of luck on her Birthday.

                            Yours sincerely,

                            B. Shankly
                            Manager.

> always be difficult to get, but perhaps the best incentives for goalscorers would be to tell them that you'd dock their wages if they didn't score.'

## On amateur preparation:

'It is amazing how many clubs still have a hit and miss approach. If all the teams and all the players concentrated fully on preparing for a match, the game would be better.

'Instead you see experienced players doing things on the field that a schoolboy could tell them was wrong.

'In matches this season I've seen internationals losing balls in midfield positions that led to goals against them, when they were ideally placed to pass.

'When I see ability not being used it angers me immensely. I've seen teams playing well and winning, who then changed their style by going into their shell.

'They tried to close up the game instead of realising that their play has been good enough to get them in front and doesn't need changing.

'Many well known players can't seem to release the ball at the right time, and this is a talent being wasted.

'I've seen a team arrive for a big game only 25 minutes before kick-off. It simply shouldn't be allowed.'

### 22 November 1975

## The day Shanks went onto The Kop unannounced. Bill had fulfilled a promise

Following his first visit on to the Kop, Bill Shankly revealed he had taken a trip down Memory Lane while fulfilling a promise he once made to the fans at Anfield.

'When I was a boy I used to watch Celtic and Rangers play, with 100,000 people there,' he said.

'That was nothing to us and I was in it again on Saturday.

'The wheel had turned full circle only this time it was with a red and white scarf. I got one from a boy and brought it home.

'I promised to go on the Kop long ago and to see the games from all parts of Anfield. It has taken a long time to get round to going.

'You get a view of the game, but the pitch looks different. It looked wider and bigger and it was difficult to judge what was going on at the other end.

'At first the people were surprised to see me, but when I went in the Coventry team were coming out, at eight minutes to three, and people were concentrating on that of course. Then all of a sudden it struck them that I was walking and talking to people there.

'I am a citizen of Liverpool and I wanted to go there and see these people who have done so much for me. The handshakes are real, they aren't false.

'The jostling was not too bad, but there were a lot of kids around in the 10-years old bracket and some of them wouldn't see the game at all. That surprised me.

'It was an enjoyable day, and not as tiring as one would think. I will be going again.'

**7 January 1976**

## Burnley haven't contacted me, says Shankly

Rumours that Clarets manager Jimmy Adamson had resigned, to be replaced by Shankly, were ruled out:

'I have heard nothing at all from Burnley and I deal with things as they come along. They are not the only club my name has been linked with.

'I have had a number of offers, one from a really big club was a staggering affair but it necessitated total involvement and that does not interest me.

Heroes of '65: Fans at the FA Cup homecoming outside Lime Street Station

## Desperate Cup final plea that didn't fall on deaf ears

**From Denise Watterson, Rainford, St Helens**

I would like to tell you of my experience when I met Bill Shankly.

I used to go to all the games home and away in the early 1960's and sometimes got tickets from the players before an away game.

I started off going by myself to the away games but soon met up with people who were as fanatical as myself.

When an England v Scotland game came up on 10 April, 1965, I thought I would love to go, but wondered how I could get a ticket. After one Liverpool home game I waited for Mr Shankly to come out of the ground and asked him how I would get a ticket for the international.

He asked me who I was going with and I said by myself and that I was going down on the Friday morning so I would be able to go to the Spurs v Liverpool game on the Friday night.

He gave me a ticket there and then.

He told me to go to the players' entrance at Tottenham where someone would give me a ticket as it

## Burnley haven't contacted me, says Shankly

THE MOST improbable rumour of the season came last night with the suggestion that Burnley, whose manager Jimmy Adamson has resigned, were looking to former Liverpool manager Bill Shankly, as his replacement.

Mr Shankly has shown no inclination to move back into club management, despite a number of inquiries—and Burnley are hardly the club who might be considered best

"There was another one from a club which is not terribly big just now, but that could become a big club again. I have done little jobs in the way of advice to several people. That sort of thing always interests me."

**2 April 1976**

### Return for Shankly – as a director?

In his Saturday radio programme, Shankly had indicated his interest in a boardroom position. Horace Yates, meanwhile, found the Scot unwilling to fully commit his future ambitions.

"I have had one offer. I didn't fancy it at the time. It did not suit me.

"I have been to many grounds, locally and elsewhere and received a good welcome. I have discussed this subject with many people without committing myself.

"I feel that anything I can do to help I am willing to do. I am never short of something, but it is not always convenient to go to some places.

"Just put it that I am interested in doing something for football."

was very expensive in London. I waited before the game and was given two tickets for the Spurs match.

I had never been to Wembley before and it was a great experience and a great game. Ian St John was playing for Scotland and Peter Thompson for England. I was in the middle of the Scottish fans and they were great.

When we reached the Cup final the next month, my dad and I both had season tickets for the Kemlyn Road, but not everyone qualified for a Cup final ticket. They were so hard to get hold of. My dad said I should go because I had followed them

everywhere.

As a last resort I wrote to Mr Shankly on Tuesday, 20th April, 1965 stating that I was the young girl (just 18) who went to the international game to see two of our players, but couldn't get a ticket to see all of our lads play in the FA Cup final. I hadn't really wanted to ask him. I felt it wasn't fair because everyone would be doing so, but I was desperate.

On the Thursday, guess what popped through the letter box? A ticket from Mr Shankly.

He was the best. I still have the same two season tickets, but now go with my daughter and hope to introduce the grandchildren shortly.

> **16 September 1976**

## 'It was never my intention to make a complete break ...'

Shankly's autobiography was now looming and unhappily some of his frustrations inevitably came out. He said:

"I still wanted to help Liverpool because the club has become my life. But I wasn't given the chance.

"I have a pension scheme and I had a testimonial, which was marvellous, an unforgettable evening, but I was willing to work for the club for nothing more than my pension. I was willing to help in any capacity.

"It is scandalous and outrageous that I should have to write these things about the club I helped build into what it is today. If the situation had been reversed I would have invited people to games.

"It would have been a wonderful honour to have been made a director of Liverpool FC, but I didn't go round saying, "I would like to do this and that." That's begging – and I'm not a beggar!

"It was never my intention to have a complete break with Liverpool, but at the same time I wasn't going to put my nose in where it wasn't wanted. Maybe I was an embarrassment to some people."

In reference to his new book, Shankly referred to the fact that he had not been asked by Liverpool to see their away matches and also stopped going to the Melwood training ground.

He said: "That situation has not changed. My book is 99 per

**Shoulder high: Shankly loved to put local people in the spotlight**

## Unsung hero makes a young fan's day

**From Derek Hensley, Widnes, Cheshire**

During the early 1970's my niece was a patient at Alder Hey Hospital. All the children in the ward were very sick and visitors were allowed at all times, and Bill Shankly was often to be seen chatting to the children and their parents.

On one of these visits he told a young supporter that he would get some of the team to visit, then went off to make a phone call. Very quickly footballers began to assemble. Unfortunately, some were dressed in casual gear and Shanks sent them off to put on their suits,

telling them that they were representing Liverpool Football Club.

Upon their return they introduced themselves to a delighted little lad. On another occasion the television in the ward had broken and when Shanks heard about this, a replacement was quickly installed. Shanks had done it again!

Finally, whilst visiting my niece with my young son, who was and still is a keen supporter of Liverpool Football Club, Bill Shankly arrived to visit the children. My son was thrilled to meet Bill and today is the proud possessor of the great Shankly's autograph.

This man did such a lot to cheer the lives of these very sick children and did so without fuss or fanfare and should long be remembered for his unsung kindness.

## Blue was the colour for thoughtful Shanks

**From Eric Hoare,
Bootle, Merseyside**

In the 1960s when colour TV first came out I worked for DER TV rentals. My boss had agreed to supply Liverpool FC with a colour TV on match days in the VIP lounge, so it was my job to take the TV and set it up.

One Wednesday night Liverpool had a European Cup tie and so I was setting up the TV in an empty lounge before the game. The picture on the TV showed a boat sailing in a blue sea, when suddenly a voice behind me said: "What a beautiful colour that blue is."

I turned around and it was Bill Shankly who had come in with a cup of tea and sandwich. Being an Evertonian, I suddenly wished I had a tape recorder to record what he had just said. He then asked: "Have you got a ticket for the game?"

I replied no, not telling him I was an Evertonian. He told me to wait, went away and came back with a ticket and said: "Now you have."

I ended up sitting with the 'gods' watching Liverpool win 3–0

After the game I went back to the lounge and when the VIPs had watched the highlights in 'wonderful colour' I collected the TV and took it back to work.

On reflection, I suppose Bill Shankly saw me as a man working late who deserved a ticket. He must have had many things to do before the game, but still found time to get me a ticket. What other football manager would have done that?

**Just the ticket: Shanks signs a ball for a local football team**

## 'ON REFLECTION, I SUPPOSE BILL SHANKLY SAW ME AS A MAN WORKING LATE WHO DESERVED A TICKET. HE MUST HAVE HAD MANY THINGS TO DO BEFORE THE GAME, BUT STILL FOUND TIME TO GET ME A TICKET'

➤ cent about people and one per cent of criticism. That one per cent is fair comment about fact, about what has happened. But people have dived in to talk about that one per cent.

'I have not written anything derogatory about anyone. I have just stated the facts.'

**16 December 1976**

### Bill Shankly 'may join Derby'

It was only natural that Shanks would continue to be linked with other clubs. It was reported that Derby County wanted the former Liverpool boss for an advisory role at the Baseball Ground. Bill was quoted as saying:

'I am seriously thinking about this offer.

'I envisage going to the Baseball Ground once or twice a week, but that does not affect Colin Murphy's position at all. I'm not being pushed for a decision. It's not like being asked to get a spade out and dig the road.'

Further details revealed Shankly's restlessness, having been out of the game for over two years:

'I would feel as if I were part of the game again without having the worries of a manager. When you are manager you have more worries than the Prime Minister – and he's got enough.

'I'd be helping with the training and playing side of the club, working on little details like where to eat and what time to go to bed and so on.

'I could come and go as I please, maybe going just one day a week, which suits me fine. I go to the games anyway, so I wouldn't be away from home any more than I am now.

'But I would feel as if I were part of something.

'I've been in football 43 years and sometimes I get a bit moody and fidgety.

'Going to the games is fine but having been involved it's better if you go with the official party.' ➤

> ### 18 January 1977

### 'Make Shankly a director' campaign is called off

The campaign to make Bill Shankly a director of Liverpool Football Club was dropped, at the request of Mr Shankly himself. But petition organiser Mr Sam Leach said he would continue collecting signatures to present to the former Liverpool manager as a personal memento. He said:

'I am confident we can reach the target of 250,000 signatures we originally said. Mr Shankly asked me to call the campaign off because he feels it may do Liverpool FC great harm and I do appreciate his reasons. But at least we have made our point and asked the question which needed to be asked.'

### 30 April 1977

### A big welcome from Anfield's former idol

Bill Shankly was the star attraction at a special fundraising evening for Dr Barnado's in Liverpool. He said: "Dr Barnado's is a fantastic organisation. It is a pity that special fundraising events have to be held. The Government should help more."

### 22 October 1977

### A soccer revolution

Bill continued to write his football Echo column, a tremendous platform for him to air his views which were still keenly sought by the fans.

### On coaching in England:

'One season, five of us went from Anfield to spend a week at Lilleshall – I went with Bob Paisley, Reuben Bennett, Joe Fagan and Ronnie Moran. We had

## Standing up for those who couldn't pay their way

**From Ernie Ashley, Woolton, Liverpool**

I have wonderful memories of the great Bill Shankly. He arrived at Anfield in December 1959 and had an incredibly close relationship with Reds supporters. Along with a few lads from Huyton, we never missed a game, home or away, for many years. We saw every game that Shanks was involved in during his time at Anfield.

On many occasions we would meet and talk to him on the train, especially on the way to London games. On one occasion, as we

prepared to play Arsenal at Highbury in the 60's, a couple of us managed to get in his first class carriage. He was with Bob Paisley and Joe Fagan. He welcomed us in, of course, and the five of us started talking about football.

Suddenly two railway inspectors, who had these three young lads by the scruff of their necks, walked past the compartment.

Shanks saw this, and opened the door and said: "What are you doing treating them like that for?"

The inspectors replied: "They have no tickets Mr Shankly. They bunked on the train at Lime Street."

Shanks knew they were going to the game because they were wearing Red scarves. Bill reached for his

Making us a part of it: On the pitch with the fans and the 1973 title

wallet and asked the inspectors how much the fares were. He paid for the three of them to have a return fare, of course. He asked the lads if they had tickets for the match and they said they didn't, but planned to try and get in.

Shanks reached into his inside coat pocket and gave them a ticket each. The inspectors were just shaking their heads, but Shanks repeated that there had been no need to treat these boys so roughly. He had saved them from getting locked up when the train reached Crewe. I'm sure the lads will always remember that day.

Another time, one of the lads invited Bill up to his house to celebrate his brothers' 21st birthday

party in Huyton. He arrived at 9pm, but said he couldn't stay long as he wanted to be home to watch Match of the Day at 10.30pm. In the hour he stayed, everyone must have tried his white Mac on, including myself.

I have seen Bill Shankly looking for people who were out of work outside different grounds, to give them a match ticket, as long as they wore a Red scarf. Bill would often be seen in West Derby Village carrying shopping for the elderly people. A friend of mine who lives in the village told me he would often see Bill around there. If he saw someone who looked a bit down, he would often reach in his pocket and help them out. Thanks for the memories Bill; you made us all happy.

a good time. We heard all kinds of expressions.

'We even heard people saying you could make footballers.

'We heard all the jargon and saw the functions they were trying.

'And we left convinced that our ideas were better than theirs.

'As I always say, football is a simple game, and that is the way it should stay.'

## On the importance of mind games:

'Psychology is a crucial point. An example is the use you make of information on opposing teams.

'At Liverpool we gathered information about teams and players, but we did not use it so as to frighten our own players.

'Don Revie, apparently, gave his players a dossier to study on their opponents.

'My approach was exactly the opposite.

'Imagine giving a player a dossier on Tom Finney!

'It would have frightened him to death!

'We would mention the names of Best, Charlton and Law in our tactical talks, but that was all.

'We wouldn't go to great lengths about them.

'Our attitude was that if the football machine was working, the opposition might get caught up in it and would be crushed by it.'

## Shankly's tips on how to manage a winning team:

'I have tried to give some guidelines as to the things I would like to see done.

• Choose your system and pick the players to fit it.
• Keep the language simple.
• Remember that the people who matter most are the ordinary people, the supporters.
• Always ask advice from those who have closest experience of the game.'

### 18 November 1977

#### It's extra time for Shanks – and he wants to go on

The Liverpool Echo produced a feature on retirement – focusing on Shankly, in which he said:

'Every day for me is still a cup final day and nobody, no matter what they try to do or say, will ever take that away.

'Everything I do from signing autographs to cleaning the car I do with enthusiasm and with a certain amount of pressure behind it.

'I have always driven myself all along the line and I'm not going to stop now just because I'm retired.

'Keeping fit is the most important thing of all. If you are physically fit, you are mentally alert as well.

'I was an athlete and fitness was in my blood. I'm still only 11 stone 13 lbs – just 3 lbs heavier than I was when I was playing.

'Ambition kept me going – if you have no ambition you might as well go into your coffin now.

'I have had offers almost every month since I packed in from chairmen and vice-chairmen of I don't-know-how-many football clubs, but for one reason or

another the jobs were just not suitable.

'Many of them meant travelling too far away and while I would like to travel around with a club I don't like to spend a night away from home and I don't want full-

Up for a game: Shankly on the Barnfield Drive pitches in West Derby

### Honour to have met the superstar who never forgot his roots

**From Gerald Murphy, Stoneycroft, Liverpool**

My memory of Bill Shankly has its origins in the early 1960s when Liverpool was emerging as one of the true centres of style, fashion and culture in the English-speaking world let alone a centre of football excellence.

Bill Shankly's house in West Derby was quite close to where I lived in Norris Green and he was known for being seen around West Derby village and playing football himself on the Barnfield Drive pitches, now known as the "Shankly Fields".

In those days it was possible to go to Liverpool FC's training ground at Melwood and gain entrance to watch the players train.

It must have been half term when I went with a group of friends and my autograph book. We saw players like Gerry Byrne and Alf Arrowsmith,

St John and Ron Yeats.

What struck me was the size of the players and their technical ability. They used to wear baseball boots in those days for training and I saw a Liverpool full-back step over the ball and flick it off the back of his heel in a perfect arc over his head, the kind of thing they do in TV adverts today and everybody gasps as though they invented it.

It was while watching this exhibition that I first saw Bill Shankly in the flesh, emerging from the wooden pavilion and changing rooms. The moment we caught sight of him, we all ran across the field to get his autograph. It did occur to me that we were running across the field like Beatles fans to a man who was over 45 at the time. The fact was, Shankly was a star.

I was a good runner and I made it over to him first. As I approached I realised he was not a big man. He was about my size, 5' 7" or so. As I got near I became aware of a kind of force around the man. He half turned towards us running kids and simply said: "Go easy lads," and we all pulled up almost bouncing off the aura he had around him.

He looked almost saintly with clear skin and white hair. He gave us all the autographs we wanted and that was it. You realised you didn't need anything else. You had been in the presence of true greatness.

Years later and in the year before he died, I was playing with the big lads on Barnfield Drive recreation ground, just by where Shankly lived in his house which famously backed on to Everton's Bellefield training ground. Across the field I saw a figure in a bright red tracksuit playing a match with the smallest of kids on the field. It looked like a proper game and the guy in the red tracksuit was organising it and playing properly. I asked one of the lads I was playing with whether that was who I thought it was and he

confirmed it was.

It was a wonderful example of the dedication of a great man to his chosen medium of expression ,but it was also sadly poignant. Shankly had been out of the game for a while but never without a game - as long as the kids still played on Barnfield Drive pitches anyway. It was that image that I used as the central image in my tribute song to Bill Shankly, 'The Green Fields of his Home' (see below) commissioned by sports editor Ken Rogers on behalf of the Liverpool Echo when he launched the Bill Shankly Memorial Award many years ago.

Shankly was at home on a well cut level playing field, like Melwood, Barnfield Drive, Anfield, Wembley and around his Scottish home Glenbuck. It was my honour to have witnessed his presence.

### The Green Fields of his home
By G. Murphy

**I**
He was a miner
A Scottish miner
Who wondered far away
From Glenbuck, Galloway
And came to England
To play in England
Far from those green fields
Of his home

**II**
He wrote a story
In deeds of glory
His teams victorious
In matches glorious
He brought us trophies
Such shining trophies
Back to that green field
On Anfield road

**Middle**
He had a dream of how the game should be
Played with dignity
Scottish gallantry
Had a dream that would make history
In those seven hills of Rome

**III**
Oh I would see him
We aye would see him
His eyes were clear and bright
His heart was red and white
He spoke of football, majestic football
And those green fields of his home

**Middle 2**
Now o'er those green fields where football is played
You will hear them say
They play Shankly's way
O'er those green fields up in Galloway
And those seven hills of Rome

**IV**
He was a miner, a Scottish miner
Who wondered far away
From Glenbuck, Galloway
But I still see him, I think I see him
In those green fields
Of his home
Oh, in those green fields
Of his home

> 'HE LOOKED ALMOST SAINTLY WITH CLEAR SKIN AND WHITE HAIR. HE GAVE US ALL THE AUTOGRAPHS WE WANTED AND THAT WAS IT. YOU REALISED YOU DIDN'T NEED ANYTHING ELSE. YOU HAD BEEN IN THE PRESENCE OF TRUE GREATNESS'

time involvement.

'I want to get involved in an advisory capacity with a football club using my knowledge and experience and be one of the boys again. It would take 10 years off my age.'

**13 January 1978**

### Shankly . . . and the 'enemies' who became friends

The first match Bill Shankly attended after relinquishing control of affairs at Anfield was at Maine Road, Manchester, he recalled in an Echo interview. The club announced his presence over the loudspeakers – and the entire crowd gave him an ovation.

"That," said Shanks, "meant more to me than ten thousand pounds."

Two weeks before, when Everton played Nottingham Forest at the City Ground, someone spotted him making his way to his seat and as the word got around, everyone around the directors' box stood and applauded (see picture below).

"It was fantastic," said Bill. "This sort of thing is one of the bonuses for me. Wherever I go, the people make me welcome. I was elated to think that I can be a club's opponent, I can fight them for years, and when I have finished fighting them I can go back and get such a reception.'

On his growing relationship with Everton FC he added: "Everton were my closest rivals, to a degree that bordered on enmity. Yet at the first match I went to at Goodison Park after I had finished with Liverpool I got a tremendous reception.

"That was a tremendous feeling of elation – that here were my deadliest enemies, when battle was over saying hello. Since that day I have been able to get tickets from Everton, and have enjoyed the hospitality of the club as I have at all the other football grounds.

"Everton's training ground is close to where I live, and their former manager Billy Bingham invited me to go to the training ground if I wanted to. When Gordon Lee took over, he made a point of renewing the invitation.

"Two days after I had finished at Anfield I injured my shoulder. In fact I nearly broke my neck. I was getting out of the bath at Anfield and I slipped and fell on the concrete. All the blood drained out of my veins. Since then I have had to have regular treatment, and I have gone to Bellefield for it because it is convenient.

"Liverpool don't have a full-time physiotherapist, and it would have been more difficult to go there.

"Everton's physio, Jim McGregor, comes from the same part of Scotland as myself, and we have struck up a good friendship. I have regular treatment from him and for that I am appreciative."

On criticism of young football supporters being branded as hooligans Shanks said:

"At the FA Cup semi-final between Liverpool and Everton at Maine Road last season, I was in a seat at the corner of the stand behind the goal. With the rain there was water dripping on me throughout the match. There was nowhere to go for a cup of tea or a cup of Oxo.

"Near to where I was there

**Football supporter: Clipboard in hand, Shankly poses with a local team**

## Holy day when I met the messiah

**From Gerard Edwards, Stockbridge Village, Liverpool**

My personal memory of the legendary Bill Shankly was in the early Sixties. When I was 14, I supported Liverpool and followed them home and away. I even went to the training ground at Melwood to watch them train and to get autographs. You could gain entry into Melwood and I only lived two miles away.

I went to watch the Reds train and approached Bill Shankly and asked for his autograph. Before he signed he said: "Aye laddie, shouldn't you be at school?"

I replied: "It's a holy day Mr Shankly. We are given a day's holiday." Mr Shankly said: "Well you learn a lot today laddie."

Then he signed his autograph over the picture of him walking the team out at the Liverpool v Leeds FA Cup final in 1965.

I still have that small book and fond memory of Bill Shankly.

## Shankly Boy

**From Helen Hayes, Liverpool**

A very long time ago, I wrote words to the tune of 'Danny Boy'. Here we go . . .

*Oh 'Shankly Boy'*
*The fans are all*
*behind you in the Kop*
*And in the terrace too!*
*And even those who*
*can't get in to see you*
*We will be cheering*
*outside as well*
*And when it's one*
*And you shall be*
*returning regardless of the score*
*You wait and see, you'll find us here*
*Awaiting your arrival*
*Oh! 'Shankly Boy'*
*Oh! 'Shankly Boy'*
*We love you so!*

I will always remember going to see our team return to the city after a losing Cup final. Shankly spoke on St George's Plateau and said to his team: "Just look at this?" The town was crowded with banners and flags everywhere. He said: "Well imagine what you'll get when you win!'

## Lost and found – reaching out and touching people

**From Joan Maloney, Fazakerley**

The great man will never be forgotten. In 1975, my son aged five was taken to his first professional match by his dad, a Liverpool fanatic. It was Shankly's testimonial and my son was wearing a family heirloom; a red and white football scarf.

However, my son lost the scarf somewhere in the ground and we were all devastated.

We decided to put an advert in the Liverpool Echo under the 'lost and found' column.

The scarf originally belonged to my sister in law who died at the age of 31. She was an avid Liverpool supporter.

It was Nessie who spotted the advert feature in the Football Echo. The next morning, Bill rang to offer one of his scarves.

My husband and son were invited to Bill's home and they were given a scarf belonging to Shanks and had their photograph taken with the great man. This was featured on the front page of the following Saturday's Echo.

We have two lovely photographs to prove that, yes, Shanks did reach out and touch the people.

Thirty years on, we have never forgotten and it is still a great story to be told.

He was a lovely man who will always be regarded as a legend.

He was a man who made my family happy.

**Lost and found: Shanks stepped in when a precious scarf went missing**

were little boys and girls with singlets on. They had spent all their money to get there, and they were soaked too.

"Then someone comes out in the media and says: 'We don't want them – they're hooligans.' That really appalls me.

"Don't they realise that without these people there would be no game?

"Don't they realise that throughout the country there are people who will spend all their money and do without a pair of shoes to support their team?"

**10 April 1978**

### Shankly won't get involved

Blackpool were the latest club to approach Shankly about their vacant manager's position – but only until the end of the season. Shanks was annoyed by the approach.

He said: "This man from Blackpool spoke to me but I don't want to get involved in their problems.

"I'm a free man now and enjoying my life. I'm prepared to help a club – but a club of my choice on my terms.

"I don't want to commit myself to anything at this stage."

**8 February 1979**

### Shanks' visit just the tonic for injured Ian

'Football-mad Ian Braithwaite just could not believe it when his long-standing hero Bill Shankly walked into hospital to see him,' reported the Echo.

'Fourteen-years-old Ian, of Maxwell Road, Tuebrook, Liverpool, has been at Alder Hey Children's Hospital for the past fortnight undergoing traction treatment.

'He injured his spine just before Christmas playing for the Lister Under-16's football team.

'The team's manager, Mr Alf Thompson, thought it would be a

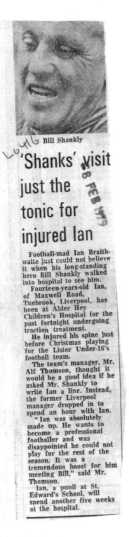

Bill Shankly

L646

8 FEB 1979

### 'Shanks' visit just the tonic for injured Ian

Football-mad Ian Braithwaite just could not believe it when his long-standing hero Bill Shankly walked into hospital to see him.

Fourteen-years-old Ian, of Maxwell Road, Tuebrook, Liverpool, has been at Alder Hey Children's Hospital for the past fortnight undergoing traction treatment.

He injured his spine just before Christmas playing for the Lister Under-16's football team.

The team's manager, Mr. Alf Thomson, thought it would be a good idea if he asked Mr. Shankly to write Ian a line. Instead, the former Liverpool manager dropped in to spend an hour with Ian.

"Ian was absolutely made up. He wants to become a professional footballer and was disappointed he could not play for the rest of the season. It was a tremendous boost for him meeting Bill," said Mr. Thomson.

Ian, a pupil at St. Edward's School, will spend another five weeks at the hospital.

good idea if he asked Mr Shankly to write Ian a line.

'Instead, the former Liverpool manager dropped in to spend an hour with Ian.

"Ian was absolutely made up. He wants to become a professional footballer and was disappointed he could not play for the rest of the season. It was a tremendous boost for him meeting Bill," said Mr Thompson.

'Ian, a pupil at St Edward's School, will spend another five weeks at the hospital.'

**18 August 1979**

## We must get back to soccer sanity, warns Shankly

On being asked who Liverpool's best player was in the 1979 Charity Shield, Shankly said:

---

## He gave so much to the people – Reds and Blues loved him

**From John Owens, Norton Cross, Runcorn**

My memories of the "greatest man that ever lived" were of the fact that I was one of those kids (I am now 56) who approached his door all those years ago in Bellefield Avenue. His daughter came out and Bill followed to take the time to not only sign an autograph, but give me a glass of orange juice because it was a warm day. What a man! He gave so much to the people. Reds and Blues loved him.

---

## He fulfilled his dream by being part of the Kop

**From John Pritchard, Liverpool**

My fondest memory of Bill Shankly was the day he stood on the Kop among his fans.

It was during a league game against Nottingham Forest.

The Kop started to chant "Shankly, Shankly give us a song" and all went quiet to see if he would respond.

Shanks just stood there with a red and white scarf on and laughed.

He fulfilled his dream by being part of the Kop among the fans who loved him.

A personal tour of Anfield
and pictures of the players

**Marie Boxx, Workington,
Cumbria**

I was encouraged to contribute my thoughts about Bill Shankly by Bill Watson who was a friend of Shanks when he was the manager of Workington. Bill Watson's friendship with Shanks continued when he was the manager of Liverpool.

I was fortunate to meet Shankly on three occasions between 1967-69. Bill Watson was invited down to Anfield by Shanks and I was asked if I would like to go along. We met Bill on the Saturday morning prior to a game against Newcastle.

First of all, he gave us a tour of Anfield, the dressing rooms, the trophy room, the famous Boot Room and his office.

I can remember quite clearly while we were sitting in his office he reached down and took an envelope from a drawer in his desk. He opened the envelope and took out individual photographs of the Liverpool players and showed them to us. He then put them back into the envelope, reached over his desk and gave them to me.

Next we were taken to Melwood to look at the training facilities before dropping him off at the end of his road so he could get ready for the game that afternoon. We were given tickets.

The second time I visited with Bill Watson, we were waiting outside before a game with West Ham United when Bill Shankly waved us inside where he had tickets for us. Shankly asked what I had in my hand. It was a team photo of Liverpool. He just took the photo off me and left us standing outside the West Ham dressing room while he went into the Liverpool one.

When he returned, Bobby Moore was going into the visitors' dressing room. He spotted Shankly and said: "Hello Bill."

Shankly muttered: "You'll get

"Liverpool", I said. "Liverpool is the best player. I think they didn't understand me, but it was my way of saying that Liverpool doesn't have any individual players like other teams.

"The Arsenal are a good side, a capable side, but they depend on Liam Brady, Liverpool depend on each other.

"It's collective, everyone working for each other. It's a kind of socialism. I'm not being political, but pure socialism; everyone doing what they can for the rest."

## Happy memories of derby day battles

Shankly recalled his favourite memories of the Merseyside derby following his retirement.

He said: "I have a lot of happy derby game memories. Look at the results since Liverpool returned to the First Division and you'll see why.

"We have beaten Everton more often than they have beaten us.

"I can see every goal that was scored.

"Every time they got one it was like having a knife in my back. When we got one I was soaring with the astronauts.

"There are no thrills like derby thrills because they mean so much to so many.

"The city is split in half and you get so much banter, so many arguments and bets that a week before a game seems a long, long time.

"I have always wanted to win them all, even when it was Liverpool reserves against Everton reserves.

'SHANKS CAME OUT OF THE LIVERPOOL DRESSING ROOM WAVING THE MATCHDAY PROGRAMME AND POINTING TO THE FRONT COVER OF THE FOOTBALL LEAGUE REVIEW WHICH USED TO BE A FEATURE INSIDE. THERE WAS A PHOTOGRAPH OF THE WORKINGTON JUNIOR SUPPORTERS AND HE HAD SPOTTED ME IN THE MIDDLE OF THEM'

"Everton came to Anfield and beat us 4-0 in 1964-65, but it didn't take long to put that right. We beat them 5-0 the following season - revenge with interest.

"The hardest and most thrilling was Liverpool's 3-2 win in 1970-71. It is like a bad dream to Everton fans. They were in their seventh heaven when they were two-up, but we never gave up.

"With players such as Liverpool had, I knew Everton could be hit

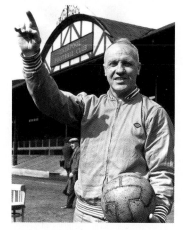

by a whirlwind - and they were.

"Then there was Brian Hall nipping in at Old Trafford to hit the goal that sent us to Wembley in 1971. That was wonderful.

"I'll never forget the rubbing we gave Everton in the Charity Shield. Records show that we won 1-0, but we gave them a pasting, and it turned out to be the best thing we did for Everton.

"Off they went to break transfer records by signing Alan Ball. Ball transformed them and put them back on the rails.

"Victory is like champagne, but defeat is a bitter pill. Thankfully we did not have many of them."

**19 September, 1979**

### Night of the 'Red Mountains'

Liverpool's all-red kit has long been famous as a weapon against all-comers. On this day Shanks spoke about its origins when he said: "The first big European game at Anfield in my reign was against Anderlecht, one of the

nothing today, son," before handing me my photograph signed by the Liverpool team. I still have that photograph hanging in my Liverpool room.

I am not quite sure who we were playing when Bill Shankly shouted Alun Evans over to get his photograph taken with me. Liverpool had just signed Evans and he was the first £100,000 teenager. Sorry to say, Bill Watson's camera didn't have a flash and the photo did not come out.

The third and last occasion I met Shanks was a game against Tottenham. Once again we were taken inside. This time Shanks came

out of the Liverpool dressing room waving the matchday programme and pointing to the front cover of the Football League Review which used to be a feature inside. There was a photograph of the Workington junior supporters and he had spotted me in the middle of them. Once again we were given tickets, and went on to beat Tottenham.

I am pleased to say I am still an avid Liverpool supporter and travel down to Anfield for all the home games with supporters from LFC Ambelside and District branch (a 320-mile round trip).

Walk On.

Friends and rivals: Shankly shaking hands with Arsenal keeper Bob Wilson

'HE SEEMED TO BE A MAN THAT WOULD DO ANYTHING HE COULD FOR THEM. SO IT WAS ONLY FITTING THAT THE ONLY NAME THAT WOULD DO OUR DOG PROUD - WITH THE STATURE THE BRITISH BULL DOG HAS IN THE DOG WORLD - WOULD BE SHANKLY'

## British Bulldog Shanks' name will live on forever

**From Colin Sumpter, Old Swan, Liverpool**

Growing up in Liverpool, you were either a Red or a Blue. No other team ever mattered.

Dalglish, Rush, Molby and Barnes were just a few of the heroes that graced the kerbs and lampposts of your local street. But even they weren't the names your dad, granddad or uncle used to shout about, the reason why Liverpool FC was so great. 'He'd never get in to 'His' team!' or "He' would never stand for that from him!' were just some of the quotes you grew up with. The 'He' they were talking about was the Great Bill Shankly.

Years and years of watching football games on the TV with your dad, granddad or uncle were always compared to the Shankly years. How Shankly would have played against that team! What Shankly would have said about that! Why Shankly wouldn't have stood for that - and my dad and granddad are both Blues. That in its own right shows the greatness the man had. It wasn't just Liverpool fans who adored him, Everton supporters also applauded this man's love for the game.

For generations to come, the man's legendary status will live not only in this city but throughout the world of football.

People remember their heroes and legends in many different ways. Some have houses, monuments or objects named after them. Some name their kids after them. This is how we all show our appreciation and respect to them.

As many people have in the past and still do now, I named a pet after him. My wife and I bought a British Bulldog a couple of years ago and when asked what we were going to call it, there was no hesitation in answering Shankly!

Being only 31 years young and not ever having the chance to see the great man at Liverpool - due to him retiring when I was born in 1974 - I've only been able to read extracts about him or watch footage of past interviews, but still I find myself drawn towards the aura of greatness that surrounded this man. The vision he had for Liverpool FC and the love and interaction he had with the fans, was truly unique. He seemed to be a man who would do anything he could for them. So it was only fitting that the only name that would do our dog proud – with the stature the British Bulldog has in the dog world – would be Shankly. This is our way of showing our appreciation to the man who brought us the Liverpool Way.

P.S We also have a cat called Paisley, but that's another story for another book, maybe!

best teams on the continent, with eight internationals in the side.

'We played in all red for the first time and I said to my wife Nessie afterwards: 'We looked like mountains.'

"That was the beginning of the all-red strip and it was kept ever since."

### 20 November 1979

### Keegan puts a happy Shankly to the sword

Kevin Keegan was devoted to Shankly, the man who put him on a top class football stage. Bill was invited to London where Kevin was due to receive a special award, a "Sword of Honour" on behalf of Souvenir Press. Shankly made the presentation, but was stunned when Keegan immediately handed the sword back and devoted it to his former boss.

Bill declared: "This is the greatest gesture since the world began and this is the greatest present I have ever had in my life, and that includes my wife!"

Keegan said: "The moment I heard the boss was going to present the award I made up my mind to give the sword to him.

"If I had not met Bill Shankly I would never have got the award in the first place. He made me and my giving it back to him comes right from the heart. He made me believe I could play football. " As the picture above shows, Shanks did indeed treasure such gifts hoarding them in his house.

**Shankly the dog: Even younger fans ensure the great man's name lives on**

## September 1979

### 'When soccer went to war' interviews

Shankly was playing for Preston when war broke out. He at first worked in a factory in the Preston area, helping to make bombers.

It was a reserved occupation but after a few months he joined the RAF and was stationed all over the country, from as far apart as Glasgow and Yarmouth.

In a series of interviews with local journalist Ann Cummings, Shankly reminisced: 'We had a regional league and you played wherever you were.

"I played in the war-time Cup final at Wembley in front of 75,000 people. We (Preston) met Blackburn and it was Tom Finney's first game at 17. He shook the life out of them! It was a 1-1 draw and we went to their ground and beat them to win it."

'He remembers being on a junior NCO's course at Arbroath and a cold, bitter wind coming in from the North Sea. "There was haddock and chips to eat – great during a time of food rationing!"

'Mr Shankly was also in the RAF boxing team, where he fought as a middleweight, and helped win the Duke of Portland Cup in the Services League. "I gave the cup to the chairman of Preston North End."

'He also played in the Air Force team with players like Peter Doherty, Stanley Matthews and George Harwick.

"During the week at camp you would get a game of football and you trained during light nights.

"When you finished duties you'd do things to keep fit. As well as being in the boxing team, I went on cross country runs.

"Nobody enjoyed the war. There was always the tension there. But it was a situation where people had to make the best of it."'

Talking about his days as a player was something he had touched upon in a special *Liverpool Echo* publication a few years earlier.

Ready to take on the enemy: Shankly's playing career was interrupted by the war

> In an article entitled 'It's Glenbuck To Glory – The Shankly Way!', journalist Charles Lambert charted Shankly's playing career:

'The Third Division (North) was a tough place for a 17-year-old and Bill wasn't a regular in the Carlisle first team. But he was there often enough to be noticed and one club that took particular notice of his powerful displays at wing-half was Preston North End.

'After a year at Carlisle, he moved to Lancashire, signing for Preston in July, 1933 for £500.

'Within four months he was in the first team and stayed there until 1949 – a run interrupted only by war service in the RAF.

'But although Shankly made his name as a player with Preston, helping them to promotion to the First Division in 1934 and to two Wembley finals – they won the Cup in 1938 – he went within a whisker of missing his chance to join the club at all.

Shankly recalled: "I turned them down because they only offered 10 shillings a week more than I was getting at Carlisle. But my brother Alec said it wasn't the money I should sign for, it was the chance.

"The Preston official had already left to catch a train to Newcastle but we caught up with him at the station. I signed for Preston on the train between Carlisle and Newcastle, got off it at Haltwhistle and caught a bus back to Carlisle."

'Shankly was capped five times by Scotland and would have earned more honours but for the outbreak of war. Shankly did his war service at a number of camps in England and Scotland, represented the RAF several times at football and boxed for his camp as a middleweight.

'Five years after his wedding in 1944, Shankly's playing career was over and he handed over the number four shirt of Preston to Tommy Docherty'

But who knows - if he hadn't have caught the train then the course of history and ultimately of Liverpool Football Club might have been very different!

**Walk on: Rare pictures of Shankly the player from the family collection. Enjoying a leisurely stroll with colleagues and (left) keeping fit**

### ▶ 1 December, 1979

### Turning back the Anfield clock twenty years

The Football Echo ran a lengthy article looking back at Shankly's appointment. He recalled the following memories:

### An air of depression about the place

'Anfield was different when I came. The Kop was open, the present day stands had not been built.

'Gates had dropped to about 21,000 and there was an air of depression about the place. I remember when I came over to Liverpool with my wife to have a look around, we went to the training ground. It was like a wilderness, with only one pitch, a tumbledown shed for the lads to change in and an old air raid shelter still there because nobody could be bothered to pull it down!

'All you could say was that it was there! But that was Liverpool, a hell of a lot of potential and not much else except the people.'

### Scousers full of Celtic pride like me

'They were fantastic, full of a kind of 'Celtic' pride and were just wanting something to be proud of.

'I've always identified with Liverpool people and I promised myself that we'd build something they could always be proud of.'

### Huddersfield could have won more than Liverpool

'If the board at Huddersfield (now in the Fourth Division!) had been ambitious, we would have won even more than Liverpool did.

'Look at the players I had there in those days: Dennis Law, Ray Wilson, Ken Taylor, the Yorkshire

## Taken under Shanks' wing for the perfect Wembley day

From Mark Fitzgerald, Huyton

It was my first-ever trip to Wembley, and 13 years old, you could imagine how made up I must have been because I was the only one out of all my mates with a ticket.

Tickets were like gold as usual and I was one of the lucky ones. We made our way to London on the Friday to stay with my uncle in Westminster and to make the most of the atmosphere.

London was packed out with Liverpool fans and Geordies. We were up early on the Saturday morning to go up to Wembley. I was carrying the 12 cans of Newcastle Brown ale for my uncle. He was carrying the banner.

When we got off the tube at Wembley the atmosphere was brilliant as we walked down Wembley Way, mixing with the Geordies. My uncle was drinking his cans, and just walking around having a look at the stadium and taking everything in.

Getting closer to kick off, I wanted to go into the ground to see what it was like. My uncle said he wanted to wait for the players' coach to come. When the coach did arrive, it was like being in the Kop.

Everyone wanted to get a look at the team. People were getting crushed, and we managed to get round to the big black gates where the coaches went in. The coach came to a standstill because of the entire crowd. The fans were going crazy, singing and pushing. All the players were waving out of the windows, laughing. That's when the police came on horses to break the crowd up.

The next thing I remember was being knocked over by a horse, leaving me lying on the ground clutching the six remaining cans of Newcastle Brown. The police horse was kicking and stamping on my legs. That's when I noticed the players banging on the window for the policeman to gain control and my uncle was having a go at this copper,

**Shanks' last hurrah: Liverpool's 3-0 demolition of Newcastle**

Shanks gave fan Mark Fitzgerald a pitch-side view of the 1974 final

'WE WERE UP EARLY ON THE
SATURDAY MORNING TO GO UP
TO WEMBLEY. I WAS CARRYING
THE 12 CANS OF NEWCASTLE
BROWN ALE FOR MY UNCLE.
HE WAS CARRYING THE BANNER'

cricketer, Bill McGarry, Ray Wood and several more. But Huddersfield was a seller's market. I wanted them to buy Yeats and St John, but they wouldn't find the money. That was the difference.'

### I was offered the Kop job eight years earlier!

'Do you know, I was offered the job at Anfield eight years earlier. I was invited over to Liverpool and asked if I would be the manager and I said right away: "Who picks the team?"

'In those days the manager recommended the players and the board approved his decision, so I said: "No. You don't want a manager. You'd best find someone else."

'That was the first thing I asked when Mr Williams offered me the job in 1959 and it's true to say I was the first genuine manager Liverpool ever had.'

### What if I had accepted the job then?

'What would have happened if Bill Shankly had come to Liverpool eight years earlier? He himself has no doubts. "We would have conquerered the world," he says with fire darting from his eyes. "I was 36 then and at my best. I helped Carlisle to take 62 points in a season and later at Grimsby, we got 66 from 42 games.

"When we won the Second Division championship, the shareholders gave us a silver cigarette box. I said to them: 'Do you think we have won something? This is nothing – it's only the start and now we're going after the real prizes.

"We won the First Division and the FA Cup and the League again and then we went after Europe. "

### No man is more important than the team

'They were wonderful days, because it was all new and

people didn't expect you to win trophies all the time. In the sixties the atmosphere was unbelievable ... I only wish I could start all over again.

'Football is a team game and no man is more important than the team.

'Manager, coach, director, player, tea lady or ball boy, they're all part of the team and they've got to be the best there is. There's no room for prima donnas.

'I tell you this, our great team of the sixties were paid the same money to a penny piece. There was no one man who got more than another. That's the way it must be.'

**18 December 1980**

### Bill Shankly's Game of Mastermind!

It was revealed that Shankly had helped Altrincham in their FA Cup preparations over the past two seasons – this in light of their forthcoming third-round tie with . . . Liverpool.

'I've always been a great admirer of Bill, and at the start of last season I asked if he would be willing to give us a hand,' Altrincham manager Tony Sanders, an Evertonian, told the Echo's Ian Hargraves.

'He's been a tremendous help and we could never thank him enough. What he's done for us has strengthened us in so many ways and also saved us a great deal of money.

**Reaching out: Saluting the people who made it happen**

hitting him with his banner.

Then a St John's first aid man picked me up. He took me through the big black gates into the famous players' tunnel. I couldn't believe this was happening to me. I sat down against the wall and that's when the great Bill Shankly came over to me. He put his hands around my face and in that famous rough Jock accent, said: "Are you alright, son' and rubbed my hair. Then one by one

watched all the players walk past me and into the changing rooms. I couldn't believe my luck.

I was taken into the First Aid room next to the players' changing rooms. Once there, the nurse bandaged me up and then the St John's ambulance lad came to pick me up. Asking who I was with, I gave my uncle's name, so he could come and meet me, but he never turned up.

Because of this, he then took me

**Our leader: Shanks addresses the crowd at the 1974 homecoming**

'Newcastle were undressed!' Keegan's famous goal makes it 3-0

'SHANKLY CAME OVER TO ME. HE PUT HIS HANDS AROUND MY FACE AND IN THAT FAMOUS ROUGH JOCK ACCENT SAID: 'ARE YOU ALRIGHT SON' AND RUBBED MY HAIR'

> 'He's not been to a great many of our matches, but his advice on training schedules and preparation for matches has also been invaluable. He also taught us the most vital thing of all – how to believe in ourselves.'

QUOTE
**Cup heroes better geared than most clubs in First Division—Shanks**

Shankly clearly enjoyed his work with the non-League side. It was just another exciting football challenge to him. He said: "Altrincham are a fine club with a nice, clean tidy ground. They now have all the ingredients needed for success, a good manager, a plan that works, a good training schedule and the right approach to their matches."

"One of the things he's always preached has been the importance of continuity," says Mr Sanders. "If a player was left out of the side and came to ask him why, he would reply 'I've not dropped you son. You dropped yourself. If you'd have played harder (or better) you'd still be in the team.'"

## Panic on the line

Broadcaster Bill Bothwell recalled Shankly's radio debut with him soon after he joined the Reds:

'I had been asked on a Saturday morning by producer Angus McKay...if I could get Bill to come to the microphone and talk about that day's match.

'Angus was in London, I was in the Manchester studio and Bill...he was at Anfield. His first reaction to my call was "what time?"

"Oh, around 12.30," I said.

"No use," said Bill. "I always go for my dinner at midday."

out of the players' tunnel and along the track along the pitch. After walking about 20 yards, he told me to sit next to him against the white wall that used to go right around the ground. What a speck I had, and I hadn't even got my ticket out my pocket yet. I must have had one of the best specks in the ground, close to the build-up before the game. Then the teams came out, and I must have been just a few yards from the managers and players walking out onto the pitch.

The rest is history. That was one fantastic weekend. The two ambulance lads finished off the cans of Newcastle Brown and I made my way back to Westminster on my own, Cup final ticket in my pocket and not finding my uncle until the Sunday.

But the thing I will never forget is the man himself, Bill Shankly, coming over to me, making sure I was okay. That was him all over. He was all for the fans, and will never be forgotten, my hero. Memories of Bill Shankly will stay with me forever.

"Come on, Bill," I said. "As one Scot to another...in fact as one Scot to two others," since Angus McKay was also wreathed in heather.

'And so the pact was made.

'Bill would turn up in the BBC Liverpool studios in St John's Lane around 12.15 and I would interview him down the line in Manchester.

"What's he like?" asked Angus McKay.

"The first question should be the only one I'll need," I replied. "Ask him about Liverpool and he'll talk all day."

'And so the scene was set.

'But when we started calling up Bill about 12.15 we were met by total silence from the Liverpool studio.

'Time raced by. Seconds before the interview was due to start the producer said: "Take a chance and ask the first question."

'Which I did. And back came the rolling Rs of Glenbuck. Bill had been there all the time, but was too deep in his thoughts about the forthcoming match to answer our calls.

'And that, I'm afraid, is how the interview went.

'To every question the answer was 'Yes' or 'No.'

'I was panic-stricken. What could I ask next? And my questions became more and more rhetorical, needing little more than the monosyllabic answer I was getting.

'But that was Bill before a match. Bill after a match, or even 24 hours before one was a lot more loquacious.'

## A helping hand for the next generation

Speaking to the Echo in 1980, Shankly touched on the responsibility that we all have to pass on a creed of life to the next generation.

He always found time for children and young people and saw them as holding the key to a better future.

He said: 'I love youngsters. I can always find time to talk to

My hero: Mark Thomas in Bill Shankly's office in 1972

## A photo to treasure from a memorable day with Shanks

From Mark Thomas, Bidston, Birkenhead

In November 1972, my dear dad was tragically killed in an accident at work. I was only 12 years old at the time. A month later, his work mates arranged for me to visit Anfield to meet some of the Reds' stars of the time.

When I arrived, I was given a guided tour of the stadium, and was able to meet my heroes along the way. I met Ian Callaghan, Steve Heighway and Ray Clemence in the players' lounge, Emlyn Hughes and Kevin Keegan in the treatment room and Bob Paisley (then our trainer), who was with Reuben Bennett in the famous Boot Room.

Eventually, I was invited into Bill Shankly's office to meet him. The great man ruffled my hair, chatted to me, signed my autograph book and then sat me in his chair to have our photograph taken together. The photograph has given me so much pleasure over the years and is a great source of pride to this day. Shanks will always be my football hero.

## Nessie invited us in as Shanks finished his bath

From Michael Daley,
West Derby, Liverpool

I used to live in Winterburn Heights, which overlooked Melwood. It was a short walk to Bill's house. In the mid-Seventies my mate Mick Corcoran and myself used to go to his house and ask him for tickets when Liverpool were away in the FA Cup.

He always gave us two tickets without fail for a number of years. When Liverpool played Everton in the 1977 semi-final, he said it was: "A pig of a ground and no semi-final should be played there."

His wife Nessie always took us inside the house and sat us down. We went one Sunday and he had been playing on Barnfield Drive playing fields, now the Bill Shankly playing fields. Nessie said he was in the bath, as he had been playing football there. This was three or four years after he retired!

We sat in the living room and waited about 20 minutes for him. When he came downstairs he said: "Hello boys, I have been expecting you." We used to buy Nessie chocolates and she really appreciated that.

I also have a friend called Chris Medway who has a bar in Salou, Spain dedicated to Shanks. I have sent a postcard of the bar.

them or sign an autograph. I never turned a kid away if I could help it because basically I'm sorry for them.

'I look at them and think: "What are you going to be when you grow up?" What is their destiny? I think it is a terrible thing if a grown-up doesn't help a youngster because kids can be hit terribly hard if an older person goes against them.

'Many times each day, the front door bell rings at my West Derby home. Standing on the doorstep will be a kid, or a group of kids, real Liverpool types, who ask: "Can I speak to Bill?" It's never 'Mr Shankly' but I don't mind.

'My wife Ness has hundreds of photographs of me holding the FA Cup and I sign one of them personally for the kid and give it to him. 'Best wishes to Jim or Joe or Jackie or whatever his name is.'

'There is one group of kids, four or five of them who have come up every day for the last couple of weeks while they are on holiday. They ask me what I'm doing and whether I can come out to play football.

'They've had their autographed photographs by now, of course, but I usually end up by giving them their bus fares home to Gillmoss. I don't know how they found out where I live but so many of them do.

'If I can help a kid along, I will. They're heart-broken if you snub them and that I will never do. There were always kids knocking around Anfield when I was there. They're the future Liverpool supporters and they're real people to me.'

Bellefield memories: In the garden and (right) Shanks' house in later years

The Spanish Kop! The bar devoted to Shankly in Salou

### ► Salutes keep rolling in for a true great

Tributes came from a variety of footballing figures in the Liverpool Daily Post and Echo during Shankly's retirement from the game. Here are a selection from a variety of sources and Liverpool figures who knew the great man inside out.

### In a class of his own as a man and a manager

'Any praise for Bill Shankly cannot be too high. For me he was a great manager and certainly the best motivator – and he was so funny with it as well.

'One minute he would give you a roasting and the next he would be telling you that you were the greatest player in the world. But he never let any outsiders do that to his players.

'Bill Shankly is everything to me as a manager. His overall influence on me has been tremendous and he means everything to me. And as a man and a manager, he is just in a class of his own. There is nobody else like him and there never will be.'

**Emlyn Hughes**

### He gave me confidence to believe in myself

'I will always be grateful to him. He made me the player I was.

'I came down from Scotland as a raw youth and this man gave me the confidence to believe in myself when at first I wondered if I was going to make it or not.

'I was with him for 11 years and I'm a good listener and a lot of things he said and has done I try to copy.

'But there will never be another like him. He was his own man.

"No matter what anyone said he wouldn't change his mind and luckily for him it came right.'

**Ron Yeats** ►

### 'Hiya son, give us a kick of your ball!'

From Michael Withe, Waterloo

My brief, but everlasting memory of Bill Shankly occurred in June 1972 when I was sitting my A-Levels at St Edward's College in Sandfield Park, which was only separated from Mr Shankly's home in Bellefield Avenue by a 10-12 feet high wall and what was then mainly a dirt-track road.

Having sat an exam one morning, my friends and I had lunch and after a 'brief' revision period, decided to go and have a football kick-about on the fields at the far end of Bellefield Avenue (now the Bill Shankly Memorial ground). Ours was a 'rugby' school.

Over the years, the wall had fallen into disrepair which meant that there was now a gap to climb through and a 100-yard walk to the pitches, rather than a one mile journey via Eaton Road. I climbed through first and one of my friends kicked a ball through the gap to me and I started strolling along with the ball at my feet on the pavement opposite Mr Shankly's house.

As I was opposite the house, Bill appeared. His driveway was only short and the front of his car was almost touching the house. He had to walk around the rear of the car in order to get to the driver's door. Suddenly he shouted over to me: "Hiya son, over 'ere."

My immediate reaction was to 'freeze' in disbelief that he was actually talking to me and although I was only mesmerised for a fraction of a second, it felt like an eternity and I can only assume that it was instinct to kick the ball over to him. He trapped it, kicked it back to me, gave a wave and continued round to get in the car.

I still don't know whether I stopped the ball or just let it roll past me as I was agog with amazement that the man who most Liverpool fans, including myself, looked upon as 'God' would speak to me, a complete stranger.

I cherish this memory to this day (I'm now 51) and to me it still serves to illustrate that this great man was a "people's man" who could, by a simple action lasting only a second, leave an indelible memory.

It is a pity that some of today's managers cannot take a leaf out of his book and be as pleasant and as inviting as him as well as being able to live in a humble home in the heart of the community.

**Back to you son! Shanks couldn't resist a kick-around**

Just another medal: With Nessie outside Buckingham Palace

> ## From Scottish football to the Mecca of football

'Bill Shankly is a man who has done more than anybody to build my career and I will be eternally grateful to him. He took me from the obscurity of Scottish football and brought me to the Mecca of football.

'He was a tremendous leader of men and a tremendous example of what a manager should be. The experience of having worked with him for 10 years has helped me enormously in my steps to become a successful manager.

'One of his philosophies in life was that whatever you put into the game you get out and I am delighted he is getting the rewards and respect he deserves.'

**Ian St John**

## He made dreams come true and he always put the people first

### From Mrs Rose Walsh, Woodchurch, Wirral

My family and I have our wonderful memories of Bill Shankly. I wrote to Bill to ask him if I could leave a book at the club for him to sign for my sons Robert and William.

I put my phone number on the letter and Bill telephoned me and invited my sons to go to his house at Bellefield Avenue with the book.

What a man he was, a truly amazing person. When he spoke to you, you just listened. He kept in touch by phone and invited us to his home. We used to send gifts to his grandchildren, soft woollen toys and teddy bears, all in red and white of course.

He even sent me a birthday telegraph and photographs. One time I was quite ill and losing weight and went to see him with my sons. He put his hands on my shoulders and I felt a tremendous surge through my body. Afterwards I got better and felt stronger. I told Bill he had healing hands and made me better.

He said he was sorry to leave LFC, but once he had made the statement he couldn't go back on his word. He reached into a drawer and let us see his OBE before throwing it back into the drawer. He said: "That's where it belongs," as if it was nothing. I told him that if he went into politics, everyone would follow him because he was like a messiah.

He really should have been given a knighthood along with Bob Paisley. Bill was a real people's person. He loved everyone. I asked him why his three-piece suit was blue and he said it was Scottish.

I have a lot to thank him for, along with my family. He made dreams come true and always put the people first. We have Liverpool plates on our wall and photos of my sons Robert and William, taken with Bill when he was manager. They are treasures. I am 78 now and I could talk football all day.

## Everything was pushed to one side for Liverpool FC

'I have always found Bill a very good friend – very straight, very honest. His retirement was a great loss to the game but I am glad he got out at the top. The pressures of managing a team like Liverpool - or Leeds - and keeping them at the top are tremendous.

'Bill just lives for football and such enthusiasm can damage one's health. Everything was pushed to one side for Liverpool FC.

'He could make players believe they were better than they were. His tremendous enthusiasm used to rub off on the players, the staff and the supporters.

'If he had a failing, it was the fact that he could not see anything outside Liverpool Football Club. He only ever talked about Liverpool, the staff and its players. Talk about anything else and he did not want to know!

'Possibly he hurt a few people over the years. But I would sooner have someone say something to my face, whatever it was, than have them talk about me behind my back.

'With Bill he would get it off his chest and that was the end of the matter.'

**Former Leeds and England boss Don Revie**

### It had to be all or nothing with him

'He is a unique man. They don't come in pairs. I've known Bill for 43 years and he hasn't changed in any shape or form. He just wants to win.

'He has no bad players and never played in a bad team. He had all the confidence in the world. The most wonderful thing about him was that he was the nicest bigot in the game.

'His love affair with the Kop is the most marvellous thing in football. It's something which is good for the game. Bill would never adapt. He was a wing-half when they called them that and they attacked and defended. Lots of people like myself compromised as we got older and played tucked in behind the centre-half. But not Bill. It had to be all or nothing with him.

'He was the same as a manager – he would not compromise. He had to be Bill Shankly or nothing.

'He is a lovely character. He's part of the football scene. People say the game will miss him, but he's still there, larger than life. Wherever football is played, he is there.'

### The master at work and a happy birthday

Mr and Mrs G Moss,
Huyton, Liverpool

This picture (above) shows the master at work. The late, great Bill Shankly taking time out at Melwood training ground to sign his autograph for our son George Moss Junior before going off to Wembley to play Leeds United in the 1965 F.A Cup final which coincidentally they won on the 1st May, 1965, our son's ninth birthday.

### I kept a picture of my mentor in my headmaster's office

From Peter J Barnes, Liverpool

In May 1968 I was a 21-year-old chemistry student and a Liverpool fanatic, working as part of my degree course just outside London. On weekends when I couldn't get home, I'd try to get a match in London, often Arsenal, as my flat mate was a supporter and could give me a lift to Highbury.

I had been concerned during the

previous season that both Gordon Milne and my all-time hero (Sir) Roger Hunt were probably coming towards the end of their Anfield careers and I wanted to ensure the club was planning for the future. I wrote to Bill Shankly, congratulating the club on a good season and recommend he take a close look at Allan Clarke, who was showing great promise as a Fulham striker and also Arsenal's Jon Sammels who was becoming a fine attacking midfield player. In my view, I told him these two players would be ideal buys for our club.

Imagine how delighted I was, a couple of weeks later, to receive a reply from the great man. He had quite obviously typed it up himself on club-headed notepaper. It read:

*Dear Peter,*
*Received your letter with your comments and good wishes, thanks very much indeed.*
*The boys did quite well last season, but not well enough. To be successful, we have to win something every season. The two players you mention can play a bit. If we can get men to buy, we will buy.*
*Sincerely,*

*W. Shankly, Manager*

I have treasured this letter ever since (I am now 59). I was so impressed that such a busy man, at the top of a very competitive profession, should take the time and interest to reply to me when no doubt he received hundreds, if not thousands of similar letters each season. His gesture spoke volumes to

me about the importance of staying connected with 'ordinary people,' no matter how rich or famous you become in life.

Bill's honesty, common sense, humour, the fierce pride he imbued in all of us coupled with this tremendous ability to relate to the people made him a truly unique character.

After graduating, I began my 35-year career in teaching, and continued my support of the 'Mighty Reds.' I retired last summer, having been head teacher of one of the

largest comprehensive schools in Liverpool for nearly 18 years (see my picture above). Throughout my time in headship, a role not without its fair share of stresses and pressures, a large photograph of Bill hung in my office. I told people he was my mentor. The photo provoked many conversations with children, parents, education officials and anyone who visited me in the course of a working week. Furthermore it acted as a constant reminder to me of the basic human values exhibited by the man himself and represented a standard to which all of us aspire.

P.S. To my knowledge, Bill never pursued my recommendation of Clarke and Sammels, though he did agree they 'could play a bit!' That was some consolation.

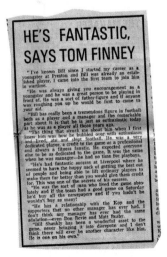

playing in front of. He was a sort of father-figure and if anyone was roughing you up he would be first to come to your aid.

'Bill has really been a tremendous figure in football both as a player and a manager and the remarkable part about it is that he is just as enthusiastic

'BILL'S HONESTY, COMMON SENSE, HUMOUR, THE FIERCE PRIDE HE IMBUED IN ALL OF US COUPLED WITH THIS TREMENDOUS ABILITY TO RELATE TO THE PEOPLE MADE HIM A TRULY UNIQUE CHARACTER'

today as he was as a player all those years ago.

'The thing that struck me about him when I first knew him was how he bubbled over with enthusiasm and lived, ate and slept football. He was a very dedicated player, a credit to the game as a professional and always a fitness fanatic. He expected everyone else to be as dedicated to the game. It was the same when he was manager – he had no time for playboys.

'He's had fantastic success at Liverpool where he seemed to have the happy knack of getting the best out of people and being able to lift ordinary players to make them far better than you would give them credit for. This was one of the secrets of his success.

'He was the sort of man who lived the game absolutely and if the team had a good game on the Saturday he'd buy all the newspapers and if you hadn't he wouldn't buy as many!

'He has a relationship with the Kop and the supporters that no other manager has ever had. I don't think any manager has ever had the same adulation – even Don Revie and Matt Busby.

'Bill Shankly has been a wonderful asset to the game, never bringing it into disrepute and I don't think there will ever be another character like him. He is one on his own.'

## The force of the man's character had an affect on everyone

No one has made more first team appearances for Liverpool than Ian Callaghan. He played under Shankly and revealed his thoughts on his former boss in his autobiography 'The Ian Callaghan Story' which featured as a series in the local papers.

He wrote: 'Bill Shankly has had a massive influence on me. Not only on my football career but on the way I live. He's moulded me as a person, and the effect of Shanks on me ranges from how

## The great Shanks even remembered my face

*From Seanie Walsh, Irby, Wirral*

I was only one of the hundreds of thousands of people who were touched by the great man. I was lucky to have met him not once but three times. The first time I did not have a camera, but I made sure I did the next time I had the opportunity.

I used to travel from Waterford, Ireland to Anfield to watch the Reds. My journey started in 1969 and like everyone else I was totally shocked when Bill decided to retire. How was he going to be replaced?

Shortly after he retired I had met Bill or Mr Shankly as I called him to ask him to pose for a photo. I was just like a kid (I was 23 then) who could not believe I had met my hero. Not only did he pose, but he had remembered me from the previous time I had met him (without camera).

He said: "I see my little Irish lads are back again. Nice to see you." It was the day (04/01/1975) we began our defence of the FA Cup, which we had won under Bill the previous May against Newcastle. We had just beaten Stoke City 2–0. Believe it or not (we were really cheeky Irish lads) we sneaked into Anfield after that game. Bob Paisley was being interviewed by the BBC and we had our photo taken with Bob and the FA Cup. Not many people were that lucky to have met the two greatest Liverpool managers of all time, all in the space of 20 minutes. Of course, people back home would not believe me, until I produced the photos. What memories!

I have lived on the Wirral since 1987 and still go to Anfield with some of my old friends from Waterford, who regularly visit Liverpool. I'm 54 now and I'm delighted to be able to share my memories.

Seanie Walsh treasures his pictures of himself with the great man

'I COULD NOT BELIEVE I HAD MET MY HERO. NOT ONLY DID HE POSE, BUT HE HAD REMEMBERED ME FROM THE PREVIOUS TIME I HAD MET HIM. HE SAID: 'I SEE MY LITTLE IRISH LADS ARE BACK AGAIN. NICE TO SEE YOU'

Streets ahead: The fans hold a party for 'Shankly The Great'

## We invited Shanks to our party and he didn't let us down

From Sheila O'Hare, Liverpool

My favourite memory of Bill Shankly was in 1974. We held a street party in Tiber Street off Lodge Lane in honour of Liverpool's win in the FA Cup and invited Shanks to come. We never thought he would come. The kids were so looking forward to seeing the 'Great Shanks,' when he suddenly walked down the street with Nessie. Who would believe that he would come? It shows what he thought of the fans.

to prepare for a match to my general outlook on life.

'I would challenge anyone not to be affected, even moved, by the sheer force of the man's character. Yes, he was outrageous at times – but he was always straight. He was an irresistible mixture.

'His enthusiasm for the game was incredible. He would hammer home points to us again and again and again. He was repetitive sometimes to the extreme that he would bore you with what he was saying because you'd heard it all before. But that was not a weakness. It was a strength, because Shanks made sure that what he was saying got home to us. It all rubbed off.

'By the weight of his personality he became the leader – and we all responded to him. Not only the players, but the training staff, the office staff, the groundsman. Everyone.

'Although I never experienced a tongue-lashing from him, I know he wiped the floor with several players, really giving them a mouthful. Yet, within an hour or so, it was all forgotten.

'He didn't just pretend to forget. He did it sincerely, and he'd even start praising the player he'd had a go at.

'And he was very protective of his players. He even told us not to read newspapers, his reasoning being that if we had been given praise, we'd get big-headed, and if we got some stick from the Press it would be bad for our confidence and do us no good at all.

'But Shanks would read the papers and remember what was said. I can't count the number of times he's slated journalists to their face about what they'd written. Yet, as with the players, he would never harbour grudges or make enemies. In fact, I doubt it anyone in football has been so much in demand by the Press and television. They respected him as much as we did.

'The greatest thing he said to me was: 'You're a young man when you finish this game. You've

got a full life ahead of you when you stop playing, but the rewards you can get while you are in it are tremendous, so give your all to the game.'

'That is so true. And although he always preached a total commitment to football, he didn't ask you to be a monk. You could still have your nights out and your enjoyment. It was a case of getting the balance right.

'His psychology was one of his greatest assets as a manager. He knew how to say things, when to say things and what to say to get the best out of a player...to motivate him, to inspire him, or to reassure him.

'I had an early experience of this during my first summer as a

professional when he telephoned me to tell me he had signed another right winger and told me not to worry about it. He demonstrated this quality again, many years later, on the night I was presented with the Football of the Year award in May, 1974.

'The boss and I travelled from our hotel at St Albans, where we were staying prior to meeting Newcastle in the FA Cup final. Needless to say, I was a bit nervous thinking about this big gala occasion and all the personalities that would be present.

'As we were about to enter the room and be announced to the guests, Shanks said to me: 'Just remember...you get out of this game only what you put into it.' That was fantastic timing...it really calmed me down.

'There will never be another Bill Shankly. He's a one-off, and for what he's done at Liverpool he

## The day new boss upstaged singing duo

From Stevie Faye, Whiston

Once upon a time, I was on a show at Liverpool's Supporters Club. Shanks had just been named manager. The duo were finishing their last number.

They took their final bow and Shanks walked in. The crowd stood up and cheered and clapped their hands. The singers thought it was for them. They did two more songs as an encore until they twigged.

Shanks was a man I knew very well, (a man's man). I asked him for his red and white tie. I still have it framed. There will never be another Bill Shankly.

will go down in history as one of the most successful and greatest managers of all time.

'Needless to say, I feel privileged to have played under him longer than any other player.

'In five, 10, 15, 20 years from now, when his deeds are still being talked of in glowing terms, I will be able to cling to the reality of Shanks. Because I'm sure the Bill Shankly story, just like Robin Hood, will change in the telling. But me, and the other players who have played under him, will never forget him as he really was.

'He breathed fire when it was necessary, but he was also very thoughtful and, at times, gentle. He hated defeat, but in victory was always glowing in his praise for the opposition. He was a proud and honest man.'

### 7 March 1981

## Shanks samples a world of darkness

**Shanks samples a world of darkness**

BILL Shankly and ballet star Margaret Barbieri had their eyes opened to the world of the blind at a special exhibition held in Liverpool.

The former Liverpool manager, who regularly helps collect money for the Royal Society for the Blind on Merseyside, and Sadlers Wells ballerina Miss Barbieri wore blindfolds and special spectacles to simulate stages of blindness at an exhibition by the Radio 4 'In Touch' programme team.

And the fearless Shanks had to give up after a few paces. "I was afraid of falling," he said.

At the Anglican Cathedral's Western Rooms, where the exhibition is on again today, they also tried out various aids for the blind, recommended by the blind presenters of the weekly programme for the visually handicapped.

Yesterday's visit also provided a thrill for young pupils at the Royal School for the Blind in Liverpool.

Lyn Marsden, of Walton and Karen Sproston, of Runcorn, danced for Miss Barbieri.

And ten-year-old Christopher Roberts and his eleven-year-old school friends Darren Tilson and Lee Ramsden displayed their soccer skills before their hero.

Sharing the triumphs: A young fan helps Shanks to show off the Manager of the Year trophy to the Kop

'SHANKS WAS A MAN I KNEW VERY WELL. I ASKED HIM FOR HIS RED AND WHITE TIE. I STILL HAVE IT FRAMED. THERE WILL NEVER BE ANOTHER BILL SHANKLY'

In what was to be the last year of his life, Shankly was still actively supporting local charities and businesses.

In March, 1981, he teamed up with ballet star Margaret Barbieri to 'have their eyes opened to the world of the blind' at a special exhibition held in Liverpool.

'The former Liverpool boss, who regularly collected money for the Royal Society for the Blind on Merseyside joined the Sadlers Wells ballerina in wearing a blindfold and special spectacles to simulate stages of blindness at an exhibition by the Radio 4 'In Touch' programme team.

And even the fearless Shanks had to give up after a few paces.

He said: "I was afraid of falling."

Two young pupils at the Royal School for the Blind in Liverpool also had their dream come true.

Ten-year-olds Darren Tilson and Lee Ramsden displayed their soccer skills before their hero.

## Importance of the right food at the right time

In the modern era, the value of eating healthily is well documented. That was not always the case during the Shankly era. However, in further proof that he was a man ahead of his time, Liverpool's former manager spoke intelligently about a footballer's diet when he looked back on his career in an interview with the Liverpool Echo – even if the time-honoured fascination for steak dinners still held firm!

## Tea, toast and honey and straight to bed

Shankly told the Echo: 'When I took a physiotherapy course before I became a manager, I learned some valuable things.

'Notably about the heart, the intake of food for an athlete and particularly the timing of meals before a match. I put this into use.

'When I came to Liverpool, I stopped the system of players

He was the closest thing to God on earth

From Sue Costello,
Rainhill, Merseyside

I was 17 years old when we faced Newcastle in the FA Cup final at Wembley in 1974. I had been to as many matches as I could afford that season, home and away, so when we reached the Cup final I just had to go!

Unfortunately I wasn't a season ticket holder and they were always given priority when we played in the 'big' games. I was bitterly disappointed, so my late father – a great LFC supporter – suggested I write to Shanks and explain my situation, which I did.

I told him that I couldn't afford a season ticket but this didn't mean I didn't love Liverpool FC as much as the next Kopite. I told him I had begged and borrowed to attend the games and that I deserved to go to the final. I pleaded with him to help me.

A few days later, a letter arrived from the man himself. Inside was a compliment slip which said: 'To Sue, best wishes Bill Shankly' and attached were two Cup final tickets. My dad was so proud of me, but mum worried about me going to Wembley. Dad had been in 1965 and he told her I would be fine. I was, it was one of the best days of my life.

Shankly was the greatest. Nobody will ever equal him as a man or a football manager. He was our folklore, he gave us our dreams - and as far as I am concerned he was the closest thing to God on earth.

Leader of the pack: Shankly is the man in front as he leads out Liverpool to face Brian Clough's Leeds in the 1974 Charity Shield. Despite his busy job he found time to help fans out with tickets

## Passion that you can't switch on and off

From W Booth, Melling

I can recall when I was going to Anfield in the 60s and 70s. I had a mate whose name was Johnny Walker. He sadly passed away, but he was a great character, well known to all at Anfield. All Reds supporters knew him. One day we were walking along Walton Lane, when Bill Shankly pulled up in his car and called Johnny over. He said to Johnny: "Do me a favour and promise me you won't run on the pitch today, and I will give you two tickets for the derby game."

"Yes Bill, okay, honest Bill," said Johnny.'

The drink and his emotions got the better of Johnny, and off he went, over the Kop wall, dodging the coppers, with his bald head and red beard. Of course, he forgot about his promise to Shanks. All Bill could do was put his hands over his eyes and sigh.

Johnny Walker was an institution who could run on the pitch and mingle with the team, and the dignitaries etc. He would even roll up his coat, put it on the penalty spot, and take a penalty against Ray Clemence.

Johnny and Bill were passionate and you cannot switch that on and off.

› having a big meal on the night before a game.

'I adopted the pattern of taking them away on a Friday night, timing the journey to reach the hotel about 10pm, where the players had tea, toast and honey and then straight to bed.

...about in Huddersfield—one day Shankly played ...

# RIGHT FOOD RIGHT TIME

**FOOD**

When I took a physio-therapy course before I became a manager, I learned some valuable things.

Notably about the heart, the intake of food for an athlete and particularly the timing of meals before a match. I put this into use.

When I came to Liverpool, I stopped the system of players having a big meal on the night before a game. I adopted the pattern of taking them away on a Friday night, timing the journey to reach the hotel about 10 p.m., where the players had tea, toast and honey and then straight to bed.

On the day of the match, three hours before kick-off, they could have a steak, or chicken, or poached eggs. They did not have a cooked breakfast as well.

It was a simple diet and the word "simple" came into most of my football thinking in training and playing ...

A taste for discipline: Shankly enforced a strict eating routine before games

'On the day of the match, three hours before kick-off, they could have a steak or chicken or poached eggs. They did not have a cooked breakfast as well.

'It was a simple diet and the word 'simple' came into most of my football thinking in training and playing as well.

'I ate the same sort of food all my life and I've always been a fitness fanatic.

'The food players had before a match is to preserve their strength, not build it up.

'Players find what suits them best by trial and error.

'If their demand fell within the limits I laid down, that was all right.

'I also expected them to eat properly when they were not at the club, not to eat stupid things when they were out of our control.

'Most of them did that but I invariably knew when any of them had stepped off the rails in any way..

'In any case, it usually told on their performance.'

> ### Classic sayings

The Liverpool Echo also published some classic Shankly sayings in 1981.

### 'It's a sort of shrine – it isn't a football ground'

Shanks after a hard-fought 1-1 result away from home: 'The best side drew!'

To the journalist who suggested that Liverpool were possibly struggling a bit: 'Aye – here we are – struggling at the top of Division One . . .'

After a shock defeat by Blackpool: 'The Football League are not going to believe this one.'

On the fans at Anfield: 'The word 'fanatic' has been used many times . . . but I think there must be another word for the Anfield spectators.

'I think it's more than fanatacism. It's a religion with them. The thousands who come here to worship . . . it's a sort of shrine - it isn't a football ground.'

### 'We annihilated England. It was a massacre. We beat them 5-4'

To an interpreter surrounded by excited, noisy Italian journalists: 'Just tell them that I totally disagree with whatever they are saying.'

To Alan Ball after the player had signed for Everton: 'Don't worry Alan, you'll be playing NEAR a great side.'

On a wartime England v Scotland international: 'We absolutely annihilated England. It was a massacre. We beat them 5-4.'

On the problems of professional football: 'Some of these lads suffer setbacks that would break the heart of a concrete floor!'

## 'World Cup Willie' 1945-2006

Paul Coyle, Kirkby

Johnnie Coyle was my brother. He was the one responsible for me following the Reds from an early age as my father was not interested in attending the matches (what you might call an 'armchair supporter!' – and a blue-nose to boot!).

Johnnie took me on the Kop for the first time for a reserve game against Bury…still I got my first glimpse of an up-and-coming goalie by the name of Ray Clemence!

That was in the Sixties. I remember he had a movie camera, which he took to Melwood to film the players training. I'll never forget inviting our mates round to watch footage on the big screen (in the front room!) of Roger Hunt, Emlyn Hughes, Ian St John and (my personal favourite) Peter Thompson training.

In those days they didn't mind spectators going and watching. You could stand next to Bill Shankly and the Boot Room staff and chat without questions asked! A far cry from the footballing world of today.

A docker for most of his life, he of course earned a nickname…'World Cup Willie!'

I can only assume this was because he bore an uncanny resemblance to the famous 1966 mascot, which was popular at the time. This could be confusing for us kids when one of his mates off the dock would telephone him and ask for 'Willie!' We would say 'who??' until we were used to it!!

Along with 499 of his comrades he was sacked by the MD & HC in 1996, and I remember how proud he was when Robbie Fowler displayed his support for the 500 lifting his top to reveal the doCKers T-shirt that famous night, nice one Robbie!

I suppose the biggest thrill of Johnnie's life had to be when he ran on the pitch at the end of the 1974 FA Cup final and along with fellow supporters kissed Shankly's feet.

We were watching the final on telly when I spotted our Johnnie running towards Bill with arms wide open. I couldn't believe it was him, and it wasn't till the highlights later that night that our suspicions were confirmed.

The next morning we excitingly told him how we'd seen him on the pitch kissing the great man's feet. He looked at us all as if he was dreaming, disbelieving almost. When we showed him the back of the Mirror he made us buy ALL the Sunday newspapers. He wrote to each paper for the prints of the photos on the back pages (and more).

About a week later he visited Shankly's house to present Bill's wife with a big bunch of flowers. Bill wasn't in but Johnnie was invited inside by Nessie for a 'nice cup of tea' and left our phone number with her. She said she would make sure Bill got it.

The next day we all sat round the phone waiting for it to ring. When it did ring the first time it was one of my sisters. We all screamed, 'GET OFF THE LINE! SHANKLY'S RINGING!' there was no doubt in our minds he would ring, such was

## 'THERE WAS NO DOUBT IN OUR MINDS THAT HE WOULD RING, SUCH WAS THE BELIEF IN THE MAN WHEN HE SAID HE WAS GOING TO DO SOMETHING HE WOULD DO JUST THAT'

Wembley delight: On the pitch with Shanks in '74

> To Tommy Smith, who explained that his bandaged knee was grazed: 'What d'ye mean YOUR knee. That's Liverpool's knee!'

To the barber who asked: 'anything off the top?' in 1968: 'Aye, Everton!'

On handing over the number four shirt of Preston North End to Tommy Docherty: 'I told Tommy not to worry. That shirt knows where to take ye!'

On disclipine of players: 'I set them an example. I am modelling my players now on what I did, the way I approached football in my playing days. I trained like a slave and I played like a slave.'

On his appointment to Liverpool: 'They didn't have to sell Liverpool to me. I had been there before, heard the noise and seen the enthusiasm of their fans. It's a big city and I knew there was room for two big clubs, not just Everton, who were Merseyside's only First Division team in those days.'

### 'Brian Clough's worse than the rain in Manchester . . .'

On Manchester United's Paddy Crerand: 'Now boys, Crerand's deceptive. He's slower than you think!'

'Believe you are the best and make sure you are. In my time, we always said we had the best two teams on Merseyside, Liverpool and Liverpool reserves.'

---

the belief in the man when he said he was going to do something you believed he would do just that. And such was the measure of the man that was Shankly, he didn't disappoint!

We recorded the conversation on a crappy tape recorder (you remember the type?) where Shanks thanked Johnnie for the flowers and engaged in idle chitchat!

Needless to say, many playing times finally caught up with that tape, and of course there were no facilities to make copies of it back then so it has gone now. However, he managed to get signed photos for all his family…except our Ste and me?

But he said, 'I've got something much better for you two…'

He then produced a copy of the book, 'A Tribute To Shanks' and sure enough, there in the acknowledgements were the names of John, Paul and Stephen Coyle.

The pride swelled.

Sadly, after being diagnosed with lung cancer in April 2005, he passed away on Saturday, 11th February, 2006.

When we were kids, our Ste and me believed he was 'King of the Kop' and to all his family and friends he always will be.

Goodnight 'Willie' and God Bless!

(You got to meet Shanks again you lucky b*****d!)

In memory of my brother Johnnie and Bill Shankly, two socialists who loved Liverpool. R.I.P.

'Brian Clough's worse than the rain in Manchester. At least God stops that occasionally!'

'There's Man Utd and Man City at the bottom of Division One and by God, they'll take some shifting.'

Tommy Docherty: "You have to say Tony Hateley's good in the air." Shankly: "Aye, so was Douglas Bader and he had a wooden leg."

'Dixie would be amazed to know that even in death he could draw a bigger crowd to Goodison than Everton on a Saturday.' (At Dixie Dean's funeral)

## Turning rags into Anfield riches

Bob Paisley was constantly asked about Shankly. In another interview in 1981, he told the Echo about Shanks' (and Liverpool's) philosophy about picking players from lower down the divisions and turning them into top quality stars – a phenomenon that is largely absent from the modern Anfield era.

He said: 'After a particularly tough Saturday game, perhaps after we had lost a vital match, the atmosphere would be electric at Anfield all over the weekend. You kept away from Bill at those times if you could.

'But on Monday morning, he would bounce out at Melwood in his tracksuit, the pressures over, his eyes shining like a schoolboy because he was going to have a five-a-side game.

'He loved buying players from a lower division and grooming them into Liverpool players.

## Trophy delight that made me kiss Shanks' feet

**From Dave Brown, Liverpool**

It certainly wasn't planned. I hadn't woken up that morning in August 1974 and thought: "I must get on to the Wembley pitch this afternoon and kiss Bill Shankly's feet!" What happened was instinctive really, just some crazy spur-of-the-moment thing when I did something out of character.

I went to the Liverpool v Leeds Charity Shield with my mate Kelvin and we knew that it was the last time Bill Shankly would ever lead a Liverpool team out. Bob Paisley had been appointed as his successor but the club was kind enough to allow Bill to lead the team out for one final time.

The game will probably be remembered more for the incident when Kevin Keegan and Billy Bremner were sent off than for anything I did. It finished in a 1-1 draw but there was no extra time and it went straight to a penalty shoot-out. Liverpool won that 6-5 and the team had been up to collect the Shield and were walking round the stadium to show the trophy off to the fans.

They came towards us and I seem to remember saying to Kelvin something like, "I'm off. I'm going for it" and next second I was over the barrier and on to the running track that surrounded the pitch, over a small fence and I didn't stop running until I was right next to the boss.

I said: "Thanks for another trophy, Bill" and just fell to my knees and made as if to kiss his feet. It was only then that I realised Kelvin had followed me. I think Bill was a little taken aback but it wasn't a subservient gesture and he knew that. He said: "There's no need for that, son" but he knew I wasn't being

**Crying game: The press cameras capture the moment as emotional fans run on to the pitch to greet Shankly**

'He had total belief that he would be able to do that because he passionately felt the Liverpool training system was the best in the world - simple but the best.

'So it was no surprise to him that players like Kevin Keegan, Ray Clemence, Larry Lloyd and others succeeded. He didn't always go to see these players before he signed them. It was Joe and I who recommended the club to sign Keegan and Clemence.

'He always wanted to be totally involved in all things Liverpool. His passion and honesty for the game were there for all to see.'

**13 June 1981**

### Shankly signs on

Shanks became a director just months before he died - of a new truck and bus assembly plant!

As well as remaining involved with charities and the Merseyside football world, he was keen to give his support to local businesses. The motivation was the same for all three - helping the 'people'.

Together with close friend Joe Mercer, Shanks was to play a vital role in 'motivating the 1,000 workforce to win contracts for a wide range of vehicles, mainly for the export market.'

After touring the Thorn's factory site in Skelmersdale, Shanks told the Echo: 'It is just what the area wants - more jobs and a vote of confidence in its work people.'

**Shankly was happy to support worthy causes and stand up for the people of Merseyside throughout his working life – and retirement. Speaking passionately about Liverpool and his own life was something he continued to do right until the end . . .**

disrespectful and that's about the moment when the picture must have been taken, as he and Kelvin hauled me back to my feet.

I can't remember exactly what I said next but it was something along the lines of: "Thanks again" to which he replied: "Aye, no problem, son" in that distinct Ayrshire accent of his. Then Kelvin and I wandered back to where we had come from and as we jumped back on to the terrace I remember Kelvin saying: "I can't believe we just did that."

Neither could I to be honest. I didn't realise until I saw the picture that Brian Hall was walking past at the moment I went down on my knees. He had a grin on his face though and I know Bill saw the funny side of the situation too. I suppose I just wanted to say thanks for everything he did for us.

I'm surprised we weren't stopped really but all they seemed to have at the time at Wembley was some sort of uniformed commissionaires as security. There's one of them in the corner of the picture and he is grinning too. I don't think anyone would have caught us anyway by the time they had reacted to what we did but nobody bothered us on our way back to the terrace either.

It was a mad thing to do really and I certainly had some explaining to do to family and friends. But more than 30 years later I treasure that picture. Something to talk to the grandchildren about I suppose. I wouldn't have done it to anyone else but there was nobody else like Bill Shankly. I suppose that's why I did it because he was such a special man who always had time for the guys who stood on the Kop and followed the team around.

Born leaders: Shankly
didn't trust politicians
but he was happy to
speak to former Labour
Prime Minister Harold
Wilson in this photograph

# INTERVIEW

ONLY TWO MONTHS BEFORE BILL SHANKLY DIED
HE GAVE LIVERPOOL ECHO READERS A RARE
INSIGHT INTO HIS STATE OF MIND AS HE COPED
WITH LIFE AFTER LIVERPOOL FOOTBALL CLUB

**13 July 1981**

**The last interview**

Shankly discussed his life with Echo Woman's Page editor Moya Jones – seven years after he quit as Liverpool boss, and sadly just two months before he died. Although he was his usual passionate self and talked poignantly about the love of his family and his adopted city, there was a sense of melancholy and restlessness in his tone ...

# Making the decision to get out of the club was the biggest problem for me

> '**FOR MOST THE BIGGEST PROBLEM IS ADJUSTMENT. THEY'VE GOT MY SYMPATHY. THE BIG THING IS TO TRY AND GET A HOBBY, DEVELOP A DAILY ROUTINE. A PLACE TO GO EVERY DAY**'

## Make me an offer I can only refuse

Shankly was flooded with offers to return to the game but there was no way the great man was going to be tempted back:

"They didn't do anything for me. Deep down my heart is still with Liverpool. I didn't want to commit myself to anyone else."

## I'd rather be Walking On than jogging every day

I must have run twice as far in the last seven years as I did when I was playing. Walking done properly, briskly, is possibly more beneficial to most than jogging. Jogging's monotonous.
I know. I go jogging every day.

**Football crazy: In 1979 he was still playing on what are now called the Bill Shankly Memorial Playing Fields**

Retirement – the word should be struck from the record. It makes people feel older than they are. For me the biggest problem was making the decision to get out. I'd fought long hard battles to straighten the club out and be successful. For most the biggest problem is adjustment. They've got my sympathy. The big thing is to try and get a hobby, develop a daily routine. A place to go every day.

## The magic of Melwood

In the early days I went down to Melwood every day for training. That lasted a season then I stopped going. Felt I was intruding.

I still go to Melwood but only for a sauna and a bath, a dip in Melwood's magic waters.

Melwood means more to me than any other part of Liverpool. It was where Liverpool was made. The first time I saw the place, an overgrown, neglected place it was too, I said to Ness: 'I'm going to see Melwood reborn, cultivated. I did. Every inch of it.' If someone took Melwood from me. . .

(He broke mid-sentence, clearly seeing such a scenario as something he could never cope with).

'MELWOOD MEANS MORE TO ME THAN
ANY OTHER PART OF LIVERPOOL.
IT WAS WHERE LIVERPOOL WAS MADE.
THE FIRST TIME I SAW THE PLACE,
AN OVERGROWN, NEGLECTED PLACE
IT WAS TOO, I SAID TO NESS:
'I'M GOING TO SEE MELWOOD REBORN,
CULTIVATED'. I DID. EVERY INCH OF IT.
IF SOMEONE TOOK MELWOOD
FROM ME . . .'

## Holidays in Liverpool suit me fine these days

The last holiday we had was a couple of years ago in Glasgow. Ness cannot take long journeys and there's everything I want right here. Travelling's a great waste of time and the older you get the less time you've got to waste.

## I don't like saying no to people

I could be out every day, make speeches two, three times a week but it gets a bit much. I'm just sorry when I have to say no.

Jolly holidays: At Butlins (top) and relaxing in Blackpool

## Modern managers

I hear them, see them, they talk like Gods and they haven't won a thing. Some of these top jobs I could sit and do with my eyes shut.

## I don't trust politicians ...

I can't stand politics – should be disbanded. Full of a lot of people who don't impress me as men who are capable of making important decisions. Politics today are a battle, a tug of war. At the club I wanted everyone working together. Football is a form of socialism with everybody helping each other. Politically there are two or three teams playing in Britain today. There should only be one, all fighting for Britain not fighting against each other. Politicians spend their time trying to drag each other down. That's not my way.

## ... but I would have trusted my life to Ian St John and Ron Yeats

I would have trusted my life to those two. Both were stone certainties. I told the board at the time when there was quibbling over the signings – £37,500 and £30,000, big money in those days – not only will they take us out of the Second Division but they'll win the FA Cup for us. And they did, but not until they'd won the league championship.

Bill's stalwarts: Ron Yeats (top) and Ian St John lifting the FA Cup in '65

## We're still living in the same house we moved into when we came to Liverpool

I regret Ness had to bear the brunt of my being away so much. During my time, 27 years as a manager, 17 as a player, I was so single minded. I never asked for money. I came to Liverpool to make a success of the job, for the club and for this city.

Now when I hear of the money that's bandied about, the thousands of pounds a week people hold out for, it makes my blood boil. There are men with tennis courts and swimming pools who haven't even got a championship medal, not one.

Maybe I didn't get enough out of it for my family. I regret I didn't give Ness more. We're still living in the same house we moved into when we came to Liverpool. But at least it's a home, not a house, and I'm not looking for a Buckingham Palace.

And perhaps the family are all right after all. They've all got a place to live and something to eat, and I've got five bonny grandchildren, all girls, and every one with a Scouse accent. Now what more could a man want?

A real family home: Shankly and Nessie's house in Huddersfield

# 'THE ATTITUDE OF THE PEOPLE OF LIVERPOOL TOWARDS ME AND MY FAMILY IS STRONGER NOW THAN IT EVER WAS'

## My love affair with the city

I thank God for the wonderful people of Merseyside. The attitude of the people of Liverpool towards me and my family is stronger now than it ever was. I never cheated them and they've never let me down.

Leading light: Shankly switches on the city Christmas lights and (below) catches a first glimpse of the fans as the team arrives at Allerton station for the 1971 homecoming

## Shankly's unique recipe for success

Shankly's unique recipe for success proved fascinating reading in the Liverpool Echo. Every modern manager should be encouraged to read the thoughts of this football genius. Shankly saw everything so clearly ...

'WE REALISED AT LIVERPOOL THAT YOU CAN SCORE A GOAL BY PLAYING FROM THE BACK. WE LEARNED THIS FROM PLAYING THE LATINS IN EUROPE'

# The system we devised was to confuse the opposition – that was the secret!

A football match is like a relay race. We realised at Liverpool that you can score a goal by playing from the back.

We learned this through playing the Latins in Europe. It might be cat and mouse for a while, waiting for that opening to appear. It's all very simple

really – but it's effective.

Improvisation! If your players can improvise and adjust to what's happening, you've got a chance.

'THAT'S WHY KENNY DALGLISH WAS AN INSTANT SUCCESS. KENNY WAS THE KIND OF PLAYER WHO COULD EXPLOIT THAT KIND OF THING TO THE FULL'

It's vital you conserve energy – making the opposition do all the chasing. When you play over 60 games a season, you can't afford to be running flat out all the time.

The system we devised was designed to confuse the opposition. And it was economical. You want everyone to do their share.

The important thing is that everyone can control the ball and do the basic things. It's control and pass – control and pass.

If you delay, the opposition are suddenly all behind the ball. So you are looking for somebody who can control it instantly and give a forward pass. And that gives you more space.

You see some teams playing and it seems as if nobody wants the ball. They turn their back on each other. But at Liverpool, there is always somebody to help you.

That's why Kenny Dalglish was an instant success. He came to a club and he had choices. Kenny was the

kind of player who could exploit that kind of thing to the full.

So this is the secret. Get it. Give an early pass. Switch the ball around. You might not seem to be getting very far, but the opposition pattern is changing. And the space opens up for the final pass.

All the players must understand that when they've delivered a pass, you've only just started. You have to back up and look to help somebody else.

## Training tricks

The initial training period should take a long time – about five and a half weeks. You need to be cautious in the initial stages. You don't go out and tear people to pieces in three or four days.

You don't put them in the sand or in the hills or on the road. You train them on the grass where they play and you take it easy. If you saw Liverpool training in the early stages in my day, you might think they were lazy. The build-up was gradual, relying on experience.

I never asked players to stretch their legs until they were ready. Injuries can be caused if the initial period is wrong. If a man breaks down two months into the season, it might be because of his initial training.

It should be a patient approach. Ray Clemence once pulled a muscle kicking balls too early into his training. It affected him for a long time and he eventually missed a few games. It cost us the League that season.

You don't let them sprint too early or kick the ball too early. Caution is the key. You train hard, yes, but only when you are ready.

Glass act: It might look like a joke, and there were plenty of those up his sleeve, but Shankly gives a new reinforced window product a serious test

## Anfield psychology

I always tried to have a joke up my sleeve to boost our lads and knock down the opposition. We took our football seriously, but we always tried to get a laugh out of the team talks. And I would always keep a few bombs for the Saturday.

I might say to the old guy on the Anfield door: "Here's a box of toilet rolls. Hand them to the opposition when they come through the door." Often, I'd say it just as our opponents were walking in.

We didn't lose many, but when we did, we were always ready to learn. We were always confident, but we were never over-confident. Being cocky is a form of ignorance. It means you are talking too much and if you are guilty of that, an opponent will bring you down to earth.

**Head boy:** Shankly uses the technology of the day to get some heading practice!

## Woolly jumpers and bus trips were key to our success story

During serious training a football player sweats. But you must still wear a sweater or top to train in, particularly if it's a cold day.

This is to cover and protect your kidneys. If you haven't worn one, you must put it on as soon as training is finished to keep warm.

Instead of stripping, training and showering at Melwood – eating there and then going home – we stripped at Anfield and went down by bus. When it's pre-season and you are hot and perspiring, you don't want to be leaping into the bath five minutes after you've finished. If you do, you'll sweat all day.

After training, I encouraged the boys to have a cup of tea and even a walk around. It takes 15 minutes or so to get to Anfield from West Derby. About 40 minutes would have passed from training until they actually got into the bath.

This is probably one of the reasons why we were always fitter than the rest. Most of the other clubs report directly to their training grounds, strip there and come straight off the pitch into a hot bath which I always disagreed with.

Our lads never felt uncomfortable. They never had their lunch with sweat pouring off them. In my opinion, this was very important and a key part of Liverpool's fitness. It actually prevented injuries from happening.

Just the ticket: Shankly believed the bus trip to Melwood was invaluable

## Training was based on basic skills – exhaustion and recovery

Footballers normally train for an hour and a half, but it doesn't mean they work for an hour and a half. Some might be demonstrating a function while the others are watching.

And then it's your turn. It's not how long you train, but what you put into it. If you train properly, 35 minutes a day might do.

We built Liverpool's training on exhaustion and recovery with little areas of two-a-side, three-a-side and five-a-side in which you work hard like a boxer, twisting and turning. Training was based on basic skills – control, passing, vision, awareness.

If you are fit, you have a tremendous advantage over everybody else.

It's important to try and give everyone a touch of the ball as quickly as possible once the match starts. If it comes to you, you chest it down simple and you roll it to your mate. It doesn't look much, but it's something.

If you try to do something clever and it breaks down, it can take the confidence out of you.

That's not my way.

# We kept fear away from our players

After all the training was complete on Fridays, we always had a talk about the impending game. All the players and subs attended.

One of the staff would have watched the opposition and would bring their report in. All I wanted to know was the formation. Was it 4-4-2, 4-3-3 or whatever. And did any of the opposing players have any little characteristics that we might want to stifle?

I never ever discussed the

'IF IT COMES TO YOU, YOU CHEST IT DOWN SIMPLE AND YOU ROLL IT TO YOUR MATE. IT DOESN'T LOOK MUCH, BUT IT'S SOMETHING'

opposition at length. The last thing you want to do is build up your opponents and frighten your own players. We might have been playing Manchester United that weekend, but I wasn't going to be singing the praises of the opposition. I can remember overhearing one of the lads coming out of a meeting and saying: "Are Best, Law and Charlton not playing?"

That made me smile. In the main, we were only concerned about us and our collective approach. The message was: 'Keep everything simple. Be patient, even if it takes 89 minutes to score. The number of times we won a match at the death was unbelievable. And when you sneak one like that, it's heartbreaking for the opposition.'

# *The Shankly* LEGACY

THE TRUE VALUE OF A MAN CAN BE MEASURED BY WHAT HE LEAVES BEHIND. WHEN BILL SHANKLY DIED, HE LEFT A LASTING LEGACY THAT WILL BE PASSED ON TO GENERATIONS . . .

The Shankly story came to an end in 1981, just months after Liverpool had claimed their third European Cup under Shanks' former right-hand man Bob Paisley. The death of Anfield's much-loved and legendary figure prompted an emotional outpouring of grief on a massive scale as fans and big names from the football world clamoured to pay tribute to the great man. Liverpool had lost a glorious son but the message was loud and clear: The Shankly spirit was alive and well and here to stay ...

## Liverpool Echo

31,565     29 SEP 1981   TUESDAY, SEPTEMBER 29, 1961     12p

# HIS LEGACY

## Shankly ... 'Symbol of courage, determination and success ...'

By Alf Green and Carolyn Taylor

BILL SHANKLY, the legend of Anfield, died to-day — and Merseyside was plunged into mourning.

For Shankly described as the manager of the century by Liverpool's chairman John Smith, he had become "an outstanding symbol of guts, determination and success who fought for the good name of his adopted city at every opportunity.

The words are those of the Lord Mayor of Liverpool, Councillor Cyril Carr, himself a patient in Broadgreen Hospital, where Mr. Shankly died.

The Lord Mayor, who was in the same ward as Mr. Shankly for a time, spoke this morning of the great feeling of loss that everybody had suffered.

In a special message telephoned to the Echo from his hospital bed, the Lord Mayor said:

### Worshipped

"Bill Shankly was worshipped in Liverpool. He and I have been in the same ward. I witnessed some of his brave fight for life.

"He was more to this city than a great football manager. He was an outstanding symbol of courage, determination and success.

"He fought for his adopted city and in spite of the hero worship he received he remained a human and approachable

**SHANKS**

**MAN OF THE PEOPLE**

□ The Echo is producing a special 12-page tribute to Bill Shankly which will be out to-morrow.

"Shanks — Man of the
... will never

arrived on Merseyside, Bill Shankly inspired a series of interviews, feature articles and pictures which collected together form a remarkable insight

## The Kop song he never forgot

SINGER Gerry Marsden has a million and one happy memories of his many meetings with his friend Bill Shankly.

"He was a great man, a brilliant man. His company was a pleasure to me, his charisma, fantastic. He'll be sadly missed," said Gerry.

"One of his fondest recollections was on his wedding day. Instead of leaving for his honeymoon, Gerry decided to stay over for the Liverpool match against Juventus.

"I rang Bill and told him I wasn't going away and asked if he'd any tickets for the match," recalled Gerry.

"He said there weren't any left, but I couldn't

## An honest man, a decent man

Sir John Moores said: "Bill Shankly made Liverpool F.C. Before he became manager they were a very ordinary club. With Shankly in charge they became a great club, winning everything worth winning. On this son Park and to our training ground at Bellefield. We will sorely miss his wit and his wisdom."

"Shankly was an honest man, a decent man. He believed in himself and he

motivating players amounted to genius and that is a rare commodity in any field.

"Since his retirement he had been a frequent and welcome visitor to Goodison Park and to our training ground at Bellefield. We will sorely miss his wit and his wisdom."

Club treasurer N Black reme "Shanks" being pr with the unique some years ago in his

"He handed it ov because he said he think of a more place for it than t That's the sort of was. His death has

# The day the Kop lost a MESSIAH

BILL SHANKLY died on 29 September 1981. He had truly made the people happy during his glorious Anfield reign.

Now they were desperately sad. Their football messiah was gone.

The whole of Merseyside mourned. Indeed the world football family came together as one to reflect on the legacy of arguably the greatest football manager of all time.

Bob Paisley, his staunch right-hand man, had gone on to win more trophies.

Indeed, Bob claimed the Holy Grail of soccer that Shanks had so desperately wanted to win – The European Cup. More than that, Bob won it three times.

But none of it would have been possible without Bill Shankly and Bob, his great friend, would have been the first to hammer home that message.

Shankly took a club that had spent eight frustrating years in the wilderness that was the old Second Division and turned it into a world-renowned entity.

He turned a tumbledown stadium into Fortress Anfield.

He saw football's Promised Land and led his people into it.

Those people were the fans he respected and adored.

In return, never has a manager been so idolised. Never has a football force been so magnetic.

Shankly could stand in front of 200,000 swaying, roaring followers

on the steps of Liverpool's St. George's Hall and command silence by simply raising his hand above his head. When he walked in front of the Kop celebrating another triumph, hands pressed together as if in personal praise of the men and women standing before him, it took the beautiful game onto another level of intimacy and total respect.

He never forgot his roots. He was unique and everyone knew that there would never be another like him.

The Liverpool Echo, in its leader column, paid him the perfect tribute. (Turn to next page...)

Former football manager Bill Shankly died at 01.20 today in Liverpool's Broadgreen Hospital.

Bad news day: Fans outside Anfield as the flag flies at half mast to mark Shanks' death

## 26 September 1981

### Shanks suffers a heart attack

Shankly was admitted to a general ward of Broadgreen Hospital just three days before he died - but his condition was thought to be not too serious according to an Echo report.

'Former Liverpool FC manager Bill Shankly was rushed to a hospital today after suffering a heart attack.

'The legendary 'Shanks' (67) was being detained in Broadgreen Hospital but a spokesman said he was not on the danger list. "He was brought in this morning shortly after breakfast time, following a mild heart attack," said the spokesman this afternoon. "At the moment he is satisfactory and resting. It is difficult to say how long he will be in but it will probably be for a week or so, so that doctors can give him tests. He is being nursed in an ordinary ward because that is where he wanted to be."

## 29 September 1981

### Shankly is dead

The Liverpool Daily Post broke the shattering news on Tuesday, September 29. Their front page story recorded the official hospital statement:

"Mr Shankly suffered a cardiac arrest at 12.30am and was certified dead at 1.20."

The report continued: 'Shanks had been battling for life since he suffered a heart attack early on Saturday morning. He had been making good progress until his condition deteriorated yesterday morning and he was transferred to the Intensive Care Unit. His wife Nessie was by his side when he died.'

"BILL SHANKLY IS DEAD.
BUT HIS MEMORY WILL NEVER DIE.
'AS LONG AS PEOPLE TALK OF FOOTBALL
AND OF GREAT DEEDS AND OF GREAT MEN,
THE NAME OF BILL SHANKLY WILL LIVE ON.
'THEY WILL SPEAK OF HIM WITH AWE AND
AFFECTION. FOR "SHANKS" WAS NOT JUST
A SOCCER GENIUS, A CHARISMATIC,
INSPIRATIONAL FORCE.
'HE WON CUPS AND TITLES, YES.
HE ALSO WON THE HEARTS OF MEN AND
WOMEN AND CHILDREN THE WORLD OVER.
'HE WALKED WITH THE HIGH AND THE
MIGHTY, BUT WAS NEVER DELUDED BY
GRANDEUR. HIS LOVE WAS ROOTED DEEPLY
AMONG THE ORDINARY FOLK OF
LIVERPOOL.
'HE ENRICHED THIS CITY IMMEASURABLY
AND TODAY, AS WE MOURN HIS DEATH,
WE ARE ALSO THANKFUL FOR THE LIFE
AND MEMORY OF A SPLENDID MAN.'

- Liverpool Echo Tribute

'IT'S A GREAT TRAGEDY FOR LIVERPOOL. I HOPE THAT THE CLUB CAN DO SOMETHING TO PAY A LASTING TRIBUTE TO HIM, NAMING A STAND OR SOMETHING IN HIS MEMORY'

Bearing up: (from left) Emlyn Hughes, Ray Clemence, Ian St John and Ron Yeats carry the coffin

## One of the greatest – I am deeply shocked

"Bill was one of the greatest managers there has ever been. I am deeply, deeply shocked. Although I knew just how seriously ill he was, the news has still come as a great blow."

**Bob Paisley**

## He convinced me I would make it

"He was exceptional in every way. The bonus for me is that I worked with him for six years and a little bit of Bill Shankly lives on in me. He made me believe in myself and convinced me I would make it to the top.

"I doubted my ability at the start, but he never did. It's a great tragedy for Liverpool. I hope that the club can do something to pay a lasting tribute to him, naming a stand or something in his memory."

**Kevin Keegan**

## His motivation could move mountains

"He was a great man. You could not talk to him, you listened. His motivation could move mountains."

**Ron Yeats**

## Shanks set the standards

"You pick up experience from all the people you work with – but Shanks set the standards."

**Roy Evans**

## He achieved success through dedication

"It is a sad loss for football and it has come like a bolt out of the blue. Bill was a one-off. He was an honest, down-to-earth character and such a wonderful fellow for the game. He achieved success by sheer hard work and dedication.

"He had no time for skivers and expected people to uphold the good name of football and dedicate themselves to the game and that is how he had such respect from the players. He always spoke the truth, no matter how much it hurt, and had no time for present-day jargon."

**Tom Finney**

"It's such a shock. I owe him everything. I can't bring myself round to accept he won't pick up the phone when I dial."

**John Toshack**

"He was a great man, a brilliant man. His company was a pleasure to me, his charisma, fantastic. He'll be sadly missed. One of my fondest recollections was on my wedding day. Instead of leaving for my honeymoon, I decided to stay over for the Liverpool v Juventus game.

"I rang Bill and asked if he'd any tickets. He said there weren't any left, but I could have his seat and my wife could have his wife's. We saw the match from the box. That's the kind of man he was. He'd help anyone out."

"Another great moment was when we were in the States and invited to appear on the popular Ed Sullivan Show. At the same time, the Liverpool squad were touring the country, so I suggested they come along too.

"And in front of 60 million viewers across America, we all sang You'll Never Walk Alone. And there in the middle of us all, with the worst voice in the world, bless him, was Shanks. He never forgot that, and he used to mention it everytime I saw him."

**Gerry Marsden**

"Bill was the most outstanding and most dynamic manager of the century. He can only be compared with giants like Herbert Chapman – and Bill worked in a much more competitive and intense atmosphere."

**Liverpool chairman John Smith**

All together: The people queue to pay their tribute at Anfield Crematorium

Leaving home: The hearse carrying Shanks' coffin in West Derby village, close to his house

'IN FRONT OF 60 MILLION VIEWERS ACROSS AMERICA, WE ALL SANG YOU'LL NEVER WALK ALONE. AND THERE IN THE MIDDLE OF US ALL, WITH THE WORST VOICE IN THE WORLD, BLESS HIM, WAS SHANKS'

"Bill Shankly made Liverpool FC. Before he became manager they were a very ordinary club. With Shankly in charge they became a great club, winning everything worth winning. On the foundations he laid Bob Paisley has been able to continue that success.

"Shankly was an honest man, a decent man.

"He believed in himself and he could make players believe in themselves and discover unexpected levels of skill and effort.

"He was a tough man to deal with but very straight. He loved his players like a father, but perhaps a Victorian father, because if they let him down he could be very tough. He certainly knew how to manage men.

"His death has shocked me – after all he was quite a young man – and it is a great loss to Liverpool FC, to the city, and to football."

**Sir John Moores**

"Bill Shankly was a great manager and a great character. His skills in choosing, coaching and motivating players amounted to genius and that is a rare commodity in any field.

"Since his retirement he had been a frequent and welcome visitor to Goodison Park and to our training ground at Bellefield. We will sorely miss his wit and his wisdom."

**Philip Carter,
Everton chairman**

"He was more to this city than a great football manager.

"He was an outstanding symbol of guts, determination and success who fought for the good name of his adopted city at every opportunity.

"He fought for his adopted city and in spite of the hero worship he received he remained a human and approachable man.

"This city will never forget him. Bill Shankly will never walk alone."

**Lord Mayor of Liverpool,
Councillor Cyril Carr**

**The fans also bombarded the Liverpool Daily Post and Echo with tributes. Two such salutes were from former players who didn't make it, but who were still captivated by the Shankly magic . . .**

In 1960 as a 15-year-old, I was brought to Liverpool by Bill Shankly from Aberdeen, to sign as an apprentice professional. I was his first signing.

The next five years were the happiest of my life and although I never appeared in the first team, the impression Bill Shankly made on me during the five years I spent at Liverpool has stayed with me always, and indeed shaped my life since.

When he transferred me to Aberdeen in 1965, I was very upset that I was going to be leaving. Bill could see the disappointment and said: "Son, you're the 12th best player in the world." I asked what he meant by that outrageous statement. He replied: "There's the Liverpool first team, then you, because you are the leading scorer in the reserves." It was 1965.

I left Liverpool with those words ringing in my ears. After a year with Aberdeen I went to South Africa on a two-year contract with one of the top South African clubs. Three years passed since I had seen Shanks, yet on my return to the UK I called to see him. I had no trade, no qualifications and no club. At 23 my future looked bleak.

Bill picked up the phone and persuaded Dave Russell, the Tranmere Rovers manager, to give me a month's trial. As a result I got a two-year contract, eventually bought a house and settled on the Wirral.

Today I am living in a good house, have two cars and a very successful business career. I still try to apply the Shankly standards to my everyday life, and but for his help when I needed it, who knows what my future would have been. I will always be grateful and proud to have crossed his path.

**George Scott,
Spital, Wirral**

Bob Paisley and ex-player Willie Stevenson at Anfield where Bill's ashes were scattered

A prayer for Shanks: Fans pay their respects. Above right: Nessie with mourners

## A man with true grit who was a true Red

I'll never forget his Cagney strut.

I was privileged and proud to be on Liverpool's books for three years from the age of 15, during Bill Shankly's reign.

Regretfully, left football prematurely but I will always have the greatest affection for the great man.

One Saturday morning I had to be at Anfield for an A-team away game. I arrived early and it was very quiet.

I sat in the dressing room, biding my time when suddenly I heard footsteps coming closer and someone whistling "You'll Never Walk Alone."

It was Shanks.

"Morning Mr Shankly."

"Morning son, how are you?"

We talked football for about 10 minutes, then he said: "You must win today son," (his teams always had to win).

Then, he strutted down the corridor in that Cagney-like style, continuing to whistle what else but "You'll Never Walk Alone" – a man with true grit who was a true Red.

P.S. We did win.

**J. Carroll, Liverpool 15**

### 8 October 1981

## Nessie has the final word – Bill was proud to be a Scouser

Bill's widow expressed her gratitude to thousands of grieving fans:

**"I would like to express my deepest thanks to the people of Merseyside for their thoughts and prayers during the last week. Bill was proud to be an adopted Liverpudlian. He loved this city and its people, and the tributes and condolences were a real comfort to myself and family during a sad and difficult time."**

**merseymart**

**OUR CITY UNITES IN MOURNING**

Thank you: Nessie was comforted by the many messages of sympathy sent

**The Reds played twice at Anfield in the space of four days after Shankly's death. Both occasions allowed the Anfield faithful to pay tribute to their hero . . .**

### October 1, 1981

### Silent Anfield pays homage

Oulu Palloseura were the visitors in a European Cup first round second leg tie the night after Shankly's death. The Daily Post reported: 'Anfield stood in silent tribute last night as thousands of Liverpool supporters paid homage to former manager, Bill Shankly. Both the Reds and their Finnish European Cup opponents, Oulu Palloseura, wore black arm bands for the occasion.

'The Kop sang: "We all agree, call it the Shankly" as a reference to suggestions of making one of the stands a Shankly memorial. For most of the second half, the Kop simply sang the word "Shankly" to the tune of Amazing Grace.

'A banner in the middle of the crowd summed up the feelings of thousands: "King Shankly Lives".

'Liverpool skipper Phil Thompson paid tribute to the fans who turned up to pay their respects to Bill Shankly.

'He said: "It was a very fitting tribute to a great man and a great manager. Shankly would have been thrilled with this. The crowd, the singing, the goals."'

'Tribute in silence to man of the people' (October 1, 1981 – Daily Post) by Andy Morgan:

'Never before can Anfield have been so quiet, so subdued.

'For an arena that has created a reputation for its uninhibited raucousness, the sight of more than 20,000 people standing mute had a surreal feel to it.

'People stand in silence so rarely that it is hard to know what to do. Stare at your shoes, stare at the opposite stand or just look at the head in front of you?

'The thousands at Anfield last night generally did none of these

'YOU'LL NEVER WALK ALONE SPILLED FROM THE SPEAKERS BUT THE ACCOMPANIMENT WAS HALF-HEARTED. WHEN THE MINUTE'S SILENCE WAS CALLED FOR, THE KOP QUIETENED. THE PLAYERS STOOD RIGID'

Messages outside the Holiday Inn in Liverpool and (right) Echo tributes

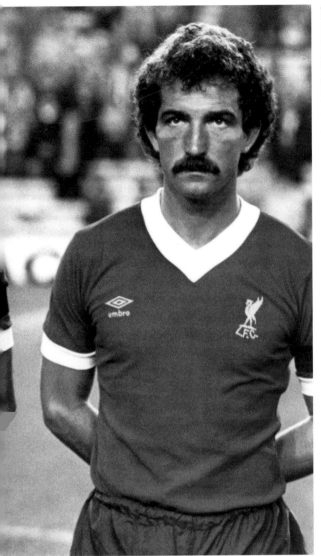

Sammy Lee, Ray Kennedy and Graeme Souness observe the minute's silence against Oulu Palloseura at Anfield. The Reds went on to win 7-0. Above: An Echo notice about Shanks' estate

The Kop flag flies at half mast during the day in tribute to Shankly

things. They seemed to be gazing into the inky Liverpool night, remembering with warmth those magical nights at the shrine when Shankly, the people's man, had applauded them for their loyalty. Now, they were silently flicking through their memories.

'Shankly would probably not have approved of the minute's silence before the Oulu Palloseura game last night.

'But when one of the game's greatest has gone, it is hard not to observe custom, to have a communal silence in which to reflect on his contribution.

'For a community so closely bound as the Anfield fans, staff and players, no other opportunity would have allowed so many members of this soccer tribe to come together and inwardly recall those times Shankly had raised the string of trophies to the Kop for their approval.

'Or when he stood outside the Picton Library, fist clenched like a Roman general, when the side he had helped build first won the European Cup under Bob Paisley.

'Before the minute's silence, the crowd had a melancholy air to it. Shankly's death was a sad event but all chagrin was tempered with the memories of what he had done for the game and the city. In such circumstances, it was impossible to be grief stricken.

'A few men in the Main Stand and the Kop wore black arm bands. Some draped black over rosettes. One young supporter, probably only a child when Shankly first came to Anfield, had swopped his customary red for an entire wardrobe of black.

'The team announcements, normally greeted with rapture, barely raised a murmur. All minds were clearly on the 60 seconds when thousands would focus on one subject alone.

'You'll Never Walk Alone spilled from the speakers but the accompaniment was half-hearted.

'When the minute's silence was called for, the Kop quietened within seconds.

'The players stood rigid, with only the occasional thoughtless photographer ferreting about and pricking the solemnity.'

## October 1 1981

### Fitting tribute to an Anfield legend

'Liverpool captain Phil Thompson made a point of turning to the Kop and clapping them as he ran off the pitch after their European Cup game at Anfield,' reported the Liverpool Echo.

'"I just thought it was fabulous the way they paid tribute to Shanks," he explained afterwards. "I wanted to let them know the players appreciated it.

'"When we stood for the minute's silence the only sound you heard was the clicking of the cameras. It was all a fitting tribute to Shanks."

'A crowd of 20,789 turned up not just to watch the expected demolition by Liverpool of the Finns. They came to pay their respects to their old friend, Bill Shankly.

'They chanted his name, they sang "There's only one Bill Shankly," and "Oh, Shankly we love you" and waved banners, one of which bore his name, "King Shanks".

'Before the kick-off the players, wearing black arm bands, lined up on the pitch and stood to observe a minute's silence in respect of the legendary figure's memory. For the last 20 minutes of the match the singing of Shanks' praises continued virtually non-stop. The fans kept chanting his name and sang: "You'll always be our king."

### Fitting tribute to an Anfield legend

LIVERPOOL captain Phil Thompson made a point of turning to the Kop and clapping them as he ran off the pitch after last night's European Cup game at Anfield.

" I just thought it was fabulous the way they paid tribute to Shanks," he explained afterwards. " I wanted to let them know the players appreciated it.

" When we stood for the minute's silence the only sound you heard was the clicking of the cameras. It was all a fitting tribute to Shanks."

A crowd of 20,789 turned up, not the size of those of the heady European nights of the past, but thousands more than anticipated and the atmosphere was charged with emotion.

They didn't just come to watch the expected demolition by Liverpool of the Finns, the Anfield faithful. They came to pay their respects to their old friend, Bill Shankly.

#### Waved banners

They chanted his name, they sang " There's only one Bill Shankly," and " Oh, Shankly we love you" and waved banners, one of which bore his name, "King Shanks."

Before the kick-off the players, wearing black arm-bands, lined up on the pitch and stood to observe a minute's silence in respect of the legendary figure's memory.

For the last 20 minutes of the match the singing of Shanks' praises continued virtually non-sto... kept chanting his name and sang: " You... king.

It was a tribute to the man ... this famous club. And ... approved of the 7-0 res...

Emotional day: Former Shankly star John Toshack wipes away a tear

Walk on with hope: Bob Paisley and John Toshack lead out the teams

Comeback: Terry McDermott celebrates one of his two penalty goals

**It was fitting that Swansea, managed by former Anfield favourite John Toshack, were the visitors for the first league match after Shankly's death. It proved an emotional afternoon as a packed Kop sung tribute after tribute to Shankly . . .**

## John Toshack's pride and pain

'John Toshack was set to bring his Swansea City team to Anfield, the first team to do so in the First Division since Shankly's passing,' wrote Ian Hargraves in the Liverpool Echo.

'On the eve of the game, Toshack said: "We've all been looking forward to this game since the start of the season. It's just a tragedy it has to take place in such sad circumstances.

"I owe it to Bill Shankly and Bob Paisley. Shanks has had a part to play in Swansea's success. He taught me to reach for the stars. I'm so grateful for the help he gave me over the last three years."

## The great man's name rang out loud and clear

'Swansea held their own in a thrilling match at Anfield this afternoon and it took two second-half penalties, both scored by Terry McDermott to get the home side back into the game,' wrote Ken Rogers in the Football Echo match report of October 3, 1981

'Shankly Lives Forever' proclaimed a giant banner on the Kop as the great man's name rang out loud and clear over packed Anfield before today's game.

'The teams stepped out before kick-off to observe a minute's silence, led by Bob Paisley and John Toshack.

'The Swansea manager removed his black tracksuit top to reveal a red Liverpool shirt in honour of his former boss.'

Despite going two goals down to strikes by Leighton James and Bob Latchford, the Reds rallied to draw 2-2 after a stirring fightback. Shanks would have been proud.

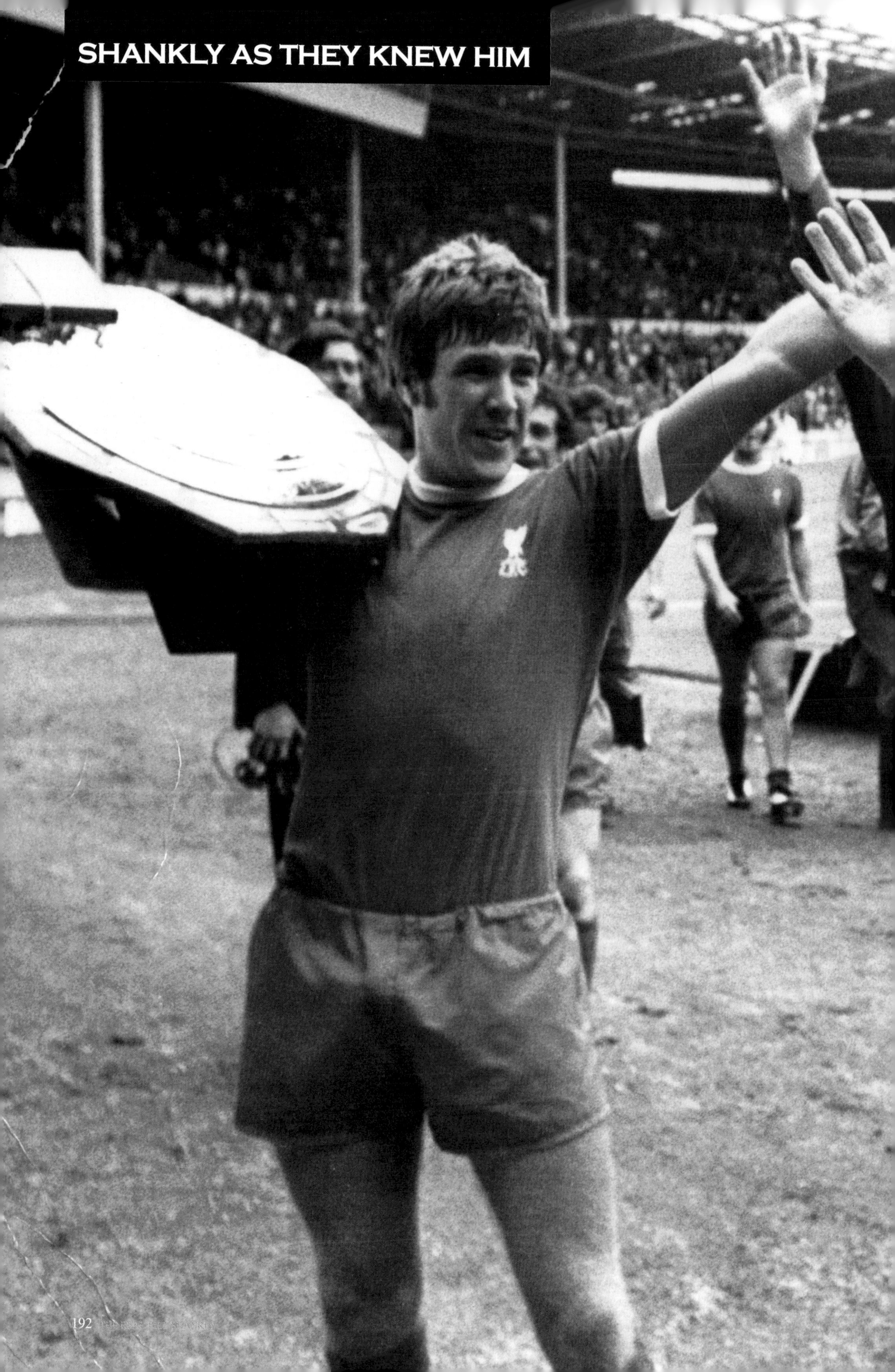

# The
# GREATEST
## of them all

NINE YEARS AFTER HE DIED, IT WAS TIME TO
TAKE STOCK AND REMEMBER AGAIN THE
MAGIC OF SHANKLY. ST. JOHN, PAISLEY, KEEGAN
AND DALGLISH WERE HAPPY TO REMINISCE

People never tire of telling and re-telling the Shankly story, often through the memories of the people who worked closely with him. Nine years after Bill died, the Liverpool Daily Post produced a series in which journalist Brian Reade, a big Liverpudlian who later became an award winning Daily Mirror columnist, talked to some key characters about the greatest of them all, including Ian St. John, Bob Paisley, Kevin Keegan and Kenny Dalglish ...

ST. JOHN on SHANKLY

Shankly was a man ahead of his time. He was the first tracksuit manager, the first to introduce modern training methods, the first manager who really worked on set-pieces. He even used to have us practice set-pieces at throw-ins.

He was the first manager who really lived with his players, spent every minute of the working day with them.

His team talks are legend. They were superb entertainment and he'd have us in stitches, but he was very clever. Behind the funny stories there was always a serious message. The stories were almost biblical in form.

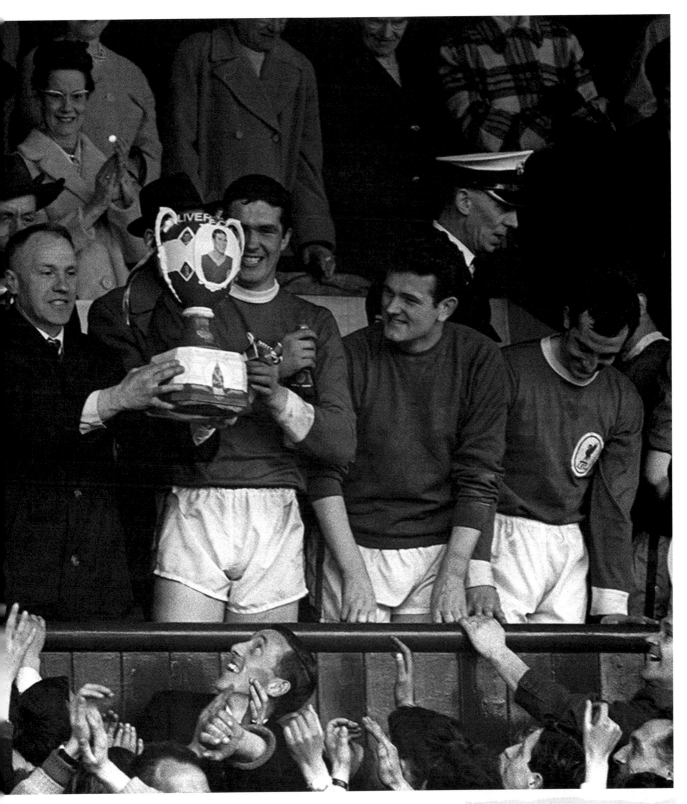

He was a role model for everyone in the game. There was no-one who had a greater love of the game. All the great managers: Revie, Nicholson, Mercer, they'd all tell you stories about Shanks, about how intense he was. He'd make even them look like layabouts.

He went too soon. Everyone misses him. I can still see him standing there like Jimmy Cagney: jacket open, hands in his pockets.

He should have got the Scotland job. He was just the man. Along with Busby he was the greatest manager of all time.

'HIS TEAM TALKS ARE LEGEND. HE'D HAVE US IN STITCHES, BUT THERE WAS ALWAYS A SERIOUS MESSAGE'

# Quitting was the death of Shanks

Bob Paisley got on his hands and knees and begged Bill Shankly not to retire.

It was July 1974, and the man who had been at the Anfield helm for 15 years and just guided them to a memorable FA Cup final victory had had enough.

Paisley was stunned. Shankly told him he would be recommending him as his successor, but Paisley told him the only job in football he wanted was to be number two to Bill Shankly. It had no effect.

'All Bill would say was: "No, I'm going to finish." It was such a shock. I told him: "You can't pack in; it'll kill you," and sad to say it eventually did,' said Bob.

'I knew this more than anyone else, because I was the closest to him in the game, and I tried harder than anyone else to persuade him to stay.

'I must have asked him a hundred times what was getting him down, but he wouldn't say, and to this day I can't tell you why he retired.

'I used to say: 'Bill, what are you going to do with yourself if you retire?' You see, he was a real loner. He didn't knock about with anyone.

'I'd go round and see Nessie to try and find out what was up, and she'd beg me to persuade him to change his mind.

'She was frightened of him lying round the house with nothing to do. I did my best, but he'd made his mind up.

'If I was pushed to give an opinion about why he went, I'd say maybe he was frightened of having another lean spell.

'He'd just won the Cup and I think he'd made up his mind to go out at the top like a class boxer. He was a boxer at heart.

'And his retirement didn't work. He went to places like Tranmere to advise, but he was on the outside of things and that wasn't good enough for Bill. He needed to be at the centre.

'Without doubt he made a big mistake going so soon. He should have known it wouldn't do him any good, and of course it all got a bit too much for us at Anfield.

'He started going to games and being a bit critical of things, saying he wouldn't have done this and that if he'd been there.

'I'd say to him: 'Do what you want, Bill. If you want to come training, come training.' I took a risk and it all got too much for him.

'He'd come down to Melwood and the lads would be a bit overawed by his presence. I didn't mind at first, but it got ridiculous. Sadly, for the benefit of the club, he had to stay away.'

'When Bill arrived he upset a few people because he was a very straightforward man. But he knew his

Warning: Paisley tried to talk Shankly out of quitting for his own good

Three wise men: The formidable trio of Bob Paisley, Bill Shankly and Joe Fagan

# We were nothing before he came

business. He was a great manager. But, as I say, not everyone liked his style, especially the directors.

"You see, in the late 50s we were a happy-go-lucky, slap-happy crowd. The height of the directors' ambitions was to get into the First Division and they'd have been quite happy just to get there and go along three or four places off the bottom.

'But Bill was determined to change things and so was I. We talked a lot and made our plans. We got on like a house on fire.

'You see, I always gave Bill a straight answer and he liked that. He'd always ask my opinion and respect it because I was straight with him. We never once had an argument.

'Bill always accepted criticism from people he respected. He was good at his job and he expected other people to be the same.

'So we both decided in the early days that Liverpool were going places under us.

'And Bill would tell the board this, and his ambition would frighten them. They didn't want the boat rocked, and they didn't know how to handle Bill.

'But Bill was so dedicated to football and Liverpool that they just had to give him a chance. Football was the only thing he'd seen. He couldn't relax. It was all football, football, football.

'The board would try and knock down some of his ideas, but he'd convince them they were wrong. He always got his own way, and then when he got success they had to leave him alone.

'The players loved him, of course.

He was a real rabbit and all the funny stories and the jokes were right up their street. He'd have them in stitches but there was always a serious message there and that's how he got it across.

'And, of course, he was a great psychologist. He'd tell the lads how pathetic the opposition were and 90 minutes later tell them they'd beaten the best side in the country, and they'd take it week after week because of his personality. That was what made him such a great manager. He was a great motivator.

'Sometimes it would backfire on you, mind. You see, he used to encourage all sorts of lads to come down to Anfield and receive attention for injuries. And I'll never forget one day I was in my room and I heard Bill in the corridor telling this lad: 'Ah, that's no problem, son, Bobby Paisley will sort you out. He's the greatest trainer in the world. He can fix anything. There's his room, there. Tell him I sent you.'

'And then a few moments later this poor young fella wheels himself in in a wheelchair. It was so sad. I couldn't do anything for him. But that was Bill. He'd think just by telling people something it would make them believe in themselves and they'd be alright, and it rubbed off on lots of them and made them better people.'

'He had a great knowledge of the body and it stood me in good stead as a trainer. Training was very planned. We'd discuss it every morning and then put our plans into effect right to the last detail. It was a science under Bill, training.

'If I have one criticism of Bill it was that he didn't break the great team of the 60s up earlier. He was content with what he'd done and kept faith with the players. He was a very loyal man, but I was keener to get back to winning things again.

'But I picked up a lot of knowledge from Bill that stood me in good stead as a manager. I'd pick stuff out and store it away. You had to learn from Bill. He was football crazy, and I mean crazy. He was fanatical, like no-one else I've ever met.

'If I had to sum up Bill's effect at Anfield it's quite simply that he got the whole thing going. We were nothing before he came, and look at us now. He's very sadly missed.'

'HE WAS A GREAT PSYCHOLOGIST. HE'D TELL THE LADS HOW PATHETIC THE OPPOSITION WERE AND 90 MINUTES LATER TELL THEM THEY'D BEATEN THE BEST SIDE IN THE COUNTRY, AND THEY'D TAKE IT WEEK AFTER WEEK BECAUSE OF HIS PERSONALITY'

When I first went to Hamburg I wasn't really accepted by the players. I was a big name, and I'd just replaced one of their mates.

They tried to freeze me out, and I was unhappy. Anyway, it was the second pre-season friendly game, and I had a punch-up on the pitch. In fact I knocked a fella unconscious, and got sent off.

Of course the pictures were shown on the telly all over Europe and it looked bad with this fella out cold on the floor.

It caused a big scandal. I was fined and suspended for eight weeks, and I was really low.

That night I'm sitting in my flat with the wife Jean, turning it all over in my mind and I was about to quit and go home, then the phone goes, and it was the boss.

"I've just seen the picture of that fella you nearly killed on the television son. Jesus Christ you must have really hit him. Tell me, how did you hit him?"

"Well, I hit him with a right and

**KEEGAN on SHANKLY**

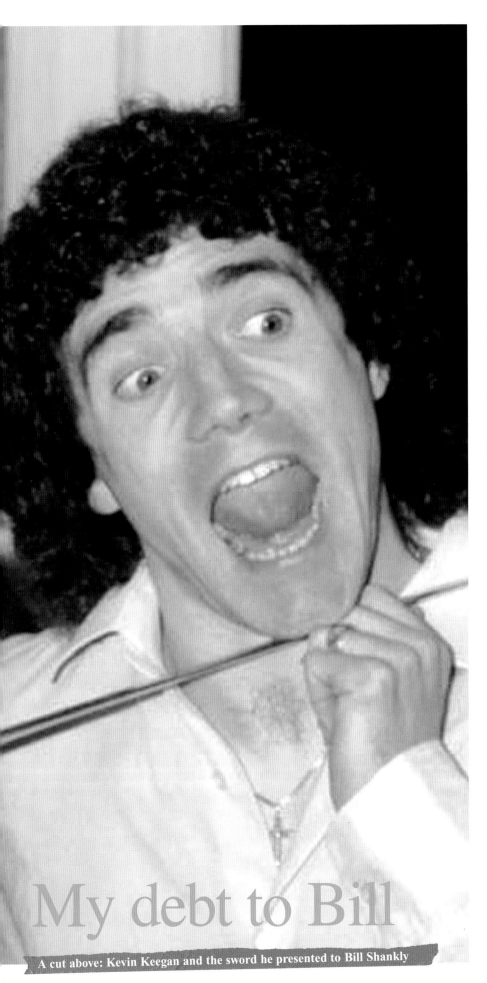

My debt to Bill

A cut above: Kevin Keegan and the sword he presented to Bill Shankly

when he was going down I caught him with a left", I said.

"Was it an uppercut son. It looked like he'd taken a good uppercut. Christ son I'm proud of you. That must have been one hell of a combination. Keep it up son, you're showing them the way out there."

He made me go through every detail of the fight with him, and he was enjoying it so much.

When I put the phone down I just killed myself laughing.

He'd cheered me up no end. The incident just didn't matter anymore.

Before the call I was on the verge of resigning. After it, I'd seen it all in a different light and there was no way I was going to give up.

Shanks had seen to that.

He'd saved my career with that phone call.

I was so sad when he died, and I realised that leaving Liverpool had killed him.

After he went it was so sad. He just became a ghost hanging round the club.

It was very difficult for the club but it could have been handled better. He should have been treated like Matt Busby. They should have found a position in the club away from the pressure.

But I can sympathise with the club in a way because his involvement would always have had to be total, and once he'd retired that could never have been.

But leaving Liverpool killed him because it was his life.

More than anything Bill taught me how to care for the human race.

He could converse with anyone from the Queen Mother to a Russian peasant. He was a very humble man. He realised Liverpool FC was all about people and he made it a people's club.

That was his greatest achievement.

To me, Bill Shankly was Liverpool. When he left the club a big part of Liverpool died.

# He made people relate to club

Bill Shankly laid the foundations of Liverpool's magnificent success. The people who came in after him have benefited tremendously from his work because he laid those foundations so strongly. He was the one who started it all.

I don't think Liverpool would be in the position they are today without his influence. He didn't just build great teams he built up a club full of great people at every level.

He was the people's man, and he made Liverpool the people's club which I think it still is today.

He identified with the people who pay to come here and the people who come have never lost that strong identity with the club,

He made people relate to the club and the people within the club relate to each other in a unique way because he was a special type of person.

He made the feeling of working for the common cause run throughout the club and the fans and

it's the same today.

He changed all this 'us' and 'them' mentality. The club since Shankly has never been about that.

Bill Shankly began the feeling that the club and the fans and all who work here are in it together. That seemed very important to people when he came here and it's just as important today.

Shrine to Shankly's Red Army: A fan's bedroom wall decorated with Liverpool stories in the '70s includes the Shankly headline: 'Everything I do for football – I do for the people. We're one big happy family'

# Shankly lives on . . .

The Twelfth Man never forgets: A different era but the banner makers of the Spion Kop know their history . . .

Shankly day: The former players salute a new generation in 1999

Museum memories: A scene from the dressing room during Shanks' days

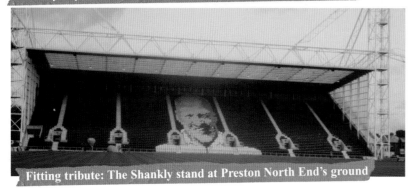

Fitting tribute: The Shankly stand at Preston North End's ground

Shankly's men: (From left) Callaghan, Lawler, Moran, Keegan, Evans, Hughes, Cormack at the Shankly flag day

Shanks would have hated this fuss! Sharing a joke

All four one: At a Shankly title celebration dinner in 2004

Walk on with hope in your hearts: Gerry Marsden and 'Colossus' Ron Yeats lead the singing at a Shanks dinner

Happy day: The famous Shankly statue is unveiled in 1997

Fans at the statue after Emlyn Hughes' death in 2004

The Liverpool family: Granddaughter Pauline joins the team picture for the 40th anniversary of the 1964 title triumph

Sons of Shankly: Phil Thompson presents Steven Gerrard with the Liverpool Echo's Bill Shankly Award

THE
BILL SHANKLY
PLAYING FIELDS

SUPPLIED & FITTED BY CORPORATE ADVERTISING

Field of dreams: The place where Shankly used to play will forever carry his name. Granddaughter Pauline is pictured with her sons Matthew and Stuart

Touching the legend: Reds on a pilgrimage to the Shankly memorial in Glenbuck

THE LEGEND
THE GENIUS
THE MAN.

...RE, 2nd SEPTEMBER 1913.
...E, 29th SEPTEMBER 1981.
...LD WITH LOVE. THANKS SHAN...
BILL SHANKLY'S ACHIEVE...
LIVERPOOL F...
LEAGUE CHAMP...

'Shankly, Shankly, Shankly, Shankly'. . . still watching over the Kop during the Rafa Benitez era

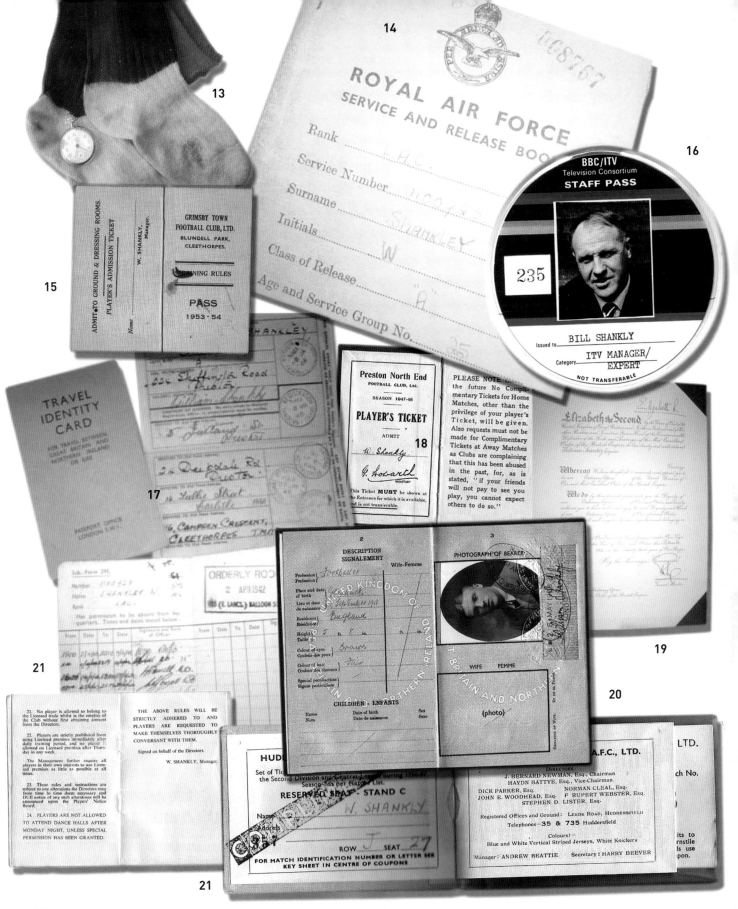

## Shankly treasures . . .

1. A certificate from the Swedish Massage and Electrical Institute.

2. Telegram from Tommy Docherty congratulating Shankly on Manager of Year award

3. Passport

4. An FA letter reporting Tommy Smith

5. Playing contracts from Preston

6. LFC season tickets

7. Shanks' old trilby!

8. A Workington FC players' handbook

9. A TV press pass

10. OBE medal

11. Shanks' tie-pins and football badges

12. Manager of the Month certificate, April 1972

13. Old football socks and stopwatch

14. RAF service and release book (with Shankly spelt wrong!)

15. Grimsby Town pass

16. ITV press pass for 1966 World Cup (Shanks was TV pundit)

17. Travel I.D

18. Preston player's ticket

19. OBE certificate

20. Stamped passport

21. Huddersfield Town season ticket

# Dear Grandy ...

# You will NEVER be forgotten

In August 1982 Liverpool secretary Peter Robinson confirmed that the Bill Shankly Memorial Gates would be ready in time for the first home League game against WBA at the end of that month:

"We considered several suggestions from design companies and we feel the one we have chosen will be a perfect memorial to Bill," said the man who had worked with him through the glory years.

Kevin Keegan said that Liverpool should have gone one better and named Anfield 'The Bill Shankly Stadium.' The former Kop hero was quite forceful in his thoughts and many thousands were on his side.

Several years later a similar argument could have been made for the "Bob Paisley Stadium."

What matters is that neither man will ever be forgotten.

The Shankly Gates have become an integral part of Anfield, standing proudly alongside the Hillsborough Memorial.

Everyone who passes through them feels that sense of passion and excitement that makes Anfield stand out as arguably the most atmospheric stadium in the country.

That stadium is part of Shankly's legacy to the Liverpudlians who adored him.

They walk through his Gates and stand proudly by his statue behind the Kop and feel the power and magnetism.

Bill won the Second Division Championship (1962) and three League Championships (1964, 1966 and 1973). He was the first Liverpool manager to claim the FA Cup (1965) and repeated that success in 1974 when he also became the first Reds' boss to secure a European trophy – the UEFA Cup.

But you can't judge Bill Shankly on trophies alone, as impressive as his haul was.

Everything Liverpool have today is inextricably linked with the football dream of a man who never countenanced defeat, never allowed anyone to undermine the Liverpool cause and who had a unique and highly charged relationship with the fans that has never been equalled by any manager, anywhere in the world.

He set the standards for Bob, Joe, Kenny, Roy, Graeme, Gerrard and Rafa – on and off the pitch.

You can't be manager of Liverpool without sensing the Shankly Legacy.

The real Bill Shankly was simply amazing. We hope this book stands forever as a salute to the man himself and to the club he adopted, loved and gave his heart and soul to.

*For me the book has been a special journey, one of memories and discovery. Please forgive me if my final words are spoken directly to my Grandy, the great Bill Shankly ...*

IT HAS BEEN A GREAT PRIVILEGE FOR ME TO
WRITE THIS BOOK ABOUT YOU.
I FEEL AS THOUGH I WAS GIVEN A SECOND
CHANCE TO COME CLOSE TO YOU.
ONCE YOU SAID THAT YOU HAD LIVED THE LIFE
OF A MONK AND CARRIED IT TO EXTREMES.
YOU SAID: 'THERE IS A HAPPY MEDIUM I SHOULD
HAVE TRIED TO FIND.'
I KNOW YOU REGRETTED NOT SPENDING AS
MUCH TIME WITH US AS YOU WOULD HAVE LIKED
. . . MAYBE YOU FELT A BIT GUILTY ABOUT IT.
BUT THE TRUTH IS TO ACHIEVE SOMETHING
GREAT, WHATEVER THAT MAY BE, WE HAVE TO
MAKE SACRIFICES AND IF YOU HADN'T GONE TO
EXTREMES, THEN I WOULDN'T BE WRITING THIS
BOOK ABOUT YOU 25 YEARS ON, WOULDN'T
HAVE RECEIVED THOUSANDS OF LETTERS,
EMAILS AND CALLS FROM PEOPLE WHO STILL
HOLD YOUR MEMORY SO DEAR, EVEN TODAY.

I THINK IT WAS WORTH IT.
IF IT WAS POSSIBLE TO TURN BACK TIME,
I CERTAINLY WOULDN'T WANT THINGS
TO BE ANY DIFFERENT . . .

Before this book comes to an end I would just like to say something about my granddad's retirement. Many people have conjectured and hypothesised about the reasons why he retired, implying some deeper hidden motives lay behind his decision.

Maybe they are right. I can only say that to his immediate family, he never professed privately anything other than what he declared publicly. I tend to agree with something that Brian Clough said in 1975.

"The very fact that he thought of retirement means he's tired."

He was comparatively young when he retired, but he'd given his all, not only as a player but as a manager. He had completely dedicated over 50 years of his life to the game he loved. He certainly wasn't tired of football – he never would be – but maybe the total commitment that was required as a manager had taken its toll.

Retirement was definitely not a role that he ever slipped into with ease and it may well have been a decision that he sometimes regretted; I think that is only natural for somebody who has filled every working hour with thoughts and actions centred around one thing and one thing only.

He may have been disappointed by some aspects of his retirement and initially by the way he was treated by some people. But of one thing, he was always assured, and that was the love of the people of Liverpool. If he ever felt he had been unfairly treated in some way, the Liverpool fans and their treatment of him compensated ten-fold. Seven years after his retirement and just two months previous to his death, he had this to say: "I thank God for the people of Merseyside.

The attitudes of the people of Liverpool, towards me and my family is stronger now than it ever was. I've never cheated them and they've never let me down."

'FEW MEN EVER HAD SUCH A CAPACITY FOR WARMING AND DELIGHTING THEIR FELLOWS WITHOUT BEING PHYSICALLY IN THEIR COMPANY. FOR MANY OF US HE REALLY WILL ALWAYS BE THERE'

Obviously this is the reason why he declared that he would never leave Liverpool and that he would always live among the people he had grown to love and respect. What a beautiful relationship.

As I was reading through the obituaries that were written at the time of my grandfather's death, I came across a piece written by the great sports writer Hugh McIlvanney, which appeared in 'The Observer' on October 4, 1981.

One part of the obituary particularly grabbed my attention, as it seemed to epitomise the essence of Bill Shankly and it summed up perfectly the way I and many others feel about him.

"Few men ever had such a capacity for warming and delighting their fellows without being physically in their company. For many of us he really will always be there."

Simple but accurate, just the way Grandy himself would have liked it. May his legacy live on.

*When you say Liverpool, you think Bill Shankly.*
*He made the people happy.*
*It has made me happy to pay this special salute to my granddad from his family.*

*We love you Grandy and so do the people of Liverpool.*

BILL SHANKLY
1913-1981

WALK ON ...

SELDOM IN THE HISTORY OF SPORT CAN A VILLAGE THE SIZE OF GLENBUCK
HAVE PRODUCED SO MANY WHO REACHED THE PINNACLE OF ACHIEVEMENT
IN THEIR CHOSEN SPORT. THIS MONUMENT IS DEDICATED TO THEIR MEMORY
AND TO THE MEMORY OF ONE MAN IN PARTICULAR, BILL SHANKLY.

THE LEGEND
THE GENIUS
THE MAN.

BORN - GLENBUCK, AYRSHIRE, 2nd SEPTEMBER 1913.
DIED - LIVERPOOL, 29th SEPTEMBER 1981.

FROM ANFIELD WITH LOVE. THANKS SHANK'S.

BILL SHANKLY'S ACHIEVEMENTS:

LIVERPOOL F.C. 1959 - 1974.

LEAGUE CHAMPIONS 1963/64, 1965/66, 1972/73,

RUNNERS UP 1968/69, 1973/74,

SECOND DIVISION CHAMPIONS 1961/62,

F.A. CUP WINNERS 1964/65, 1973/74,

FINALISTS 1970/71

UEFA CUP WINNERS 1972/73,

EUROPEAN CUP WINNERS CUP FINALISTS 1965/66,

SEMI-FINALISTS 1970/71,

EUROPEAN CUP SEMI-FINALISTS 1964/65.

THIS PLAQUE WAS LAID ON APRIL 27th 1997 BY

SCOTTISH COAL    LIVERPOOL AWAY SUPPORTERS CLUB    NETWORK 5

OTHER TITLES PRODUCED BY SPORT MEDIA:

'Liverpool's
5-Star Heroes'

£20.00

'A to Z of
Liverpool FC's
Greatest Pictures
- The Official
Collection'

£20.00

'Official Liverpool FC
Hall of Fame'

£20.00

'Liverpool FC
The Official Guide
2007'

£14.99

All of these titles are available to order by calling 0845 143 0001
or by sending a cheque payable to Sport Media to:
Sport Media Books, PO Box 48, Old Hall Street, L69 3EB